The Indian Partition in Literature and Films

C000152618

This book presents an examination of fictional representations, in books and films, of the 1947 Partition that led to the creation of the sovereign nation-states of India and Pakistan. While the process of representing the Partition experience through words and images began in the late 1940s, it is only in the last few decades that literary critics and film scholars have begun to analyze the work.

The emerging critical scholarship on the Partition and its aftermath has deepened our understanding of the relationship between historical trauma, collective memory, and cultural processes, and this book provides critical readings of literary and cinematic texts on the impact of the Partition both in the Punjab and in Bengal. The collection assembles studies on Anglophone writings with those on the largely unexplored vernacular works, and those which have rarely found a place in discussions on the Partition. It looks at representations of women's experiences of gendered violence in the Partition riots, and how literary texts have filled in the lack of the "human dimension" in Partition histories. The book goes on to highlight how the memory of the Partition is preserved, and how the creative arts' relation to public memory and its place within the public sphere has changed through time. Collectively, the essays present a nuanced understanding of how the experience of violence, displacement, and trauma shaped postcolonial societies and subjectivities in the Indian subcontinent.

Mapping the diverse topographies of Partition-related uncertainties and covering both well-known and lesser-known texts on the Partition, this book will be a useful contribution to studies of South Asian History, Asian Literature, and Asian Film.

Rini Bhattacharya Mehta is Assistant Professor of Comparative Literature and of Religion at the University of Illinois, USA. Mehta's teaching interests cover both literature and cinema. Her edited volume *Bollywood and Globalization* was published in 2010; she is currently working on a monograph on Indian cinema. Her articles have been published in *Comparative Studies in South Asia, Africa, and the Middle East, South Asian History and Culture*, and *Comparative American Studies*.

Debali Mookerjea-Leonard is currently Associate Professor of English and World Literature at James Madison University in Virginia, USA. She is a member of the editorial board of *Genders*. Her recently completed book is titled *The Paradox of Independence: Literature, Gender, and the Trauma of Partition*. She has contributed to anthologies, and journals including the *Journal of Commonwealth Literature, Feminist Review*, and *Social Text*.

Routledge contemporary South Asia series

The Indian Partition in Literature and Films

History, politics, and aesthetics

**Edited by
Rini Bhattacharya Mehta and
Debali Mookerjea-Leonard**

Foreword by Antoinette Burton

Routledge
Taylor & Francis Group

LONDON AND NEW YORK

First published 2015
by Routledge

2 Park Square, Milton Park, Abingdon, Oxfordshire OX14 4RN
52 Vanderbilt Avenue, New York, NY 10017

Routledge is an imprint of the Taylor & Francis Group, an informa business

First issued in paperback 2019

Copyright © 2015 Rini Bhattacharya Mehta and Debali Mookerjea-Leonard

The right of the editors to be identified as the authors of the editorial
matter, and of the authors for their individual chapters, has been asserted
in accordance with sections 77 and 78 of the Copyright, Designs and
Patents Act 1988.

All rights reserved. No part of this book may be reprinted or reproduced or
utilised in any form or by any electronic, mechanical, or other means, now
known or hereafter invented, including photocopying and recording, or in
any information storage or retrieval system, without permission in writing
from the publishers.

Notice:
Product or corporate names may be trademarks or registered trademarks,
and are used only for identification and explanation without intent to infringe.

British Library Cataloguing in Publication Data
A catalogue record for this book is available from the British Library

Library of Congress Cataloging-in-Publication Data
The Indian partition in literature and films : history, politics, and
aesthetics / edited by Rini Bhattacharya Mehta and Debali Mookerjea-Leonard.
    pages cm. – (Routledge contemporary South Asia series ; 93)
    Includes bibliographical references and index.
    1. South Asian literature (English)–History and criticism. 2. Partition,
Territorial, in literature. 3. Motion pictures–South Asia–History and
criticism. 4. India–History–Partition, 1947–In literature. 5. India–In
literature. 6. Pakistan–In literature. 7. India–In motion pictures.
8. Pakistan–In motion pictures. I. Mehta, Rini Bhattacharya, editor. II.
Mookerjea-Leonard, Debali, editor.
    PR9570.S64I53 2015
    820.9'954–dc23   2014022491

ISBN: 978-1-138-78180-1 (hbk)
ISBN: 978-0-367-32219-9 (pbk)

Typeset in Times New Roman
by Wearset Ltd, Boldon, Tyne and Wear

Contents

Contributors

Nandini Bhattacharya is Professor of English and affiliate of Film, Women's Studies and Africana Studies Programs at Texas A&M University, USA. Her interests include South Asia Studies and Indian Cinema, Transnational Feminisms, Feminist Theory, and Gender and Colonialism. From 2003 to 2006 she served as Chair of the Department of Women's and Gender Studies at the University of Toledo. She is the author of *Reading the Splendid Body: Gender and Consumerism in Eighteenth-century British Writing on India* (1998), *Slavery, Colonialism and Connoisseurship: Gender and Eighteenth-Century Literary Transnationalism* (2006), and *Hindi Cinema: Repeating the Subject* (2012).

Antoinette Burton is Professor of History and Bastian Professor of Global and Transnational Studies at the University of Illinois at Urbana-Champaign, USA, where she teaches courses on modern British history and imperialism, gender and colonialism, autobiography and the archive, approaches and methods, and world history. Her most recent publications are *A Primer for Teaching World History: Ten Design Principles* (2012), *Brown over Black: Race and the Politics of Postcolonial Citation* (2012), and *Empire in Question: Reading, Writing and Teaching British Imperialism* (2011). She was Guggenheim Fellow for 2010/2011, and served as Chair of the History Department from 2005 to 2010.

Ipshita Chanda is Professor of Comparative Literature at Jadavpur University, India; she served as Head of the Department of Comparative Literature from 2005 to 2007. Her recent monographs are *Selfing the City: Women Migrants and Their Lives in Calcutta* (2012), *Packaging Freedom Feminism and Popular Culture* (2003), and *Lights! Camera!... Taarpor? Ganamadhyam, naari, bishwayon* (2008, in Bengali). Her translations include *The Book of Night* (translation of Sibaji Bandyopadhyay's *Uttampurush Ekbachan*, 2008), *The Glory of Sri Sri Ganesh* (translation of Mahasweta Devi's Sri Sri Ganesh Mahima, 2003), and *Bitter Soil* (a volume of translations of stories by Mahasweta Devi, from Bangla into English, 1998).

Shumona Dasgupta is Assistant Professor of English and Postcolonial Literature at the University of Mary Washington, Virginia, USA and is writing a book on the representations in contemporary South Asian fiction and film of the 1947 Partition of India. The book delves into Partition texts which reveal the nexus between gender practices and the practice of violence while exploring the representation of trauma, social suffering and mourning, and the tentative survival of community in the wake of catastrophe. She has published her work in the *South Asian Review* and the *Journal of Postcolonial Writing*.

Lalita Pandit Hogan is Professor of English at the University of Wisconsin-La Crosse, USA, where she teaches Shakespeare, Critical Theory, International Literature and courses in writing. Hogan is affiliate faculty of the South Asia Center at the University of Wisconsin-Madison, USA. She is co-editor and contributing author of three books and three special issues of journals, and has published numerous articles and book chapters on Shakespeare, Tagore, Comparative Aesthetics, Goethe, R.K Narayan, as well as on numerous Hindi films, such as *Pyaasa, Jagate Raho, Omkara, Mirch Masala, Guide, Meenaxi: A Tale of Three Cities*, as well as the Iranian film, *Gabbeh*.

Patrick Hogan is Professor of English at the University of Connecticut, USA, where he teaches courses on cognitive approaches to literature and the arts, narrative across cultures, literature and culture of India, literature and philosophy, ideology and culture, history of literary theory, and post-colonial literature and film. His most recent books are *Understanding Indian Movies: Culture, Cognition, and Cinematic Imagination* (2008), *Understanding Nationalism: On Narrative, Identity, and Cognitive Science* (2009), *What Literature Teaches Us about Emotion* (2011), *Affective Narratology: The Emotional Structure of Stories* (2011), *How Authors' Minds Make Stories* (2013), and *Narrative Discourse: Authors and Narrators in Literature, Film, and Art* (2013).

Rini Bhattacharya Mehta is Assistant Professor of Comparative Literature and of Religion at the University of Illinois, USA. She has a PhD in Comparative Literature; her current research focuses on the continued evolution and synthesis of 'modernity' in the Indian subcontinent, from early forms of 'colonial modernity' to the emergent post-global modernity in India. Mehta's teaching interests cover both literature and cinema. Her edited volume *Bollywood and Globalization* was published in 2010; she is currently working on a monograph on Indian cinema. Her articles have been published in *Comparative Studies in South Asia, Africa, and the Middle East, South Asian History and Culture*, and *Comparative American Studies*.

Debali Mookerjea-Leonard holds a PhD from the University of Chicago and is currently Associate Professor of English and World Literature at James Madison University in Virginia, USA. She is a member of the editorial board of *Genders*. Her recently completed book is entitled *The Paradox of Independence: Literature, Gender, and the Trauma of Partition*. Her work has been supported by fellowships from the American Association of University Women, the American Institute of Indian Studies, and the National

Endowment for the Humanities. She has contributed to anthologies, and journals including the *Journal of Commonwealth Literature, Feminist Review*, and *Social Text*.

Sudipta Sen is Professor of History at the University of California, Davis, USA. His work focuses on the history of early colonial India and the British Empire. He is the author of *Empire of Free Trade: The English East India Company and the Making of the Colonial Marketplace* (1998) and *Distant Sovereignty: National Imperialism and the Origins of British India* (2002). His forthcoming book *Ganga: Many Pasts of an Indian River* is an exploration of the idea of a cosmic, universal river at the interstices of myth, historical geography and ecology.

Laurel Steele served as a career officer in the United States Foreign Service. She holds an undergraduate degree from the University of California, Berkeley, USA, and a doctorate from the University of Chicago, USA. She received a Fulbright grant to fund her dissertation, 'Relocating the Postcolonial Self: Place, Metaphor, Memory and the Urdu Poetry of Mustafa Zaidi (1930–1970)'. Her publications include 'The Myth of the Moth and the Flame: Insect Metaphors in Urdu Poetry' in *Insects and Texts: Spinning Webs of Wonder* and, upon the poet's centenary, 'Finding Faiz at Berkeley: Room for a Celebration' in *Pakistaniaat: A Journal of Pakistan Studies*.

Foreword

Sequels to history: Partition 3.0

Antoinette Burton

Partition will never be over. It is destined to return again and again not just as memory, but as history, politics and aesthetics as well. And despite the power of memory in shaping Partition's recurrence, it is always already anachronistic: not simply out of joint or out of time but productive of the very tensions between the "here and now" and the "then and gone" that call it into being. Partition's perpetual retake and return, to draw on a phrase in Rini Bhattacharya Mehta's essay below, takes place in realms of imagination and regimes of representation that often compete for truth – or, at the very least, vie for recognition and legitimacy among communities of "readers" (broadly speaking) who depend upon Partition memory to anchor their sense of self, to secure their attachment to the nation, and to sanction forms of contemporary state-sponsored violence in the process. This recurrent splicing is more than rehearsal or rehash or even sequel in a colloquial sense. As the essays in this collection so boldly illustrate, new scripts emerge from these familiar returns, generating new forms and figures for struggle around what Partition means in the dialectical present. In that sense, the fields of history, politics and aesthetics that come into view here are contested rather than static terrains, as narratives and genres and delivery systems (textual and visual) compete for recognition in a public sphere shaped by the uneven distribution of capital across the transnational circuits that keep arguments about Partition memory alive and profitable. How we plot them on, and against, the grids of representation inherited from the post-1947 moment and seek affinity or distance from those emplotments is the animating question of this collection.

Taken together, the essays here seek to re-boot the conversation about Partition memory by encouraging us to think more purposefully about the periodization of that work down to the present. Drawing on Partition fictions as they happened and what we might call second-generation Partition memory work – that flourishing of interest and investment in Partition representations which erupted in the 1990s – the editors have drafted contributions that strike out in new interpretive directions. Some authors populate the field with unheard voices or underexplored genres. Thus, for example, Sudipta Sen offers a reading of the short stories of Samaresh Basu to make the point of just how profoundly the protocols of history have failed to capture the full register of the habitus of expulsion and dislocation the way literary devices may do, while Laurel Steele resurrects Urdu poetry both for itself and in conversation with texts like Nehru's speech to underscore the overlap of politics and aesthetics at a particular historical moment. Others introduce a new conceptual or theoretical apparatus to decode and recode familiar representational complexes, with Patrick Hogan emphasizing the cognitive as a category of analysis and Lalita Hogan drawing upon the scholarship about emotion to make a case for the montage as a strategy of fear management.

Restarting the debate about how to think about Partition requires attention to alternative plotlines as well. Even a quick glance at this collection's table of contents indicates the emergence of *Pinjar* as just one alternative. No fewer than three contributors (Shumona Dasgupta, Patrick Hogan and Lalita Hogan) argue quite persuasively that the 1950 novel and then the 2003 film *Pinjar* seem to be serving as a new substructure for twenty-first-century apprehensions of Partition trauma. To be sure, *Pinjar* is neither sui generis nor disconnected from earlier forms and genres. And, as Ipshita Chanda reveals in her essay, it is precisely this intertextuality – as when "the literature that enters Kamleswar's text as witness to history includes Rahi Masoom Raza's *Adha Gaon*" – that makes diverse, even global, communities of readers and viewers into "the Partition audience." Whether we focus on its continuities or its ruptures, *Pinjar*, for its part, is now a contender in the arena of Partition representation. It also has, apparently, wide appeal for audiences who may be more or less familiar with older Partition stories and are in effect getting their Partition history through the film's politics and aesthetics. Like Jyotirmoyee Devi's writings for an earlier generation, *Pinjar* is a counter-history aimed both explicitly and implicitly at what Debali Mookerjea-Leonard calls the "representational deficiency" of official Partition archives, knowledge and representation. Its contemporary popularity speaks, perhaps, to a new periodization of consumption in what might be called the "Partition industry." An economy both symbolic and real, its long-term significance has yet to be fully gauged. In the meantime, this collection effectively materializes its lineaments and makes it visible as a subject ripe for analysis.

It is tempting here to imagine that what we are seeing is not just multidirectional memory – a phrase coined by the scholar Michael Rothberg to help us think through the relationships between genocide and colonialism – but a kind of *re-directional* memory as well: work that at once draws on and seeks to break from older models of emplotment because they do not speak as effectively to the exigencies of the current political, aesthetic and historical moment. Diaspora, cognition, emotion, even the resurgence of *Pinjar* – these all suggest a frustration with the methodological limits of now canonical interpretations and a hunger for new ways of thinking about trauma, displacement and exile. Yet, as welcome and as promising as these new directions are, they share a recurrent anxiety: that the deeply gendered, painfully communal violences of Partition history will not be fully or properly accounted for, as they have not rigorously been until quite recently, in historical and historiographical terms. Indeed, if re-directing Partition scholarship is what's called for, the "woman question" remains the heart of the matter. Here Rini Bhattacharya Mehta's approach is exemplary, precisely because it asks us to consider the long life of 1950s Bengali melodrama not just in shaping Partition memory narrative but in creating and sustaining audiences – who she calls "stakeholders" – who cannot necessarily part with their long-standing affective attachments to a particular complex of historical, political and aesthetic mode. If directors like Ghatak don't require them to – if they fail to re-boot the patriarchal plots and the regressive, universalizing work they rehearse – then the chances of truly re-directional memory work in and for Partition are arguably slim.

We continue to be in need of aesthetically novel, politically radical and historically innovative frameworks for understanding the centrality of sexual taboos and violence to the making of Partition fact and fiction. For in the fractious arena of Partition production, sequels will, perhaps inevitably, proliferate. Needless to say, the forms they take matter and the lines they draw between past and present have consequences for what is, in the transnational marketplace of history, politics and aesthetics, fast becoming a global Partition narrative complex. This collection signals some of the ways in which scholars are trying to intervene in that complex by acknowledging their indebtedness to previous plotlines and experimenting with new interpretive grids – all in the hope of re-imagining, resetting and restarting the debate with audiences old and new. Like all re-boots, this one is subject to critique and refit. By insisting on the recursive nature of that process, the authors here remind us of the urgency of taking continual stock and of keeping the sequel to follow always in view.

Introduction

Rini Bhattacharya Mehta and
Debali Mookerjea-Leonard

I

On June 3, 1947, All India Radio – the broadcasting corporation that was controlled by the colonial government and served the entire Indian subcontinent – became the chosen vehicle for announcing the Partition of India. The special program had four speakers: Lord Mountbatten the Viceroy, and the first Governor General of independent India; Jawaharlal Nehru, the protégé of Mohandas K. Gandhi, leader of the Indian National Congress and the future Prime Minister of India; Muhammad Ali Jinnah, leader of the Muslim League and the future Governor General of Pakistan; and Baldev Singh, the Sikh delegate, the Sikhs being the third religious majority in the Punjab region. They spoke in that order about the political decision to divide British India into two sovereign states: India and Pakistan. In geopolitical terms, lines drawn through British India were to form a peninsular India spotted with princely states and flanked by Pakistan in the east and the west. While British Indian provinces with a Muslim majority, located in the northwest, were allocated to Pakistan, two provinces with mixed populations, the Punjab in the west and Bengal in the east, were split. Thus, almost two-thirds of the original territory of the Punjab in the west and two-thirds of Bengal in the east both became part of Pakistan, as the population in these areas was predominantly Muslim. Pakistan emerged as an independent nation on August 14, and India on August 15, although the territorial extent of the two countries was as yet unknown, since it was only on August 17 that the decisions of the two Boundary Commissions (the Punjab and Bengal) regarding international borders were made public. A massive cross-border migration of population had commenced in the weeks leading up to the event, as numerous Muslim families left India for Pakistan, and Hindus and Sikhs left Pakistan for India. Most people who migrated had to take refuge in makeshift camps, which were both unsanitary and unsafe, and the refugees were often victims to sudden attacks, either by "riot mobs" or by an isolated small group. Violence bloodied both the Punjab and Bengal – communal riots exploded in Bengal in 1946 with the Muslim League's call to escalate the demand for Pakistan with "Direct Action" on August 16, the infamous Great Calcutta Killing (August 16–19) was followed by bloodbath in eastern Bengal in October, and then the violence spilled over to Bihar, and eventually, in early 1947, to the Punjab. Brutalities continued for months beyond August 1947, spreading wider and deeper on both sides of the border, into both countries. Accounts vary regarding the actual number of deaths; survivors of unimaginable violence are estimated at more than three million. This combined violence and destitution accompanying the polit-ical division of the Indian subcontinent, often glossed over in nationalist histo-ries, has lingered in the cultural memory of a large number of Indians and Pakistanis as simply "Partition."

The 1947 Partition has had a cascading impact on the economics and polity of both India and Pakistan, but two distinct sequels stand out in terms of histor-ical scope. First, the country of Pakistan failed to reconcile its two segments – East and West – and a swift but bloody civil war in 1971 resulted in East Pakistan emerging as a new nation, Bangladesh. The Bangladesh War, as it was called by the Indian government which joined East Pakistan in its fight after Pakistan bombed Indian Air Force bases, precipitated a new wave of migration and destitution along the India–East Pakistan border, recalling memories of 1947. The second sequel is the still open narrative of present-day Kashmir, a princely state with a Muslim majority bordering the British Indian Empire in the north, which became a contentious territory between India and Pakistan after its Hindu ruler, Hari Singh, signed the Instrument of Accession in October 1947 with India.

Partition emerged as the only viable answer to the conflicting nationalist aspirations of two political parties – the Indian National Congress and the Muslim League – both of which had grown powerful enough to negotiate with the British on political grounds. The Muslim League had existed since 1906, but it was only in the 1930s that it gained momentum politically. The crucial turning point came in 1936 when the Muslim League's differences with the Indian National Congress outweighed the League's differences with other Muslim parties. Indian National Congress, formed in 1885, had matured into a nationalist *tour de force* under the leadership of Gandhi between 1920 and 1938. It had always claimed an identity that was non-religious, but it had historically been incapable of defending its credentials before either Muslim or Dalit interests. Congress' compromise with the Dalits in 1932 – with Dr. Bhimrao R. Ambedkar withdrawing the demand for a separate constituency for the Dalits – was achieved through politics of a personal kind. Dr. Ambedkar gave in to a stubborn Gandhi on a hunger strike against the Dalit demand. No such compromise hap-pened between the League and Congress, and after a long stalemate between the two parties, the Pakistan Resolution – asserting the demand for Pakistan as the primary political program – was passed by the Muslim League on March 23, 1940. With the Pakistan Declaration, the issue of British India's dissociation from the British Empire became irrevocably triangulated, determining every political turn until the fateful days of August 14 and 15 arrived.

No other single word, inherited from the English and used almost unchanged except with regional accents or intonations, is laden with as much historical import in the Punjabi, Hindi/Urdu and Bengali languages as "partition."

Vernacular words such as *batwara* and *deshbhag*, used in newspapers and formal usage in place of "partition," invoked the idea of "division" without the hint of "parting." On the contrary, the words *muhajir* (migrant, in Urdu), *udbastu* (uprooted, in Bengali), and *sharanarthi* (refugee, in Hindi and Bengali) are more evocative of departure under stress. All these words, suddenly vested with new meanings in 1947, are important markers for the strange dispersal of the partition trauma; they are comparable to unnoticeable humble tombstones scattered all over the land, impossible to collect, gather, and organize for an official display in a museum. Dispersal is in fact what also happened to the survivors; the diaspora of the Hindus, Muslims, and Sikhs alike is spread all over South Asia and beyond, impossible to count, categorize, and comprehend. The British were excellent planners and even better record-keepers, and so it is no less than a surprise that the famed law and order of the British Raj turned into a bloody chaos in a matter of months, and that historians have had to mine the archives of dispersed, thinned-out memories of survivors for grains of history. It is inconceivable, for instance, that a hastily assembled unit out of the British Indian Army – the Punjab Boundary Force – was placed in charge of keeping peace from August 1 to September 1 during migration across the western border. The carnage in the Punjab – evidence enough of the dismal failure of the unit – remains impossible to quantify or even to grasp, due to the paucity of actual film records of riots and migration. The government's division for documentary productions – Information Films of India and the India News Parade – was closed down in 1946, to be reopened in 1948 by the government of independent India, renamed as Films Division. That leaves us with words – borrowed, coined, and learned under compulsion, future witnesses to the murder, rape, and dismemberment of thousands.

The immediate footfall of the Partition's representation in literature, theatre, and cinema is not insignificant. It is impossible to write a literary-cultural history of twentieth-century India, for example, without any reference to the stories of Saadat Hasan Manto (1912–1955), the poetry and fiction of Amrita Pritam (1919–2005), and the cinema of Ritwik Ghatak (1925–1976). But beyond the international fame of these figures (Manto and Pritam have been translated widely; Ghatak has been inducted into the pantheon of world cinema, albeit long after his death), there are numerous writings in vernacular literature – still largely untranslated – that addressed the unprecedented violence and destitution caused by the Partition. Ghatak was part of the acting cast in the Bengali film *Chinnamul* (*The Uprooted*, 1950), directed by Nemai Ghosh, one of the early Indian films dealing exclusively with the Partition. *Chinnamul*, a Bombay Talkies film, *Lahore* (*Hindi/Hindustani*, 1949), and *Natun Yehudi* (*The New Jew*, 1953) recall Indian cinema's earliest instances of a direct engagement with the Partition, distinct from the much more mediated and mostly subliminal traces found from the 1960s onwards. Irrespective of the sustained popularity of a literary work such as Khuswant Singh's *A Train to Pakistan* (1956), there was no sustained commentary on or interpretation of Partition in either literature or cinema. Ritwik Ghatak was the only director in the 1960s who created a cinematic aesthetic that could capture both the personal loss and the moral descent that the "refugee" status brought upon an unsuspecting middle class. But Ghatak was largely unknown outside Bengal during his lifetime; it is only recently that subtitled versions of his films became available for public consumption. What are collectively often referred to as Ghatak's Partition trilogy – *Meghe Dhaka Tara* (*The Cloud-Capped Star*, 1960), *Komal Gandhar* (*E-Flat*, 1961), and *Subarnarekha* (*The Golden River*, 1962) – were not commercial successes; they did not create a sphere of influence even in contemporary Bengali art cinema.

The anti-Sikh riots in Delhi in 1984, following the assassination of Prime Minister Indira Gandhi by her Sikh security guards, reawakened memories of Partition, and urged the necessity for the recognition of the intersections among violence, social relations, and the politics of manipulation. The revival of scholarly interest in the Partition in the late 1980s also coincided with (1) the tectonic changes in South Asian politics in the post-Cold War era, and (2) the increased significance of modern South Asia, India in particular, as a growing field of study in the US and the UK. India's moves towards economic liberalization in the 1990s had radically changed the nature of the official discourse in the country, and so in 1997 it was possible for the Indian press and media to recall both Independence and Partition in an unprecedented manner. The August 1997 issue of the weekly magazine *India Today*, for example, ran a cover story on siblings separated during the 1947 Partition riots, complete with their photographs and whereabouts in 1997. A Hindi film *Gadar: Ek Prem Katha* (*Revolt: A Love Story*, 2001) went on to become a blockbuster and one of the highest grossing films in the history of Indian cinema. Based on the true story of a Sikh man and a Muslim woman who marry during the Partition riots, only to be torn apart by the woman's family, the film rewrites the man's eventual suicide by turning him into a Bollywood-style action hero who rescues his wife from her Pakistani relatives, almost single-handedly defeating the Pakistani forces that try to intervene. The commercial success of this film may be interpreted as a validation of a neo-nationalist demonization of Pakistan and the championing of a future Indian domination by any means necessary. The 2001 film *Gadar* thus presented a view that was radically different from the slow and sporadic emergence of the memories of Partition on Indian television (Doordarshan) in the 1980s. The immensely popular television serial *Buniyaad* (*The Foundation*, 1986) and a multi-episode film *Tamas* (*Darkness*, 1987) recalled both the violence and the dispossession caused by Partition. In terms of form, *Buniyaad* retained the basics of the "development" soap opera that was already tested on Indian television viewers with *Hum Log* (*We the People*, 1984), with occasional crossing over to the cinematic melodrama that was the hallmark of Bombay-based Hindi cinema. *Tamas* was an art-theater production, with Om Puri in a lead role and directed by Govind Nihalani. Nevertheless, Doordarshan's foregrounding of a fictionalized memory of the Partition – in the form of the mellowed *Buniyaad* and the visceral *Tamas* – must be considered as an endorsed official version, resonating with the overall politics of national integration. Punjab, the region where both the narratives begin, was the Indian state most ravaged by secessionist, communal, and police violence; and half-a-dozen constitutional amendments were introduced in the 1980s to bring the state back under control by imposing the President's rule.

Academic interest in Partition has produced an inspiring body of scholarship in the past two decades. This volume is a modest contribution to the continued collective effort. The international reading of the Partition that originated in Anglo-American academia has led to the foregrounding of a different set of texts and positions. Texts such as Bapsi Sidhwa's novel *The Ice Candy Man* (1988; retitled *Cracking India* in the US and published in 1991) and its cinematic rendition in Deepa Mehta's *1947: Earth* (1998) have depended upon a global/post-global aesthetic that is still evolving. The participation of vernacular texts and narrations of the Partition from the local archives in South Asia in this global aesthetic will be the ultimate determining factor in what Partition will become to posterity.

II

In May 1942, a few months before the Quit India Movement, Gandhi called upon the British to "leave India to God. If this is too much then leave her to anarchy." And to anarchy she was left in 1947. For millions of people in the Indian subcontinent, Partition disconnected their birthplace from their homeland (and nationality); and the inter-community violence during the riots surrounding Partition compelled an estimated 12 to 15 million people to relocate to areas across the border to live among co-religionists. (It is impossible to find accurate statistics of the number of persons who migrated, or of those who did not survive the violence. Readers will note that in both cases our contributors have cited different numbers. This is because in the absence of documentary evidence on the subject, historians have offered different estimates.)

While the process of representing the Partition experience through words and images began in the late 1940s, it is only in the past few decades that literary critics and film scholars have begun to sift through the existing archive to analyze the traces left by this foundational trauma on the national imaginaries of India, Pakistan, and Bangladesh. The emerging critical scholarship on Partition and its aftermath has deepened our understanding of the relationship between historical trauma, collective memory, and cultural processes. However, its scope and potential remain limited by a near-exclusive focus on Anglophone writings of the 1980s and 1990s. This collection attempts to assemble studies on Anglophone writings with those on the largely unexplored vernacular works. It includes recent critical readings of literary and cinematic texts on the impact of Partition both in the Punjab and Bengal. It comprises essays on popular texts, as well as others which have rarely found a place in discussions on Partition. While it was our intention to include the work of writers and auteurs from India, Pakistan, and Bangladesh, it has been particularly challenging to find studies on the experience of Partition in East Pakistan/Bangladesh.

The chapters in Part I of this book, "Surviving violence," examine different dimensions of women's experience of gendered violence in the inter-community riots surrounding Partition. The "cracking" of the Indian subcontinent was marked by the abduction and violation of women that numbered in the thousands, by men of the rival community. And for many Hindu and Sikh women victims of Partition's violence, their suffering did not end with the assault on their bodies; instead it was compounded by the rejection they experienced within their families and communities upon their return "home." Debali Mookerjea-Leonard analyzes the consequences of the "touch" that rendered women "untouchable," and traces the cost, for women's bodies, of the discursive transformation of Hindu women's chastity into a prerequisite for their belonging in the new nation. She illuminates how women's participation in the national community was made conditional not only upon their residence in the right country and following the right religious faith, but also upon their maintaining the right (chaste) body. Shumona Dasgupta examines the presentation of women, in female-authored novels, as active agents of history, and their experience of Partition as violence. The texts, Dasgupta argues, make visible women's experience of violence within the "home," the family, and the nation, and expose a critical continuum between the everyday and extraordinary violence against women.

The chapters in Part II, "Borders and belonging," together examine how literary texts have filled in the lack of the "human dimension" in Partition histories for several decades as the concurrence of the "event" of Partition and the birth of the two nations continues to make the retrieval of differentiated memory a complex, mediated process. Turning away from the "high" politics of the principal actors and the geopolitical consequences of the event, fictional narratives of Partition have anticipated the many "histories from below" that have emerged in recent years. Ipshita Chanda investigates the manipulation of identity by separatist politics, and the consequent loss of plurality. She claims that it is in the process of carving out the two nations wherein lie the roots of the fundamentalist problems and the secular challenge of the present. Sudipta Sen traces important fault lines in the narrative of the Bengal partition of 1947, arguing that the uprooting of inhabitants from the villages and cities of what was to become East Pakistan, to the city of Calcutta in West Bengal, was difficult to reconcile with the linear narrative of anti-British, nationalist struggle. This political fragmentation reflected a certain loss of innocence, and compensated for such loss through the lyrical, mnemonic figure of an "undivided Bengal." The political failure in averting such a severing along sectarian lines, Sen contends, also produced a particular mode of story-telling. Laurel Steele studies the intellectual and political relocation of Urdu language and literature. Given the new political landscape, writing in Urdu became linked to a new space where Urdu was the official language: Pakistan. Steele contends that much of Urdu Partition poetry and the complicated locations of the writers provide an access to the distilled emotion and political awareness that linger in the hearts of Urdu speakers. What these poets say about Partition and its aftermath contributes to a nuanced understanding of the cultural and political divisions, and linkages, between Pakistan and India today. Nandini Bhattacharya examines the relationship between the political, on the one hand, and the aesthetic, on the other. She presents a comparison of auteurs, Guru Dutt and Ritwik Ghatak, and author, Saadat Hasan Manto, to find a way to approach the question of an early aesthetic of alienation in post-colonial India.

The chapters in Part III, "History, memory, and aesthetics," excavate how the memory of the Partition is preserved and how it is sublimated. They examine how creative arts' relation to public memory and its place within the public sphere change through time. Patrick Hogan tracks how the film *Pinjar* consciously emplots its narrative force and conflict on the substructure of the *Ramayana* and, at the same time, challenges that emplotment from within the text. It is not difficult to imagine just what the default use of this paradigm is likely to be: Pakistan is Ravana, the demon that seized both land and women, while India is Rama. The relationship between India and Pakistan in this imagination is almost necessarily belligerent. Moreover, this emplotment places blame on only one side in the Partition violence. As a result, *Pinjar* emplots South Asian history in ways that contribute to antagonistic nationalism and militarism. In another reading of the same film, Lalita Pandit Hogan examines *Pinjar*, emphasizing the impossibility of recuperating traumatic experiences in literary or cinematic representations. The impossibility is caused by both the actual nature of the horror that takes place in situations like Partition and an erasure of the subject that is inevitable. Rini Bhattacharya Mehta examines the subliminal engagements of popular Bengali films with Partition focusing on the encoding of the macro-political trauma into articulations of the private, hetero-normative world of the Bengali bourgeoisie. Using films starring the famed "romantic pair" – Uttam Kumar and Suchitra Sen – Mehta investigates the interjection and the eventual sublimation of the trauma of Partition into the romantic fantasy that this on-screen couple embody, in the context of the genre of melodrama in the golden age of Bengali cinema.

Together, the essays map the diverse topographies of Partition-related uncertainties which, we believe, are essential to a nuanced understanding of how the experience of violence, displacement, and trauma shaped postcolonial societies and subjectivities in the Indian subcontinent.

Part I
Surviving violence

Part I

Surviving violence

1 Quarantined

Women and the Partition[1]

Debali Mookerjea-Leonard

Introduction

Responding to the problem of Hindu and Sikh families' and communities' refusal to reintegrate women who were sexually violated during the Partition riots and later repatriated from Pakistan, Mahatma Gandhi addressed the issue at a prayer meeting on December 7, 1947:

> It is being said that the families of the abducted women no longer want to receive them back. It would be a barbarian husband or a barbarian parent who would say that he would not take back his wife or daughter. I do not think the women concerned had done anything wrong. They had been subjected to violence. To put a blot on them and to say that they are no longer fit to be accepted in society is unjust.
>
> (Gandhi, *Collected Works of Mahatma Gandhi* 1994, 9)[2]

On December 26, 1947, he urged his audience again:

> Even if the girl has been forced into marriage by a Muslim, even if she had been violated, I would still take her back with respect. I do not want that a single Hindu or Sikh should take up the attitude that if a girl has been abducted by a Muslim she is no longer acceptable to society.... If my daughter had been violated by a rascal and made pregnant, must I cast her and her child away?... Today we are in such an unfortunate situation that some girls say that they do not want to come back, for they know that if they return they will only face disgrace and humiliation. The parents will tell them to go away, so will the husbands.
>
> (Gandhi 1994, 117–118)

And in January 1948, the Prime Minister of India, Jawaharlal Nehru, also made a similar plea.[3] The repeated appeals, the state-sponsored homes for "unattached women," and feminist studies by Ritu Menon, Kamla Bhasin, Urvashi Butalia, and Veena Das – drawing upon oral histories and official records – testify to the prevalence of the practice by families of rejecting women abducted and/or raped in the communal (religious community-based) riots of 1946 to 1947.[4]

Contextualizing these desertions within the social production of a discourse of honor and of women's sexual purity, I examine the rejections through a reading of the Bengali feminist author Jyotirmoyee Devi's (1894–1988) short story "*Shei Chheleta*" ("That Little Boy") and novel *Epar Ganga Opar Ganga* (translated as *The River Churning*).[5] Jyotirmoyee Devi does not raise the question: Why are women's bodies subjected to a gendered form of communal hostility? Instead, she analyzes *how* women's bodies are made the preferred sites for the operation of power diffused throughout everyday domestic life. She critiques the over-emphasis on chastity and tabooed social contacts among Hindus that led to their abandoning the women abducted and/or raped during the communal riots. In doing so, her work breaks the silence surrounding the sexually victimized women that has operated as an effective denial of their citizenship. Her writings address the representational deficiency in the social and cultural historiography of the 1947 Partition of Bengal of the large-scale gendered violence.[6] For the most part, the locus of the trauma in research studies has been the loss of home-land, migration, dispossession, and refugee dilemmas. Unlike Bengali *udbastu* (refugee) fiction that deals primarily with dislocation, economic struggles, and wistfulness for a lost time and place, Jyotirmoyee Devi focuses on the society-wide repression of memory of the negotiations of national borders performed on the bodies of women. She repeatedly demands accountability for the tragic con-sequences of Partition, interrogates the meaning of Independence, and expresses skepticism about the gendered nature and class character of its privileges.

Jyotirmoyee Devi calls attention to the ellipses of history, and especially to women's histories that are inextricable from the histories of nation formation but which have been, until fairly recently, only a few glosses in the margins, if not wholly omitted. After the feminist scholarship of the past three decades, the cri-tique of the absence of gendered national histories might not seem absolutely cutting edge, but in the 1960s, at the time when Jyotirmoyee Devi's short story and novel were published, it was radical. More radical was her embedding of these histories in the context of the national struggle at a time when the euphoria of Independence had not faded. The 1991 republication of Jyotirmoyee Devi's writings under the aegis of the Jadavpur University School of Women's Studies, Calcutta, and the subsequent English translations from feminist presses like Kali for Women, Delhi, and Stree, Calcutta, vouch for the pivotal position of her work in contemporary feminist scholarship. It also coincides with the renewed interest in Partition since the 1980s.

Partition's women: "recovered" by the state, rejected in the community

Carrying forward the preliminary feminist research on Partition by Butalia, Das, Menon, and Bhasin, I suggest that it is possible to link the rejections of abducted and raped women with the social production of a discourse of honor and, espe-cially, of women's sexual purity. Imbricated in a program of Hindu cultural nationalism beginning in the nineteenth century, the discourse of women's chastity was deployed to counter issues of foreign domination.[7] Elite women confined to the private sphere were considered unsullied by British colonization, and their chastity was made a critical site of symbolic economies involving the nation, a site of pedagogy and mobilization for an embryonic collective political identity. That is to say, the nationalists engaged in a process of myth-making whereby feminine sexual purity was endowed with the status of the transcendental signifier of national virtue. (This simultaneously shielded masculine proto-nationalism from the narration of its failures.) From this period of early nationalism and high imperialism first emerges the figure of the chaste upper-caste, upper- and middle-class Hindu woman. And in her role initially as Wife, and later as Mother, it was a figure destined to function as the supreme emblem of a consolidated Hindu nationalist selfhood. This formulation of an ideal femininity did not grow out of some social pathology. Instead, it was embedded in the macrosociological dynamics of colonialism and culture, wherein the central struggle was for control over state apparatuses, property, and the law.

The Partition riots of 1946/1947 and the destabilization of community alliances that they entailed also treated women's bodies as a site for the performance of identity. According to the same patriarchal logic that resulted in the mass rape of women from the "other" religious community (Muslim), the "purity" of Hindu and Sikh women became a political prerequisite for their belonging in the new nation. (In the communal violence surrounding Partition, Hindu and Sikh women sometimes committed suicide or were murdered by male kin, and these acts – designed to thwart the rival (Muslim) community's aims to dishonor the nation by violating its women – were lauded as self-sacrifice by the woman's family.) The Hindus in India viewed Partition as the loss of territory of "ancient Bharata" (Bharata is the Sanskrit name for India). They felt that, even if the "diseased limb" of this territory could be sacrificed by the Indian National Congress leadership for the independent possession of the erstwhile colonial state apparatus, the women could not be so forfeited. And newly independent India's "national honor" demanded the repossession of national property (Hindu and Sikh women) from Pakistan.

The events around Partition – the migrations, mass killings, and abductions – spurred the state to assume responsibility for the restoration of its citizens. To enable this, the Indian state entered into an Inter-Dominion Agreement with Pakistan in November 1947 and mounted a recovery mission in early December of that year. While the territorial claim for Pakistan was viewed by the Congress as an unfortunate practical concession, the Pakistani government's demand for the return of the Muslim abductees was considered equally legitimate to the Congress' own demand for the return of Hindu and Sikh women. The violence on the part of the state during the recovery mission often led to uprooting women who had settled into life in their new homes. This uprooting was normalized as benevolence, while women's rights to self-determination regarding their future domiciles (and citizenship) were obliterated. The process of repatriation objectified the women as only bodies marked by religious affiliation, and placed these bodies under the protection of the state. In addition, the presence of abducted

Muslim women in Hindu and Sikh homes challenged the state's claims to legiti-macy in the arena of international politics, and it was therefore necessary to "return" them to Pakistan. The women were important only as objects, bodies to be recovered and returned to their "owners" in the place where they "belonged," a belonging determined by the state and which advanced the state's claims both nationally (recovery of Hindu and Sikh women) and internationally (return of Muslim women). In this chapter, I use Jyotirmoyee Devi's writings as a basis for exploring how women who were sexually abused by the rival community in the riots of Partition, unless excluded from the nation, become representative of the fallen nation.

The accumulating histories of violence and social death (exclusion from society) in the period around Partition oblige a revision of prior periods because legislations around *satidaha* (widow burning) (1829), widow remarriage (1856), the Brahmo Marriage Act (1872), the Age of Consent Bill (1891), and the Sarda Bill (1929) were not discrete moments. Rather, the rejections that abducted and/ or raped women experienced in the aftermath of the Partition riots seem less anomalous when viewed as the culmination of developments in the legal status of Indian women over the *longue durée*. South Asian gender historians have made detailed studies of the many tumultuous debates around specific colonial ordinances focusing on Hindu women. However, I urge the necessity for situat-ing these discussions in a historical continuum. Nationalist anxiety about coloni-alism manifested itself in, and intensified, gender pathologies, and the discursive developments around chastity in the colonial and nationalist era clearly had con-crete consequences for women, because their bodies were not simply sites for discourse but were also sites of patriarchal constraint and violence. The repudi-ation of abducted wives, daughters, mothers, and sisters was a dramatic demon-stration of the fact that nationalist discursive constructions of Hindu femininity held abundant scope for violence. Nor is this simply a historical issue in South Asia. The escalation of Hindu nationalist/culturalist sentiments in India urges a reassessment of this essentializing ideology for women. Reports by feminist groups on the violence in Gujarat in 2002 illustrate the transformation once again of women's bodies and sexuality during ethno-religious conflicts into an important arena for enacting emphatically modern gender pathologies. The attacks on Muslim women, mostly of childbearing age or who will soon enter their reproductive years, and the murder of children, even fetuses, adumbrates a new and, in some respects, more awful form of ethnic cleansing and partition.

In the next section of this chapter, I analyze Jyotirmoyee Devi's writings on Partition as representative texts of women's experience of social hostility fol-lowing their violation, as well as of the suffering resulting from their rejection at home and in their communities. However, I argue that this early moment of her writings is simply a moment of breaking the silence. It does not proceed much further analytically than to produce narrative and affect around the costs of an ideology with which everyone as part of the community was familiar. The raped woman lost, or was at least threatened with the loss of, her personhood through the violent event and the subsequent social death that followed as abducted women were uniformly rejected across differentials of caste and region. Jyotirmoyee Devi's writings measure the costs of that ideology.

Unfinished histories: women in *"Shei Chheleta"* and *Epar Ganga Opar Ganga*

Born in 1894, married and widowed at an early age, Jyotirmoyee Devi's life was largely structured by the cultural terrain of patriarchal nationalism. Although her access to economic privileges as the granddaughter of the Prime Minister to the Prince of Jaipur shielded her from the crises affecting the lives of propertyless Hindu widows and enabled her to pursue a literary career, she lived within the narrow circumference of rituals and prohibitions that ordered the social existence of women, and especially of widows. Embedded within this privileged social context, she nonetheless mustered a keen critique of the constructed nature of gender, and of the systemic oppression of women. Her memoirs, essays, short stories, novels, and poetry cover a wide range of subjects, from women's histories, their education and gainful employment, and Hindu women's rights, to property and divorce in the Hindu Code Bill, women in the Jaipur aristocracy, the condition of prostitutes and "untouchables," to Partition and the war in Bangladesh. Her work combines insights gleaned from a hybrid library of Indian and European intellectual/philosophical traditions. In her individual capacity as a writer and feminist, she worked towards instituting women's civil, political, and human rights.

Writing women's histories of rejection

A reading of Jyotirmoyee Devi's works suggests that the discursive developments around "ideal" womanhood in Hindu cultural nationalism, the responsibility on "the gendered and sexed female body ... to bear the burden of excessive symbolization" (Ray 2000, 135) played a significant role in the responses generated towards the female victims of Partition, and that "the violence of the Partition was folded into everyday relations" and the events of Partition "came to be incorporated into the temporal structure of relationships" (Das 2000, 220).

Jyotirmoyee Devi's writings mark a negation of the patriarchal discourse of colonialism/nationalism by exposing the brutal and isolating practices that ritualized forms of purity demanded. The compelling question animating Jyotirmoyee Devi's short story *"Shei Chheleta"*[8] and novel *Epar Ganga Opar Ganga*[9] is not so much *how* state intervention affected the lives of women, but rather *what* happened afterwards. Both focus on the reception, or non-reception, of women in the community to which they had returned (or were returned) on the basis of the religion of their fathers/brothers/husbands. Some of the questions that resonate through both texts are as follows. Why are women who were abducted, raped, and dislocated by Partition repeatedly displaced after their "recovery" to boarding schools, or to hostels for single/working women, or forced to take to begging or prostitution? What makes their reinstatement in their original families impossible? How does the symbolic burden placed on a woman by cultural nationalism produce an immediate effect on the female body? What is the status of the individual detail, and does the specific case matter?

Charting the histories of women's oppression acquires the semantics of a political project for Jyotirmoyee Devi. Questions of historical visibility or the denial thereof, the constitution of the political subject through history, and the deliberate evasions/perversion of history are central to her interests: the privilege of who gets to write, whose history is written, and how. That the state manipulates the process of the dissemination of histories – for instance, the state sanctions for undergraduate studies the work of historians with certain political biases while refusing patronage to others – constitutes the core of Jyotirmoyee Devi's critique of the writing of history in the opening chapter of the novel *Epar Ganga Opar Ganga*. (The project of history writing in the years immediately following Independence routinely focused on the overcoming of imperialism. As histories of the nationalist movement for the most part, these typically centered around a select group of ideologues from the Indian National Congress, detailing their role in the freedom struggle.) Although Jyotirmoyee Devi's counter-history in the novel incorporates a larger concern for the recuperation of obliterated narratives of other subordinated groups – class/caste – the focus is on women's absent histories. The novel analyzes with relentless intensity the condition of the female victims of Partition.

Drawing upon the ancient Sanskrit epic *Mahabharata*, the novel *Epar Ganga Opar Ganga* was originally entitled *Itihashe Stree Parva* or *The Book of Women in History* ("*Stree Parva*" or "The Book of Women" is the title of one of the books in the original epic, whose generic title is "*Itihasa*" or "History"). However, in her authorial preface, Jyotirmoyee Devi indicates that, despite its name, "The Book of Women" of the *Mahabharata* was not about sufferings specific to women, but focused on general grief and bereavement for the losses incurred in the battle of Kurukshetra. She therefore refers to the epic's "*Maushala Parva*" or "The Book of Iron Clubs" which makes an obscure mention of the abduction and rape of the Yadava women. Critical about the silences that fill the interstices of history, Jyotirmoyee Devi draws a parallel between the suppression of women's histories of oppression in Vyas' (author of the *Mahabharata*) scant attention to the predicament of the abducted and raped women in the "*Maushala Parva*" and the more recent historical context of Partition. Placing Partition on a comparable scale with the devastation of the subcontinent during the battle of Kurukshetra, and the violation of Yadava women after the death of their men in the battle, Jyotirmoyee Devi thus positions the Partition atrocities as constituting the epic of the modern Indian nation.

Hence, it is not coincidental that in *Epar Ganga Opar Ganga* the description of the student population at the women's college at Delhi where Sutara teaches, incidentally named Yajnaseni (another name for Draupadi in the *Mahabharata*), bears traces of the Indian national anthem, although mutilated to sustain the sacred geographic relevance. (The song had been composed in undivided India.) The original line naming the different provinces runs, "Punjab, Sindh, Gujarat,

Maratha, Dravir (Deccan)," while Jyotirmoyee Devi emphasizes the all-India character of the college by writing, "There were students from all parts of the split 'mahaBharata,' ... Marathi, Gujarati, Madraji (Deccanese), Punjabi women" (*maha*: great; *Bharata*: India) (Jyotirmoyee Devi 1991, 129). Conspicuously absent is the mention of Sindh (and of Sindhi women in the college), since following Partition it became Pakistani territory. The violence performed on the original line from the anthem thus becomes a metaphor for the severed subcontinent as well as for the brutalities visited upon women. Opening with Sutara Datta, Assistant Professor of History, meditating on the absences in the historical discourse, *Epar Ganga Opar Ganga* narrates the costs of the violence surrounding Partition, thus offering an account that deviates from the glorious textbook histories of the Indian freedom struggle. In telling a story that has been deleted, the novel provides a corrective, re-inscribing the obliterated, unspeakable women's bodily experience of the political division of the country as the new "*Stree Parva*," "The Book of Women."

While the constitutive nature of the violence in Punjab and Bengal may have been marked by regional specificities, Jyotirmoyee Devi takes a holistic approach towards understanding the dilemmas of women twice subjected to violence, initially sexual and later social. And, indeed, the refusal to reintegrate women within the community was not regionally specific. One of the textual strategies Jyotirmoyee Devi employs is to continuously bring together women from Bengal and Punjab, the two partitioned provinces: Raj (Punjabi) with Baruna and Sujata (Bengali) in "*Shei Chheleta*"; Sutara with Kaushalyavati, Sita Bhargava, Mataji, and other women from Punjab in *Epar Ganga Opar Ganga*.[10] Thus, Sutara's feeling of a special affinity with her Punjabi colleagues and friends at Delhi is based on a shared history of violence, homelessness, and migrancy. That said, while the subject of Jyotirmoyee Devi's Partition fictions is the rejection of sexually assaulted women, the plots do provide indications of a qualitative difference in the character of the violence in Punjab and in Bengal. The sexual and reproductive violence to which Raj's mother (Punjab) is subjected, or of which Kaushalyavati speaks, is replaced by a more cultural violence for Sutara (Bengal). I use the relative "more" because despite the focus on Sutara's social marginalization, incidents of the abduction of her sister, her friends' suicides/abductions, and her personal sexual harassment are also present. The economic struggles involved with migration transform in similar ways Raj's and Sutara's lives from those of the previous generation of home-bound elite women, obliging both to find gainful employment in civil society. This articulates the transitions in women's lives as they emerge as survivors in the public sphere; Jyotirmoyee Devi's feminist convictions are obvious in her repeated emphasis, in her fiction and essays, on the importance of women's financial independence.

Jyotirmoyee Devi's Partition victims are "deeply wounded people" (Naim 1999, 176). Raj's mother ("*Shei Chheleta*"), Sutara, Kaushalyavati, "Mataji" (*Epar Ganga Opar Ganga*) – all are exiled subjects "who in a most organic way, are tied to a history and a place but who, overwhelmed by yet another more powerful history, must live out their days elsewhere" (Naim 1999, 175–176). But the "elsewhere" Jyotirmoyee Devi's women characters encounter is not only a different country but a different life outside the domestic pale, the possibilities of which they could never have foreseen, and for which they lack required survival skills. In *"Shei Chheleta,"* history violently interjects itself into Raj's mother's sheltered existence, ravages her home, invades her body, and eventually makes her homeless. Originally from a wealthy family and married into one, later raped and with the resulting child, Raj's mother adjusts to the contingencies of life by perfecting her skills as a beggar and cultivating an ingratiating smile. Independence makes little sense in the lives of migrant women like her, for whom the freedom of the country is tethered to betrayals by their families, by the nation, and more substantially, by the loss of control over their bodies and the erosion of consent.

Since the narrative landscape in *"Shei Chheleta"* is defined by Raj, the readers are not clued into whether Raj's mother "chose" to migrate to India or was recovered on state initiative, a subject that animates the gendered critiques of the state in feminist studies on Partition. For instance, ethnographers Ritu Menon and Kamla Bhasin in *Borders and Boundaries* and Veena Das in *Critical Events* critique state policy of intervention in displacing "abducted" women, leaving no space for their exercise of preference in their citizenship. They emphasize that many of these women, far from longing to be "recovered," had married their abductors, borne children, settled in their new lives, and resisted state repatriation efforts. Sugata Bose and Ayesha Jalal, on the other hand, argue that the events of abduction and rape – long before any initiative by the state to restore them to their former communities – serve as the starting point for an erosion of consent. They suggest that some of the feminist scholarship on the "recovery" efforts undertaken by the state "miss more than a historical nuance or two in their dogged anti-statism."[11] Countering Bose and Jalal's argument, however, Martha Nussbaum indicates that the erosion of consent has a longer history, originating not with abduction and rape but with the denial in many cases of women's decisions pertaining to marriage.[12]

The debates around the "Recovery Mission," however, do not constitute the point which Jyotirmoyee Devi makes in her writings. She depicts the intense community disdain towards the women subjected to tabooed sexual contacts, the near-unlivability of their situation, and the possibility of spaces outside of middle-class domesticity for raped women, as well as the bonds fostered on a shared basis of suffering.

"Shei Chheleta"

Jyotirmoyee Devi's short story *"Shei Chheleta"* is set in mid-1950s Delhi, though its plot is structured around the communal violence preceding Partition in Lahore during 1946/1947. When the little girl Raj (or Rajkumari) and her family evacuate from Lahore during the riots under police protection, her mother is accidentally left behind. On arrival at Khasa near Amritsar – a "safe" place with Hindus and Sikhs in the majority – the family conducts a desperate but futile search for the missing woman. Eventually, they assume, from reports of suicides, arson, and communal violence, that the deserted woman was killed in the riots. That is, they conclude – notwithstanding reports of abduction and/or rape – that she died "honorably." Several years later, returning from work one evening, Raj – now living in the refugee colonies in Delhi – meets a beggar on the Delhi streets. The beggar is Raj's mother, and she is accompanied by an unfamiliar little boy – the "wrong" child. She approaches Raj and her friends Baruna and Sujata for alms. Her mother recognizes her, but Raj – the "correctly" born daughter – at first bewildered at the beggar's cross-questioning, later shrinks from the embarrassed realization that her mother – who she had told her friends was dead – had been raped in the communal violence. Withholding recognition, Raj returns home, but the memory of the Lahore riots haunts her, together with her recent vision of her abandoned, destitute mother. The presence of the little boy, however, makes it difficult for her to accept the truth, and Raj decides to confront the beggar woman the following day to clarify her suspicions. But for all her searches (and later Baruna's too) in the beggar haunts of Delhi over the next several weeks, the mother and child are not found.

Whether it is suicide or murder, the only contingency imaginatively viable for Raj's family is the abandoned woman's death, implementing a deliberate closure of the other "less respectable" and sinister possibility: her abduction and rape. While the memory of a mother, whom for several years Raj considered dead, mists her eyes, the moment of the meeting with her, when comprehension of the beggar woman's identity dawns on her, is saturated with anxiety and shame. The prospect of her mother's alternative life is far too deviant for Raj, and the fact that she is alive causes more uneasiness than the previous assumption of her death. Raj is caught in an emotional impasse: while she realizes the beggar woman's place in her life, she also desperately wants to believe that she is mistaken. Perhaps her mother's retreat may be read as "shame," as an effect of the internalization of Hindu patriarchal nationalist norms.

The conscious omission of the mother's name is intriguing: the narrator refers to her as "Raj's mother," her mother-in-law uses "Badi Bibi," meaning eldest daughter-in-law, "Bibi" is used in the Punjab, to address women; her husband calls her "Bibi"; and her brothers-in-law and their wives call her "Bibiji" ("ji" is an honorific). In addition to the routine Indian practice of identifying women by the names of their children – "Raj's mother" – this anonymity may be explained as the customary use of relational forms of address that are used to embed women in the familial to the extent that there is almost a refusal to acknowledge their individuality. In addition, the deliberate oversight may allude to Raj's mother's condition as nondescript, so that by remaining nameless she could be any among the abundant casualties of the sexual and reproductive violence associated with Partition. I add that with the exception of the three young women – Raj and her friends Baruna and Sujata – everyone else is referred to by their relationship to Raj.

Jyotirmoyee Devi's narrative technique – the use of short, crisp sentences, mostly unsentimental prose except in the third section where she recounts the

family's retreat from Lahore, frugal descriptions, short paragraphs and, hence, frequent breaks – intensifies the feel of the sad, broken lives which she narrates.

> [Raj] lay wide awake. The vision of the beggar woman returned to her – clad in a dirty salwaar kammez with a ripped chunni covering her head, a face pleading and weary, holding by the hand a boy, small and skinny like a beggar. How long had she been begging?...
>
> She felt she should say something about it to her father, or to her uncles. But what if they ask why she hadn't mentioned it before? What would she say? That she had not been able to recognize her properly! Or, ... or what?
>
> She remembered the little boy. What could she have said about him? Whose child was he? Mother's? Could Mother have come? Then why did she hide?
>
> Perhaps the woman was not her mother after all?... Yes, that was a possibility. A feeling of relief surged through her. The disquiet was fading. But from the deepest reaches of her mind, a thin dark, beggar woman with sad eyes, ill-clad, holding the hand of a small boy, gazed steadily at her, near the bushes of Queen's Park.
>
> Her mother. And that little boy who wasn't her brother.
>
> (Jyotirmoyee Devi 2002, 144–145)

The mother's repudiation by the family, embodied in Raj's intentional non-recognition, is combined with tacit encouragement from the community, in the figure of Raj's friend Baruna. Baruna trusts Raj's story insofar as the beggar woman they had met was her mother; she commiserates with Raj's loss; but when the discussion shifts to the child, she, like Raj, recoils from capitulating to the existence of another sexual life for a Mother. When the child's paternity becomes suspect, her initial compassion – "Why didn't you say so right away? You could have taken her home" (Jyotirmoyee Devi 2002, 144) – is replaced, not by a cautionary qualification but by an outright denial: "Maybe you were not able to recognize her properly, Raj. That was not your mother." Baruna's silences, together with her definitive dismissals of the possibility, almost force the victimized mother into a "discreet disappearance" (Rajan 1999, 70), since, for the survival of the community's myth of its own purity, it becomes almost imperative to isolate, or negate, the raped woman. A Hindu woman's intimacy with a Muslim man would constitute a transgression on the grounds of violation of the codes of conduct as well as a political betrayal of the nation, since it was along lines of religious faith – and the perceived impossibility of a harmonious coexistence – that a demand for a separate homeland for Muslims (Pakistan) was first raised and eventually led to partitioning the subcontinent.

The anxiety over the "wrong" children was not restricted to the families, but as studies by Menon, Bhasin, Butalia, and Das illustrate, debates were held in political circles to settle the perplexing issue of the citizenship of these children. In addition, cognizant of the social odium which women with children born from the attacks were likely to encounter, the state not only sponsored orphanages for abandoned children, but also organized clandestine mass abortions (abortion was otherwise illegal in India until 1971). It is thus important to note that, while Raj's mother must have been certain of the social contempt she would endure and perhaps had the option of terminating her pregnancy or abandoning the infant, nevertheless, she exercises her discretion in keeping him with her. In doing so, she bargains her motherhood at the cost of jeopardizing her domestic security. While the child's presence as proof of the mother's sexuality outside of marriage shatters cultural templates dictating a virtuous womanhood (funda-mental to which, as noted earlier, are monogamy and chastity) and makes impossible her re-absorption into her former family/community, the child is itself abiding proof of the failed manhood of one community. The child fathered by the Enemy is testimony to the rivals' virility in gaining control over the com-munity's women, and thus a reminder of the national humiliation.

I concur with Veena Das' contention, in her work on national honor and prac-tical kinship, that "it is the ideology of the nation which insists upon ... purifica-tion" (Das 1995, 80). However, I take issue with her position that, unlike the nation,

> practical kinship ... knew strategies by which to absorb [women and chil-dren] within the family.... [And] in the face of collective disaster the ... community showed a wide variety of strategic practices were available to cushion them from the consequences of this disaster
>
> (Das 1995, 81)

To the contrary, empirical evidence from the work of Butalia, Menon, and Bhasin, as well as my reading of Jyotirmoyee Devi's texts, finds the community and the nation operating in an expedient alliance, so that the purity of the one supplements the purity of the other. The nation not only preserves the interests of the community but also, as Benedict Anderson has pointed out, experiences itself as a community (Anderson 1991). I find it more useful to consider the "[f]amily, community and state ... as the three mediating and interlocking forces determining women's individual and collective destinies."[13] Perhaps some Hindu/Sikh women, as Das' research demonstrates, found acceptance in their original communities. Sometimes it came in exchange for their silence or after abandoning their children in the custody of social workers. However, Das, citing state-sponsored pamphlets that solicited families in an idiom of purity, to accept "reclaimed" members (Das 1995, 80), writes that "[e]ven in 1990, Menon and Bhasin (1993) found women living in camps in some cities of Punjab, either because their families had never claimed them or because they had refused to go back to their families" (Das 1995, 82). Butalia claims that, for many repatriated women,

> [T]he ashrams became permanent homes ... there they lived out their lives, with their memories, some unspeakable, some of which they were able to share with a similar community of women. And there many of them died....

As late as 1997 some women still remained in the ashram in Karnal; until
today there are women in the Gandhi Vanita Ashram in Jalandhar.

(Butalia 2000, 129)

On a different register, and with a different status from facts and raw data, but
furnishing a more textured understanding, literary writings on the horrors of Partition by Lalithambika Antherjanam, Rajinder Singh Bedi, Jyotirmoyee Devi,
and Krishna Sobti also corroborate the claim that a large number of women were
deserted by kin and community on the grounds of their loss of "purity." I will
refer briefly to another nuanced literary moment which suggests the impossibility of a return of the "normal" in structures of intimacy ruptured by the 1947
violence: Rajinder Singh Bedi's Urdu short story "Lajwanti" (Bedi 1995,
179–191).

Although many missing daughters, sisters, and wives "rescued" from Pakistan are abandoned by their natal families and affines, Sunderlal welcomes home
his abducted wife Lajwanti. His acceptance, however, is tempered with irony
because her brief absence has altered the dynamics of their marriage condensed
in the switch from "Lajo," his former nickname for her, to "*Devi*" (goddess).
The remaking of Lajwanti's raped body into the sacred, inviolable body of a
goddess pushes her beyond human contact, and constitutes a denial of her
embodiedness. Transformed into a goddess, Lajwanti is desexualized.[14] While
Sunderlal discursively annuls her sexuality, it remains the terrain of contest with
his absent adversary – the man who abducted her and with whom she lived until
she was brought to India. Sunderlal asks her whether the Other man mistreated
her, and his agitated vow of compassion is prompted, not by remorse for the pain
he had previously inflicted upon her, but rather by an unreal threat that his wife
may actually yearn for her Other life. That he transcends convention and
"pardons" Lajwanti marks out Sunderlal not only as different but also as superior to the rest of his community, and an all-forgiving godhood is something he
arrogates to *himself*. At a subterranean level he suspects that she may express her
satisfaction with the quality of her Other life – and thus shatter *his* reconstruction of their histories in separation; Lajwanti's continued presence in his life is
provisional on the repression of her past. The return of normality in their marriage is not postponed but prevented. Further, Sunderlal's anxiety that Lajwanti
may compare her life unfavourably with him to that with her abductor is rooted
in the contingency that, as Nussbaum suggests earlier, their marriage suffers
from the lack of Lajwanti's genuine consent. While at some level, he struggles
to overcome the intertwining of national identity with his wife's chastity (or lack
thereof), other patriarchal realities nourish his anxiety.

As I discussed above, through the initial accentuation of the chastity of Hindu
women as a marker of the superiority of Hindu culture, together with the later
expulsions of women in contact with the Other, the woman's body functioned as
a frontier safeguarding the nation and the community's collaborative interests. In
her study of the role of gender in the consolidation of a Hindu identity, Sangeeta
Ray also notes the scripting of difference on the body of woman by way of

embedding it in a set of regulated social and cultural practices that purport to maintain a historical continuity with the past, which the Other presumably lacks:

> The raped female body encompasses the sexual economy of desire that is denied the mythologization of the purity of one's own ethnic, religious, and national gendered subject. The inevitability of rape leaves women with the "choice" of committing suicide so that she can be accommodated within the narrative of the nation as a legitimate and pure, albeit dead, citizen. Those who survive rape are refused entry into the domestic space of the new nation.... The purity of the family mirrors the purity of the nation, and the raped woman cannot be the vehicle of the familial metaphor that enables the narration of the nation.
>
> (Ray 2000, 135–136)

Epar Ganga Opar Ganga

Ray's remark is useful in reading Jyotirmoyee Devi's later novel *Epar Ganga Opar Ganga* and, despite the anger that suffuses the work in consequence of the new national citizenry's dealings with women – including those without visible signs of violation – her optimistic aesthetic intervention opens up a textual possibility for resituating these women into the heart of middle-class domesticity.

I refer here to an excerpt from a lecture on gender injustice by former Finance Minister Professor Madhu Dandavate in which he mentioned an incident brought to his attention by Sucheta Kripalani, former Chief Minister of Uttar Pradesh. I cite the incident not because it offers a factual instance of the disenfranchisement women encountered, but more importantly, the incident may have been an inspiration for Jyotirmoyee Devi's novel. Instantiating his claim in the context of women's experiences of Partition that "in a large number of cases, [the abused and/or converted Hindu] women were not welcome in their original families," Dandavate said,

> What happened in Noakhali in Bengal during Gandhiji's peace march in that strife-ridden area is an epic to be remembered, narrated to me by the late Sucheta Kripalani, who had accompanied Gandhiji in his peace march to Noakhali, which succeeded in restoring peace there. One night Sucheta Kripalani received news that three young girls in Gandhiji's Peace Brigade were likely to be kidnapped. Along with the three young girls, she approached the Muslim landlord next door and requested him to protect the girls as his daughters. The Muslim landlord put his hand on the Koran and took a vow that he would fully protect the three girls. After a few months, peace returned to Noakhali. The members of Gandhiji's Peace Brigade then returned to their respective homes. When the three young girls who were protected by the Muslim landlord returned home, their parents told them, "You have no place in our family, as you had stayed with a Muslim for three months, forgetting that you were Hindus." "What shall we do?" asked the

girls. The parents reply was "Go onto the streets and, if need be, become prostitutes, but our doors are closed for you." Disowned by their parents, the girls took shelter in Gandhi's Ashram. They were never married and later on died unsung and unwept. This only reveals the grim story of women who had to suffer only because of the communal prejudices of a tradition-bound society.

(Dandavate 2002)

There are striking parallels between this incident and the plot of Jyotirmoyee Devi's novel, and the possibility that her daughter, Ashoka Gupta, who volunteered with Kripalani in relief work led by Gandhi in Noakhali helping abused women, mentioned the incident to her cannot be ruled out.

The novel *Epar Ganga Opar Ganga* opens with Sutara Datta, an Assistant Professor of History in a women's college, pondering over the question of omitted histories of suffering. She turns to her personal history of pain during the Noakhali riots in the autumn of 1946 and the continuing disgrace over subsequent years, and her story is then presented in a flashback. The narrative unfolds in the background of a blaze of communal violence, arson, murder, and rape in the Noakhali and Comilla districts of east Bengal subsequent to the Great Calcutta Killing in August 1946. Sutara Datta, then an adolescent, loses her parents in the communal fury: her father is murdered, her mother attempts suicide (and is eventually untraceable), and her sister Sujata is abducted. Sutara herself loses consciousness in the course of an attack. She is rescued by Tamizuddin – a Muslim family friend and neighbor to the Dattas – and his sons. Convalescing in their care for six months, she is eager to be reunited with her surviving family members (i.e., her three brothers and a sister-in-law), whereupon Tamizuddin and his sons escort her to the "safety" of Calcutta. In Calcutta, she joins her brothers and sister-in-law Bibha at the home of Bibha's parents where they have taken refuge to escape the violence of the riots. The elderly women of the household, Bibha's mother and aunts, disapprove of Sutara's presence in the family – because she spent six months living among Muslims and so is "polluted" – and hasten her further displacement. Shunned by family and the community, Sutara is sent to a Christian boarding school for women, a non-Hindu space where the student body is primarily constituted of lower castes or low-caste converts and women in situations similar to hers. She is especially unwanted at social events and Bibha's mother's routine snubs reach a peak on Bibha's sister Subha's wedding day when Sutara is fed separately and hurriedly sent home to protect other guests from her "polluting" touch. (And years later, at the suggestion of her mother, Bibha deliberately delays inviting Sutara so as to prevent her from attending Bibha's daughter Reba's wedding.)

Through the many years, Sutara's brothers either witness her humiliation mutely or pretend it did not happen (Bibha's father AmulyaBabu, brother Pramode, and sister Subha protest occasionally). In the meantime, Sutara completes her studies and finds employment teaching history at a women's college at Delhi, realizing painfully that she will never have a "home," not only because

she has no place in her brothers' affections but also because her marriage prospects are bleak (she is "polluted"). Her correspondence and occasional meetings
with her Muslim neighbors from the village, all of whom continue to cherish her
– especially Tamizuddin's wife and daughter Sakina – come to an abrupt end
when Tamizuddin's wife suggests a matrimonial alliance between her elder son
Aziz and Sutara. In Calcutta, Bibha's brother Pramode expresses his resolve to
wed Sutara, infuriating his mother, who has already arranged a match for him.
Nevertheless, Pramode goes to Delhi and proposes marriage to Sutara. The novel
ends with her bewildered acceptance.

The novel is structured in four parts; the last three, the "*Adi Parva*" (The
Book of Origins), the "*Anusashana Parva*" (The Book of the New Instructions),
and the "*Stree Parva*" (The Book of Women), derive their names from books of
the *Mahabharata*; the first short section is titled "Sutara Datta." The second,
third, and fourth sections plot Sutara's repeated dislocations; hence, the locale
for the second is a village in Noakhali, the third Calcutta, and the fourth Delhi.
Further, towards the end of the fourth section, the author hints at a future possibility of Sutara's passage to England with Pramode. Within these larger changes
of location there are smaller displacements too: Sutara is transferred from her
original home to that of her neighbors' at Noakhali; from the residence of her
extended family to the boarding school at Calcutta. Small or large, each of the
transitions also bears a permanent character; in other words, Sutara never returns
to the original site, whether it is her parents' home, her Muslim neighbors in
Noakhali, or to her brothers and extended family in Calcutta. Her perpetual
movements advance the feeling of homelessness, and each site becomes a new
place of exile. (Significantly, it is among the women refugees from West Punjab,
residing at Delhi, that Sutara, for the first time, feels the bond of community, of
being part of a shared history of violence.) As with Raj's mother in the short
story discussed above, gendered migrancy constitutes a central trope in the
novel.

The attack on Sutara, followed by her prolonged contact with the Muslim
family who sheltered her, brands her as "impure," "polluted," an Other in her
"native" community, whose material practices in the performance of daily life
are troubled by her presence. Her integration in her original community is almost
impossible because her body carries an alternative history, the imprint of another
set of practices that constitute another everyday life. The details of her life are
rendered meaningless for others, and the course of future events, the multiple
instances of psychological harassment, is determined by the single incident of
bodily violence. In stating a claim for exemplarity, Jyotirmoyee Devi furnishes a
bounty of details, but she suggests simultaneously that the details are inconsequential: Sutara, like Raj's mother, could have had a particular kind of life, she
could have had a particular kind of dignity, or she could have had no dignity, but
the moment she is sexually assaulted she becomes a non-person, the details of
whose life and personhood translate only into so many petty minutiae. The event
of violation assumes the rank of the definitive moment of Sutara's life. It determines the plot, so that the novel itself enacts the simplification of the character

socially. Sutara becomes paralyzed in deciding its conditions, in determining the status of the detail in her own life. Like Bhuvaneswari Bhaduri in Gayatri Chakravorty Spivak's essay "Can the Subaltern Speak?" (Spivak 1988, 271–313), the woman's (Sutara/Raj's mother) only practicable mode for signification is through the negation of a negation. However, eventually neither Raj's mother nor Sutara may be defined by the sexual violence they encounter.

Sutara's alterity is insupportable in the upper-caste Hindu family that had been made secure from all contact with the outside world through discourses of cultural nationalism insisting on Hindu domesticity as the sanctuary for launching (and sculpting) a Hindu national identity. It is difference that constitutes community identity – different religion, different set of customs, different foods – so that communities, like nations, "are forever haunted by their definitional others" (Parker *et al*. 1992, 5), and Sutara's position at the periphery of two rival communities makes her loyalties suspect. Thus, Jyotirmoyee Devi situates Sutara within the "woman-as-nation" paradigm, but in her writings the fallen woman is the symbolic representation of the nation. It is interesting to note that women's citizenship is contingent not only upon residence in the right country and following the right religious faith, but also upon their possessing the right (inviolate) body. In the domain of the elite home, the definitive factor for belonging was unsullied virtue.

The gender dynamics in the novel do not operate on the basis of an antagonism between men and women. Rather, excepting the gendered character of the violence during the night of the riot, the novel highlights the role of women not as "victims" of a patriarchal culture but as active in policing one another and reproducing repressive masculinity (and femininity) against women. While Jyotirmoyee Devi deems the fetish of women's bodily purity to be the cardinal cause of Sutara's miseries, she also indicates that its perpetuation was guaranteed by women who, as Nira Yuval-Davis and Floya Anthias caution, "actively participate in the process of reproducing and modifying their roles as well as being actively involved in controlling other women" (Yuval-Davis and Anthias 1989, 11).

As preservers of domestic sanctity, women were authorized to make crucial decisions in assessing other women's rectitude. In *Epar Ganga Opar Ganga*, Bibha's mother and aunts endorse the continuity of patriarchy and veto Sutara's existence because of her contact with the forbidden that disrupted her caste and religious practices. Bibha's mother monitors, with a reproving vigilance, the social and intimate contacts among family members. She orchestrates Sutara's alienation both from her brothers and from the extended family, in the name of safeguarding the future for Bibha's daughters. When Bibha's mother's efforts to isolate Sutara are defeated by her idealist son Pramode's decision to marry her, she reproaches Bibha for restoring her orphaned sister-in-law (Sutara) to her extended family in Calcutta:

> After a long silence, [Bibha's mother] turned to Bibha, "I told you repeatedly not to bring that girl [Sutara] here. Don't. Don't get her. But you persisted! You let her stay here. Good for you! Saved your face from

people's comments. A fine thing you did ruining my family; dug a canal and courted a crocodile into my backyard.... What was the point in fetching her anyway, she who had lived with those unclean non-believers [Muslims]? Whatever happened was her misfortune. She should have stayed back. There are countless women like her in that country [Pakistan]. You think she retained her religion-caste purity living with them for such a long time? Who knows what she ate! And then, what had happened? That about which no one knows. She certainly could not have remained a Hindu living with Muslims!" Anger, disappointment, and revulsion swept through [Bibha's mother] and she burst into tears.

(Jyotirmoyee Devi 1991, 243–244)

Bibha's mother, perhaps the most vocal of all, is by no means the only character in the novel to voice such sentiments. However, it is her acknowledgment of the possibility of marriage, even in its denial, that is radical. Sutara's stay with an "impure" (*mlechchha*) Muslim family realizes the worst fears of "pollution" in the upper-caste Hindu household. Her body seems to undergo a process of losing her original caste and, as a result, she is treated as a low-caste "untouchable." As the term "untouchable" suggests, she cannot inhabit the same space as the other members of the family. At the wedding of Bibha's sister Subha, elderly women who have no clue as to the exact nature of the events during the night of the attack make suggestive comments about her past, and a well-wisher warns the family that guests, especially the women, will probably refrain from participating in the wedding dinner for fear of the contagion of Sutara's contaminating presence. It is only after Sutara escapes the supervision exercised by the patriarchal family and community and migrates to a new space of economic independence that it is possible for her to establish some genuine social solidarity – a sisterhood with refugee women from West Punjab.

Jyotirmoyee Devi illustrates the modalities of women's participation in social processes "as reproducers of the boundaries of ethnic/national groups; as participating centrally in the ideological reproduction of the collectivity and as transmitters of its culture; as signifiers of national differences" (Yuval-Davis and Anthias 1989, 7). Thus, the women ensure the continuation of the ideology of purity developed in the name of an abstract national good. The question that begs itself here is that, while the national patriarchy has a stake in controlling women's sexuality ranging from material questions of property to more abstract ideas of national/community purity, why do women participate in segregating other oppressed members of their own sex? The answer lies, not in false consciousness, but perhaps in that (chaste) elite women benefited from these dissociative practices in the form of privileges which patriarchy offered. They received, for instance, a greater access to the public sphere, in exchange for endorsement of the patriarchy's views; they were even considered ethically superior, to say nothing of the experience of their empowerment.

While she is unwelcome in her native community, Sutara cannot enter into a meaningful relationship with her Muslim neighbors through marriage despite the kindness and sustenance she receives from them, because engaging with Muslims would be seen to be a betrayal of her parents' deaths, her sister's abduction, and her personal experience of violence. Jyotirmoyee Devi's presentation of Sutara's decision as a problem of love itself seems psychologically true, although official documents and feminist studies on the subject have illustrated that abducted women often married the men responsible for their abduction, bore children, and with time grew attached to their past abductors. So, why was a marriage proposal from Tamizuddin's family unthinkable for Sutara? It is important to acknowledge that marriage between the abductor and abductee was made possible, at least in many cases, because the woman was totally disempowered and at the abductor's mercy, whereas Sutara's situation in Delhi, when the marriage proposal arrives, is different. It is difficult to predict if Sutara would have been able to resist if Tamizuddin's family had abducted her or coerced her into marriage with Aziz while she was younger and living with them soon after the disaster, but years later in Delhi, educated and financially independent, her circumstances can no longer be compared with the helplessness of abducted women. Sadly, Sutara's response to the marriage proposal from Tamizuddin's family holds them guilty by association; she treats them not as individuals who sheltered her, even enduring threats from their community, but rather as part of the community that devastated her life. For her, correspondence and meetings with old Muslim friends were fine, but not the emotional commitment of marriage.

Jyotirmoyee Devi subtly reinforces the implication of Sutara's violation through such incidents as Sutara's quarantine on the night of Subha's wedding. She also alludes to Mary Magdalene, Lucretia, Amba, Draupadi, and Sita. However, it is crucial to note that in both – the short story and the novel – the event of the assault that ruptures the women's "good" past lives from the "tainted" presents and futures is not central to the narrative; and in the case of the novel it is even left slightly ambiguous.

> Didi [elder sister, Sujata] suddenly let out a sharp, shrill scream, "Ma, Ma, Mother, oh! Baba," and keeled over and fell to the ground.
>
> Their mother, unlocking the door to the cowshed, was shocked. Then she said, "I'll be there right away, dear."
>
> But Mother could not reach them [Sujata and Sutara]. Shadows had engulfed her. They were trying to seize her hand. But Mother freed herself and ran to the pond behind the house and leaped into it.
>
> The fire had set the whole area ablaze. One of the men tried to stop her, another said, "Don't bother. Let her go, that's the mother. Leave her." Didi was nowhere, had she died?
>
> What's the matter with Didi? Sutara did not see her again. She wanted to run to where Mother was, but her feet were caught in something and she stumbled.
>
> And then?
>
> (Jyotirmoyee Devi 1991, 135–136)

This sparse description retains a feel of the sinister and elicits the horror of the events, despite the somewhat euphemistic quality of Jyotirmoyee Devi's prose. Beyond this arrested narration and another mention that "Psychologically and physically Sutara was devastated" (Jyotirmoyee Devi 1991, 137), the trauma of the sexual assault resurfaces largely as a confused, nebulous memory, with scattered references to her torn and dirty clothes, her friends' suicides, drownings, and abductions. It is referred to again in Bibha's mother's words: "And then, what had happened [on the night of the attack]? That about which no one knows." Both in the short story and the novel, the staging of sexual violence remains beyond the narrated (and the narratable?). What the novelist represents are the after-effects of that trauma.

It is best, I believe, not to read/dismiss Jyotirmoyee Devi's syncopated, circumlocutive writing as reticence or as residual prudery of a post-Victorian novelist, because the use of the Bengali equivalent for "rape" is not rare in her writings, especially in her essays. Rather, the veiling of bodily trauma through language constitutes a counter-discourse to the economy of display of women. Her prose recovers something of the private pain that women suffered. In addition, her seeming reluctance to engage further with the issue of violation is not to devalue the sexual terrorization of women (she discerns the threat of sexual assault as a primary form of control over women's bodies) but, rather, not to compromise the unmitigated intensity on women's rejections in their after-lives in the community. (Or, is it possible that because Sutara was destined to re-enter the space of elite domesticity, Jyotirmoyee Devi chose to maintain its "sanctity"? And was her allegiance to that space responsible for withholding details of the attack on Sutara's body? Or, was it anxiety about her readership? Any of these contentions would diminish the potentials of her indisputably radical critique of patriarchy and, I believe, are less valid, since she was a fairly established writer at the time the novel was published.)

The initial withering away of Sutara's matrimonial possibilities, based on the single event of sexual abuse, which Bibha's mother euphemistically refers to as "other problems," illustrates how sexual violence, in a twisted way, involves a process of removing the body from circulation within the libidinal economy. Sutara is no longer allowed to desire; in fact, she is not even allowed much social agency. It is significant that between her restoration to her extended family in Calcutta and her finding employment in Delhi, she has little textual presence by way of speech. Although her condition constitutes the problematic, and she is constantly acted upon, she rarely speaks. I understand her silence not as resistance but as a metaphor for her loss of social agency through the "*theft of the body*" (italics in original) (Spillers 1987, 65–81, 87). Sutara's silence is socially structured and policed by the family: her brothers' paucity of interaction with her; by the community: her presence is unwelcome at social events; and by the state: the prohibition on biographical exchanges among students at the residential school she attends. In reinserting Sutara back into the script of middle-class domestic sexual economy, the novelist re-genders her by way of establishing a claim for a different destiny for gender, and eventually makes the details of people's lives matter once again.

Unlike Veena Das' suggestion that marriage was a strategic practice of the community through which some repatriated women were rendered invisible through absorption within the family (Das 2002, 55–83), I read Pramode's wedding proposal to Sutara neither as a community game plan nor as a fairy-tale ending, but rather as an individual act of will. Pramode and Subha, Bibha's brother and sister, witness Sutara's repeated disgrace and disenfranchisement within their family. The high points in this continuum of harassment are the quarantine on the night of Subha's wedding; the overheard gossip between their aunts insisting on Sutara's being left with the Muslims; and the deliberately delayed invitation she is sent in order to prevent her from attending her niece's wedding. (While Sutara's reinsertion within middle-class respectability might signal a compromise to the love interest – of which there is not much in the novel – Pramode's proposal is not inconsistent with character development. Both he and Subha are sensitive, even apologetic, throughout the novel, to Sutara's distress induced by the seniors in the family.) Beyond simply constituting a "happy ending" at the level of the plot, Pramode's proposal has a sharp feel of a conscious – if slightly patronizing – act of goodwill by a responsible citizen: "Very gently, Pramode asked, 'You won't say no, will you? We, Subha and I, talk about you often. We liked you a lot. Can't tell whether it's love, but we were pained by your plight. Could you try and like us?'" (Jyotirmoyee Devi 1991, 249). Perhaps not the first admission of her distress by her kinsfolk (Pramode's father, AmulyaBabu, is pained by her condition earlier on), it is nevertheless the first proactive step taken to reintegrate Sutara within the Hindu fold. Although this "restoration" within the community remains incomplete since Pramode's impending departure for England off-centers him to some degree, it nonetheless contains a possibility, if slightly contrived, of transcending community disdain through individual arbitrations.

Re-contextualizing Sutara within bourgeois domesticity, Jyotirmoyee Devi immediately undermines the happy ending by returning to themes of the solitude of socially excluded women (hinting also at their non-reproductivity):

> [Sutara] switched off the lights in her room. Stars sparkled in the dark *Chaitra* [March–April] sky. At the edges of the garden [surrounding the women's dormitory] a few Eucalyptus trees stood straight and tall, apart and lonely. Like the residents of the [women's] hostel. Solitary trees lacking shrubbery, fruits and flowers, branches and twigs. Cyclones would bend but couldn't break them.
>
> (Jyotirmoyee Devi 1991, 253)

Separated from middle-class domestic life, Sutara with her colleagues and friends working in the college and residing in the dormitory constitute a community, a women's community that disregards regional differences and sustains a group-therapeutic function through a mutual support system. From a lukewarm suggestion of women's solidarity in miniature in "*Shei Chheleta*," signaled by Raj's relief after sharing with her friend Baruna "[w]hat she had never disclosed to her near and dear ones, not even to her father, what she had concealed from her uncles, brothers, and sisters" (Jyotirmoyee Devi 1994, 143), the author develops and fine-tunes the idea in her novel. Writing in the 1960s, her recognition of the potential of feminist solidarity is exceptional, although by ultimately distancing Sutara from the collective at the women's hostel Jyotirmoyee Devi declines to advance a radical alternative to the family. In addition, while Sutara's entry into middle-class respectability marks a definitive break from the fixation with purity and routine rejections, it also weakens the possibilities of a life as a single, independent woman. The ending of the novel raises several questions: Does Sutara's reinstatement within the domestic space with its demands for women's chastity suggest potentials for its reorganization? Or, on the other hand, is the act in itself a subordination of the women's struggle to the struggle for the nation? Can it be because the nation still requires this construction to shore up its integrity?

Conclusion

An interviewee, cites Urvashi Butalia, unable to find a rationale for the orgy of brutality in which he had participated during the Partition riots, described it as temporary insanity: "[O]ne day our entire village took off to a nearby Muslim village on a killing spree. We simply went mad" (Butalia 2000, 56).

I contend that the rejections of women, on the other hand, cannot be explained using the language of insanity and catastrophe, or as an unleashing of the vulgar self. Rather, the rejections of abducted Hindu/Sikh women were motivated and even ideologically rationalized by a long and complicated history of the nationalist and patriarchal fetish on women's sexuality. Hence, I suggest the need to situate the abandonments as telos of the political, cultural, and legal debates around elite (Hindu) women's issues from the nineteenth and early twentieth centuries. A revisiting of the past, I insist, tracks the violence involved in the translation from the discursive to the visceral. Using Jyotirmoyee Devi's writings, I indicate that they offer possibilities for reconsidering the exclusive nature of community membership, the discursive violence sanctioned in the name of tradition, the recuperation of expelled bodies, and gendered citizenship as well as the exigency for women's histories not subsumed under grand titles of national history. In writing about women's oppression – the language for which, as she states in the Preface of her novel, has not yet been developed – Jyotirmoyee Devi exposes the silence surrounding uncomfortable social issues. In populating her works with women who refuse to annul the self by suicide subsequent to the event of rape, and who instead choose to survive, her woman-centered narratives differ from the dominant narrative which recommends that women choose death to dishonor. I conclude by citing a factual instance of intolerance towards raped women expressed by a major proponent of non-violence: Gandhi. Mahatma Gandhi not only advised women subjected to sexual violence in Noakhali in 1946 to consume poison, but in 1947 during the Partition riots he went further, exalting suicide, even murder, as deterrents to rape. In his speech at a prayer meeting on September 18, 1947, Gandhi responded to the news of devastating populist measures adopted in the face of communal violence in this way:

> I have heard that many women who did not want to lose their honor chose to die. Many men killed their own wives. I think that is really great, because I know that such things make India brave. After all, life and death is a transitory game.... [The women] have gone with courage. They have not sold away their honor. Not that their life was not dear to them, but they felt it was better to die than to be forcibly converted to Islam by the Muslims and allow them to assault their bodies. And so those women died. They were not just a handful, but quite a few. When I hear all these things I dance with joy that there are such brave women in India.
>
> (Gandhi 1994, 388–389)

Less than three months later, in early December 1947, Gandhi, attempting to reintegrate abducted Hindu and Sikh women within their families and communities (to prevent them from becoming wards of the state), would alter his views radically and – as cited at the beginning of this chapter – appeal to the public to accept, even respect, them.

Notes

1 This is a lightly edited version of my article published in *Comparative Studies of South Asia, Africa and the Middle East* 24:1, 2004, 35–50. © 2004 Duke University Press. All rights reserved. Reprinted by permission of Duke University Press. The paper was written under the auspices of a Doctoral Fellowship (International) from the American Association of University Women Educational Foundation. I thank Sibaji Bandyopadhyay, Lauren Berlant, Carol Breckenridge, Ann Kibbey, Spencer Leonard, Martha Nussbaum, Kumkum Sangari, Clinton Seely, Holly Shissler, and the workshop participants at the University of Chicago's Center for Gender Studies for their careful readings and comments.

2 For a detailed study of Gandhi's responses towards women subjected to violence during the communal riots around Partition, see Debali Mookerjea, "The Missing Chapter: Rewriting Partition History," Paper presented at the Third South Asian Women's Conference, University of California at Los Angeles and California State University at Northridge, Los Angeles, May 2000.

3   I am told that there is an unwillingness on the part of their relatives to accept those girls and women (who have been abducted) back in their homes. This is a most objectionable and wrong attitude to take and any social custom that supports this attitude must be condemned. These girls and women require our tender and loving care and their relatives should be proud to take them back and give them every help.

Jawaharlal Nehru, *Hindustan Times*, January 17, 1948
(Menon and Bhasin 1998, 99)

4 Menon, Ritu, and Kamla Bhasin, *Borders and Boundaries*; Menon and Bhasin, "Recovery, Rupture, Resistance: Indian State and the Abduction of Women during Partition," *Economic and Political Weekly* (April 24, 1993): WS 2–11; Urvashi

Butalia, "Community, State and Gender: On Women's Agency during Partition," *Economic and Political Weekly* (April 24, 1993): WS 12–24; and The Other Side of Silence: Voices from the Partition of India (Delhi: Viking, 1998); Veena Das, "National Honour and Practical Kinship," in Das, *Critical Events* (Delhi: Oxford University Press, 1995), 55–83.

5 "Devi" is not the author's last name. It reflects a Hindu–Bengali social convention of referring to upper-caste women as "Devi" meaning "goddess." Although the practice is now outdated, women writers from the past few generations, most of whom were from the upper castes, are habitually referred to using "Devi": "Swarnakumari Devi," "Anurupa Devi," "Ashapurna Devi," "Mahasweta Devi," etc. Since "Devi" fails to actually distinguish between writers, I use "Jyotirmoyee Devi" throughout this chapter.

6 *Seminar* (510) and the first volume of *The Trauma and the Triumph* have been devoted to the study of the impact of Partition in the East. *Seminar* 510 (2002); *The Trauma and the Triumph: Gender and Partition in Eastern India*, ed. Jashodhara Bagchi and Subhoranjan Dasgupta (Calcutta: Stree, 2003). By way of explaining the paucity of literary and historical writings from the erstwhile East Pakistan, Shelley Feldman suggests that the Partition of Bengal in 1947 was overshadowed by the contestation over Bengali cultural identity culminating in the Language Movement and followed by the demand for regional autonomy leading eventually to the liberation struggle in 1971. Shelley Feldman, "Feminist Interruptions: The Silence of East Bengal in the Story of Partition," *Interventions* 1:2 (1999), 167–182.

7 See Sibaji Bandyopadhyay, "Producing and Re-producing the New Women," *Social Scientist*, 22:1–2 (January–February 1994), 19–39; Sumanta Banerjee, *The Parlour and the Street* (Calcutta: Seagull, 1989); Uma Chakravarti, "Whatever Happened to the Vedic Dasi? Orientalism, Nationalism and a Script for the Past," in *Recasting Women: Essays in Colonial History*, ed. Kumkum Sangari and Sudesh Vaid (New Brunswick, NJ: Rutgers University Press, 1989), 27–87; Partha Chatterjee, *The Nation and its Fragments: Colonial and Postcolonial History* (Princeton, NJ: Princeton University Press, 1993); Tanika Sarkar, *Hindu Wife, Hindu Nation: Community Religion and Cultural Nationalism* (New Delhi: Permanent Black, 2001).

8 Jyotirmoyee Devi, *"Shei Chheleta,"* first published in 1961 in *Prabasi* (*Prabasi, Bhadra* 1368 BS) reprinted in *Jyotirmoyee Debir Racana-Sankalan*, vol. 2, ed. Gourkishore Ghosh (Calcutta: Dey's Publishing and School of Women's Studies, Jadavpur University, 1994). All translations from the short story are mine. Debali Mookerjea, "That Little Boy: An English Translation of Jyotirmoyee Devi's Bengali Short Story '*Shei Chheleta,*'" *Meridians* 2:2 (2002), 128–145. All page numbers are from this text.

9 Jyotirmoyee Devi, *Epar Ganga Opar Ganga*, in *Jyotirmoyee Debir Racana-Sankalan*, vol. 1, ed. Subir Roy Chowdhury and Abhijit Sen (Calcutta: Dey's Publishing and School of Women's Studies, Jadavpur University, 1991). All page numbers are from this text. Initially titled *Itihashe Stree Parva*, this novel was first published in the autumnal issue of the journal *Probashi* in 1966; it was published in book form under its present name in 1968 ("My Words," 127). The novel has been translated into English as *The River Churning* by Enakshi Chatterjee and published by Kali for Women, 1995. However, in my work I have used my own translations.

10 Set in West Punjab, Shauna Singh Baldwin's Partition novel *What the Body Remembers* (1999) uses a similar technique to project the plight of the two communities affected by communal violence and Partition (Baldwin 1999).

11 "Veena Das," Bose and Jalal claim,

> has suggested how the Indian state may have impinged on the exercise of choice by raped and abducted women by creating a legal category of "abducted women" for the purposes of its repatriation programme. While taking a strong and entirely

laudable position against the many instances of violence by the post-colonial state, she is curiously silent about the negation of consent and choice at the traumatic, violent moment of abduction and rape. By dramatizing, if not romanticizing, examples of murderers and rapists turned into besotted husbands of their former victims (such as a big, bearded Sikh weeping copiously at the border checkpoint), she presents a more benign picture of acceptance of raped women by families, and of kinship communities of victims and perpetrators alike, than is warranted by the historical evidence or the cultural context.

(Bose and Jalal 1997, 198–199)

12 Personal communication with Martha Nussbaum.
13 Menon and Bhasin, *Borders and Boundaries*, 255. Also manifest in the polemics around purity is a split between the objectives of the political state – repatriation of its citizens to the "right" country, regardless of their preferences no doubt, but more importantly of their violated condition – with that of the nation/community ensuring its purity via the chaste bodies of the women. Nira Yuval-Davis and Pnina Werbner speak theoretically of a "clear disjunction … between the nation, defined narrowly in cultural terms, and the state – the latter being the political community which both governs and grants its members citizenship." Nira Yuval-Davis and Pnina Werbner, "Introduction," in *Women, Citizenship and Difference*, ed. Nira Yuval-Davis and Pnina Werbner (London and New York: Zed Books, 1999), 12.
14 The Punjabi folk-song which the local rehabilitation committee members use to plead for acceptance of rescued women – "Do not touch lajwanti [the touch-me-not plant]/ For she will curl up and die…!" – has thus a resonance with Lajwanti's life.

Bibliography

Anderson, Benedict. *Imagined Communities: The Origin and Spread of Nationalism.* London and New York: Verso, 1991.

Bagchi, Jashidhara and Dasgupta, Subhoranjan. *The Trauma and the Triumph: Gender and Partition in Eastern India.* Kolkata: Stree, 2003.

Baldwin, Shauna Singh. *What the Body Remembers.* New York: Nan A. Talese, 1999.

Bandyopadhyay, Sibaji. "Producing and Re-producing the New Women." *Social Scientist* 22:1–2 (1994), 19–39.

Banerjee, Sumanta. *The Parlour and the Street.* Kolkata: Seagull, 1989.

Bedi, Rajinder Singh. "Lajwanti," in *India Partitioned: The Other Face of Freedom*, edited by Mushirul Hasan, 179–191. Delhi: Oxford University Press, 1995.

Bose, Sugata, and Ayesha Jalal. *Modern South Asia: History, Culture, Political Economy.* Delhi: Oxford University Press, 1997.

Butalia, Urvashi. *The Other Side of Silence: Voices from the Partition of India.* Durham, NC: Duke University Press, 2000.

Chakravarti, Uma. "Whatever Happened to the Vedic Dasi? Orientalism, Nationalism and a Script for the Past," in *Recasting Women: Essays in Colonial History*, edited by Kumkum Sangari and Sudesh Vaid, 27–87. New Brunswick, NJ: Rutgers University Press.

Chatterjee, Partha. *The Nation and its Fragments: Colonial and Postcolonial History.* Princeton, NJ: Princton University Press, 1993.

Dandavate, Madhu. "Social Roots of Gender Justice." *The Modern Rationalist* 27:2 (February 2002).

Das, Veena. *Critical Events: An Anthropological Perspective on Contemporary India.* New Delhi: Oxford University Press, 1995.

——. ed. *Violence and Subjectivity*. Berkeley: University of California Press, 2000.

Feldman, Shelley. "Feminist Interruptions: The Silence of East Bengal in the Story of Partition." *Interventions* 1:2 (1999), 167–182.

Gandhi, Mohandas K. *Collected Works of Mahatma Gandhi*, Vol. 98 (100 vols). Delhi: Publications Division, Ministry of Information and Broadcasting, Government of India, 1994.

——. *Collected Works of Mahatma Gandhi*, Vol. 96 (100 vols). New Delhi: Publications Division, Ministry of Information and Broadcasting, Government of India, 1994.

Jyotirmoyee Devi. *Jyotirmoyee Debir Racana-Sankalan*, edited by Subir Roy Chowdhury and Abhijit Sen, Vol. 1. Kolkata: Dey's Publishing and School of Women's Studies, Jadavpur University, 1991.

——. *Jyotirmoyee Debir Racana-Sankalan*, edited by Gourkishore Ghosh, Vol. 2. Kolkata: Dey's Publishing and School of Women's Studies, 1994.

Menon, Ritu, and Bhasin, Kamla. "Recovery, Rupture, Resistance: Indian State and the Abduction of Women during Partition." *Economic and Political Weekly*, April 1993, WS 2–11.

——. *Borders and Boundaries: Women in India's Partition*. New Brunswick, NJ: Rutgers University Press, 1998.

Mookerjea, Debali. "That Little Boy" *Meridians* 2:2 (2002), 128–145.

——. "Quarantined: Women and the Partition." *Comparative Studies of South Asia, Africa and the Middle East* 24:1 (2004), 33–46.

Naim, C.M. *Ambiguities of Heritage*. Karachi: City Press, 1999.

Parker, Andrew, Russo, Mary, Sommer, Doris, and Yaeger, Patricia. *Nationalisms and Sexualities*. New York: Routledge, 1992.

Rajan, Rajeswari Sundar. *Real and Imagined Women: Gender, Culture and Postcolonialism*. London: Routledge, 1999.

Ray, Sangeeta. *En-Gendering India: Woman and Nation in Colonial and Postcolonial Narratives*. Durham, NC: Duke University Press, 2000.

Sarkar, Tanika. *Hindu Wife, Hindu Nation: Community Religion and Cultural Nationalism*. New Delhi: Permanent Black, 2001.

Spillers, Hortense. "Mama's Baby, Papa's Maybe: An American Grammar Book." *Diacritics* 17:2 (1987), 65–81.

Spivak, Gayatri Chakravorty. "Can the Subaltern Speak?," in *Marxism and the Interpretation of Culture*, edited by Cary Nelson and Lawrence Grossberg, 271–313. Urbana: University of Illinois Press, 1988.

Yuval-Davis, Nira and Anthias, Floya. *Woman-Nation-State*. New York: St. Martin's Press, 1989.

2 The extraordinary and the everyday

Locating violence in women's narratives of the Partition

Shumona Dasgupta

The Partition of the Indian subcontinent into India and Pakistan with formal decolonization in 1947 led to moments of extreme violation and dislocation for many women.[1] This included brutalization by men from the "other" community, murder at the hands of men from within their own clans and families to preserve "honor," and forcible restitution to their "legitimate" families and homes by the newly formed nation-states, eager to sacrifice women's individual rights as citizens to preserve national health and wholeness. Perceived as possessions of men, and symbols of their community's honor, rape of women became a tool for ethnic cleansing and genocide, as well as dishonoring the other community and humiliating rival men. In this chapter I will argue that the coordinates of "Partition violence" should therefore be plotted by contextualizing it within what Menon and Bhasin label a "continuum of violence" against women, rather than encoding the Partition exclusively in terms of an abrupt and ultimately inexplicable historical rupture (Menon and Bhasin 1998, 60). Juxtaposing a vernacular novella written in Punjabi by Amrita Pritam entitled *Pinjar* (which translates variously as "the skeleton" or the "cage," 1950), with Shauna Singh Baldwin's Anglophone text *What the Body Remembers* (1999), demonstrates that while both of these female authored novels inscribe women as active agents of history, both also write women's experience of the Partition as violence.

Recent feminist scholarship on Partition historiography by Urvashi Butalia, Ritu Menon, Kamala Bhasin, and Veena Das has demonstrated that historically, women were some of the worst sufferers of this crisis, with thousands subjected to brutal forms of sexual violence on both sides of the border. Many also committed mass suicides, or were killed by their families in a bid to preserve the "purity" of familial, communal, and religious collectives (Butalia 2000, 90–91). According to Butalia, the estimates range from anywhere between 29,000 to 50,000 Muslim and 15,000 to 35,000 Hindu and Sikh women abducted, raped, and forced to convert. While collective memory constructs the aggressors as outsiders, historically, however, women were sometimes also abducted by men within their own communities who used the opportunity offered by the chaos to abduct and rape them. The violence which women experienced at the hands of the enemy must be juxtaposed with the violence they experienced from their own families and communities. Often fathers, husbands, and brothers killed them to prevent a fate worse than death, or bartered them to negotiate for the safe passage of the rest of the family (Kamra 2002, 140).

State-sponsored violence epitomized by The Inter-Dominion Treaty (1947) and The Abducted Person's Act (1949) was formulated with the explicit aim of recuperating abducted women and sending them back to their "proper" country, often in the face of resistance from the women/victims themselves, especially since they were asked to leave behind the children which had resulted from these forced unions. The Act of 1949 pronounced that after March 1, 1947, any woman cohabiting with a man with different religious affiliations would be regarded as "abducted." All conversions and inter-communal marriages after that date would be de-recognized by the two governments. Reformulated as a question of national honor, the woman/victim's testimonial was to be of no consequence. As Butalia points out, theoretically at the time of the Partition, both India and Pakistan gave their citizens the right to choose their nationality. However, these rights were suspended in the case of abducted women (Butalia 2000, 115–117). Such initiatives for the rescue, reclamation, and rehabilitation of abducted women were used by the fledgling Indian state for consolidating its own legitimacy as well as to constitute a subordinate place for women as both citizens and gendered subjects. According to Das,

> the circulation of the figure of the abducted woman, with its associated imagery of social disorder as sexual disorder, created the conditions of possibility in which the state could be instituted as essentially a social contract between *men* charged with keeping male violence against women in abeyance. Thus the story about abduction and recovery acts as a foundational story that authorizes a particular relation between social contract and sexual contract – the former being a contract between men to institute the political and the latter the agreement to place women within the home under the authority of the husband/father figure…. The origin of the State is then located in the rightful reinstating of proper kinship by recovering women from the other side.
>
> (V. Das 2006, 21, 230)

Many recovered women were rejected by their families anyway and spent the remainder of their lives in state-sponsored Ashrams. It was only after 1954 that India decided that abducted persons were not going to be forcibly brought to their "true" homes (Butalia 2000, 128–130).

Elsewhere, I have argued that the event was written upon the bodies of women in popular novels about Partition primarily by male Indian authors with the figure of the abducted woman operating as a discursive site consolidating Partition in the collective imaginary with "rape" emerging as the master trope.[2] These hegemonic texts attempt to rewrite ethnic conflict in terms of sexual rivalry over the possession of women by Hindu and Muslim men, while consolidating a normative national and ethnic community through a symbolic exchange of women with the figure of the chaste Hindu wife marking the limits of the text.

These novels accord an access to heroism and brief political subjecthood to their female characters only in their choice of death over dishonor, where literally the only "good" woman is a dead woman. In their inability to assimilate the figure of the abducted woman within political and domestic spaces, the death or disappearance of the abducted woman in many such hegemonic Partition novels is symptomatic of the inherent limits of nationalist imaginaries. Such Partition texts also "other" violence, which is always seen as being perpetuated by men from the "other" community, despite historical evidence to the contrary. Such a discursive move naturalizes the violence perpetuated by the institution of the family, one's own community and the State rendering it invisible, constituting, in its turn, a form of discursive violence.

Resisting the normalization of forms of intimate violence enacted against women within the private sphere in what I label "crisis fiction," both Pritam and Baldwin locate women's experience of violence at the intersections of the private/public and the personal/political domains while disrupting the "othering" of violence, and rupturing its teleological positioning in the *aftermath* of the breakdown of social order during Partition. This makes visible the female experience of violence within the sanctified parameters of "home," the family, and the nation, thereby also exposing a critical continuum between the everyday and extraordinary instances of violence against women. Here I draw upon the insights of the anthropologist Pradeep Jegannathan, who explores how "the everyday and the extraordinary practice of violence" are both "culturally constituted," to further de-center the constructed dichotomy between spectacular "eruption" and everyday "restraint," establishing a causal link between everyday violence and extraordinary eruptions during the riot or the mutiny (Jeganathan 2000, 41). Both authors describe the obsessive representation of Partition as the only historical juncture when sexualized forms of violence were perpetrated upon women, choosing to contrast such "officially" recognized violence against "other" forms of violence. While articulating a radical critique of the everyday oppressions of married life, both texts analyze how notions about what constitutes violence emerge within particular social and historical contexts, with violence itself emerging as a category within larger power relations. Home as a socio-symbolic space does not emerge as a nurturing place with inclusive modes of belonging in either text. Informed from the very beginning with a distinct son preference and the concomitant devaluation of daughters and women in general, the space of the "home" undergirds the symbolic and discursive violence which structures the worlds of these texts and enables the physical violence which women eventually experience. "Home" is represented as a prison (*pinjar*) as well as a sphere of death; both literal and metaphorical for women. Often populated with the ill and the insane, sickness and/or silence emerge as the conditions which enable women to inhabit the pathologized space of the "home."

Pinjar, a vernacular novella written in 1950 by the Punjabi author Amrita Pritam, is a radical feminist text which generates a trenchant critique of the positions of women within the institutions of the family and the postcolonial nation. One of the earliest female-authored Partition texts to focus upon the figure of the abducted woman, the novella begins with the abduction and rape of its female protagonist with the rest of the narrative recording her survival and evolution into an active and resistant figure which in itself resists the "crisis of witnessing" in many Partition texts. The body of the abducted woman with its "tainted" sexuality, the problematic site within which the boundaries between religious and ethnic identities are transgressed emerges as the site of resistance in Pritam's text. *Pinjar* underscores the literal and symbolic violence undergirding the female subject's experience of the postcolonial Indian state, and the microcosmic intimate space of the home, ultimately leading to a rejection of particular framings of both the "home" and the "nation." Written almost 50 years after Pritam's novella, Shauna Singh Baldwin's *What the Body Remembers* revisits the mass suicides of Sikh women during the Partition to save the "honor" of the family and community, and juxtaposes these "suicides" with men bragging about having "martyred" their women. Directly tying the gender pathologies which emerged during the Partition with reformations of both masculinity and femininity especially within the Sikh community during the period of high nationalism leading up to the Partition, the novel situates women's experience of violence within a problematic of female consent with female agency and victimhood operating simultaneously in the novel.

I have specifically chosen to focus upon these two authors who are Sikhs, a community uniquely positioned within what Homi Bhabha would label a "third space," neither Hindu nor Muslim, who for the most part threw in their lot with the Hindu community during Partition.[3] My work on these two writers marks a sharp disagreement with the claims of many Partition scholars that women who were marginalized and oppressed during Partition always write resistant texts, their border positioning enabling a "thick description" of history.[4] I also claim that the earlier, vernacular text (1950) offers greater radical possibilities in its critique of both patriarchy and nationalism, empathetically re-imagining an identity that transcends the Hindu/Muslim binary. In contrast, an analysis of the notions of "difference" which structure the later Anglophone text (1999) reveal the technologies of the self which structure modern, Sikh female identity.

Pinjar details the life of a young Hindu girl Pooro, kidnapped, raped, and then "married" to her oppressor.[5] Pritam sets the first half of her story in the pre-Partition era, right before the outbreak of communal violence, while locating the female experience of violence within the sanctified parameters of the "home," the family, and the community.[6] The text etches a backdrop of folk superstitions, rituals, and taboos. The extremely patriarchal setting of the novella is underlined – "Pooro's parents were resolved to lighten themselves of the burden of a daughter" and embark upon putting together a substantial dowry for her, while her pregnant mother prays for a son (Pritam 1987, 1). Even the space of women's everyday cultural practice is informed by son preference and the devaluation of daughters, and makes evident the symbolic violence which structures the world of the text. Female worth is evaluated only in terms of sexual purity and Pooro's violation by Rashida is framed by her own family's prior rejection of her and the subsequent ostracism by the Hindu community as a whole, thereby demonstrating "how a place in the home is contingent on certain regimes of the body, most important of which is chastity."[7] Unwilling to shelter an unchaste daughter, Pooro's mother encourages her to commit suicide following her escape from Rashida's clutches.[8] Her father rejects her by saying that if he did take her back, Rashida's clan would descend upon them and destroy everything that they possessed. Pooro has no other choice but to go back and cohabit with her rapist, eventually bearing his son. Rashida forces Pooro to convert to Islam prior to marrying her. Located on the margins of both Hindu and Muslim society, Pooro is given a new name "Hamida" in accordance with her newly acquired Muslim identity, with the rest of the narrative depicting the slow process of Pooro's forgiveness, even dawning "love" for her abductor.

This particular emplotment of Pooro's narrative has led earlier critics like Sujala Singh to critique Pritam's narrative for the limited ways in which it penetrates the mesh of silences which shroud articulations of a gendered experience of Partition. Singh's criticism centers on the novella's tacit endorsement of the patriarchal interpellation of Pooro/Hamida's subjectivity. In addition, despite her gestures of rebellion, Hamida is ultimately not able to escape from the predicament that she is in. Having internalized the state mandate in its very definition of an abducted person, she chooses to remain in her prison at the end (S. Singh 1994, 54–68). However, my evaluation of the text differs significantly from the critical terrain outlined therein. My subsequent analysis of the novella will endeavor to demonstrate that *Pinjar* is, in fact, a much more radical and subversive text which generates a trenchant critique of the positions of women within the institutions of the family and the newly instituted postcolonial nation.

On one hand, rape is coded as a "love story" as Pooro recognizes the inherent goodness of Rashida her abductor and the pressures which mitigate his complete responsibility in his crime against her. *Pinjar* furnishes a pre-story of economic and sexual exploitation of the Muslim *Shaikhs* by the Hindu *Sahukars* as well as contextualizing it within violent re-articulations of masculinity during the period leading up to Partition. An old family feud had led to Rashida kidnapping Pooro; the men in Pooro's family had earlier rendered Rashida's family homeless and raped the women. The deaths of young Rashida's mother and sister underline his orphan-like status within his extended family. It places him within an all-male community devoid of love and nurturance, while the older male members of his clan goad him into a reciprocal act of violence. Rashida can consolidate his position within the clan only through the performance of a particular kind of masculinity which is premised on his ability to commit violence upon the daughter of the enemy. The virile and resurgent maleness of the Muslim men in Pooro's village is similarly undergirded in their ability to sexually terrorize women of the "other" community. The reader is informed very early on that "Muslims had become very aggressive. Hindu girls never ventured out except in the broad daylight of the afternoon" (Pritam 1987, 3). This narrative strand also writes the "unspeakable" – the sexual exploitation of Muslim women by Hindu men – and points to the importance of unraveling the hegemonic "rape" script which emerges in such crisis fiction. In fact, most hegemonic, Hindu texts about

Partition strenuously resist any such possibility by depicting Muslim women as eager participants in sexual liaisons with Hindu men. When Pooro discovers that her brother's wife Lajo had been abducted during a riot, she enlists Rashida's support. Rashida willingly cooperates and actively helps her to rescue Lajo, viewing his actions as restitution for his previous crime.

On the other hand, the sudden and unexpected brutality of Pooro's abduction is also emphasized; Pooro "felt something hit her violently on her right shoulder. She reeled under the blow" (Pritam 1987, 6). Rashida not only converts and forcibly renames her; he brands her body to signify his ownership of her. *Pinjar* emphasizes the positioning of Pooro between two deaths in Rashida's home, and repeatedly indicts the "perfidious institution of marriage" (Pritam 1987, 20). She rages against "all men ... men who gnaw a woman's body like a dog gnawing a bone and like a dog consuming it" (Pritam 1987, 15). Her "love" for Rashida is an act of will, of willful forgetting that Rashida had "abducted and wronged" her (Pritam 1987, 20). She describes the child in her womb which results from this union as a "slimy white caterpillar," "maggot," and "leech" (Pritam 1987, 11). Pooro also surreptitiously meets her former fiancé Ram Chand in his fields more than once. Later, a convoy of refugees from Ram Chand's village stops at Hamida's village for the night on their way to India. Hamida goes in search of his family, offering them provisions to tide them over their arduous journey to India. The narrative underlines the disjunction between Pooro/Hamida's inner longings and the outer reality of her life: "It was a double life: Hamida by day, Pooro by night" (ibid.).

This "love story" is etched against an extremely patriarchal backdrop in which the very issues of female consent become problematic. Pooro friend's Taro, "ill since her wedding day," articulates a radical critique of the everyday oppressions of married life (Pritam 1987, 18). According to Taro, "when parents give away a daughter in marriage, they put a noose around her neck and hand the other end of the rope to the man of their choice" (ibid.). Taro, whose husband had abandoned her for another woman, compares all non-egalitarian marital relationships with prostitution, the exchange of exclusive sexual rights for "a mess of pottage and a few rags" (Pritam 1987, 19). Most marriages involved assault by an unknown man, an assault not recognized or named as "rape." Taro's words also draw attention to the corruption of the mother–daughter bond in this world. She is convinced that if she were to die, her mother would only "shed a few tears and then forget about [her]" (Pritam 1987, 18). Her words bring home to Pooro how her own mother had "become like a stepmother" and abandoned her (Pritam 1987, 16). Hence, *Pinjar* makes visible the similarity of the intimate violence which women experience within the institution of marriage and the home, linking that with sexual violence experienced by them during Partition. The emplotment of Pooro's story of violation and loss before, during, and in the aftermath of the historical coordinates of Partition makes visible the oppression of Hindu and Muslim women before, after, and during the Partition crisis.

The novella is populated with ailing and insane women. Madness and illness seem to be the primary registers within which women can inhabit the world of the text. Utterly dispossessed and emptied of all feelings, Pooro first describes herself as the "skeleton." The narrative finally contains the protest articulated by Pooro's story within a conventional love plot and it is the half-naked, nameless, mad beggar woman who suddenly shows up at Pooro's village after the outbreak of communal hostilities in the 1940s who ultimately embodies the "skeleton" of the title. A no-name woman who is described as being half-beast and half-woman roams the countryside screaming as "one possessed by the devil." Her naked, sunburnt skin is like "black parchment" and her laughter "fiendish ... hysterical" (Pritam 1987, 20–21). She eats whatever she can find and resists the well-meaning efforts of the respectable villagers to clothe and domesticate her. She lives in an empty shed on the periphery of the village. Variously described as "A living skeleton ... a lunatic skeleton ... a skeleton picked to its bones by kites and vultures," she dies giving birth to a child (Pritam 1987, 22).

Pooro astutely gauges the woman's "insanity" to be the measure of her traumatic experiences and rape. Pooro recognizes her as a symbolic double and acknowledges the madwoman's story as an alternative ending to her own:

> She dreamt of Rashida galloping away with her lying across the saddle; she dreamt of his keeping her in a gardener's shed for three nights and days and then throwing her out; she dreamt of her turning insane and running about the village lanes with a life quickening in her womb ... and then giving birth to a child under the shade of a tree. The child was exactly like Javed.
>
> (Pritam 1987, 23)

Hence, the narrative exposes the complicity of the vicious, rapacious figure of Hamida's nightmares with the kind husband of her waking moments. They are one and the same person, a fact which underlines the similarity of Pooro's story with that of the nameless woman's, as well as problematizing the Hamida/Rashida love plot even further. Hamida adopts the child; the child becomes her own, because the madwoman's story was her own. Within three days Hamida's breasts fill with milk and she is able to feed the dead woman's child "as if he were her own" (Pritam 1987, 23). Perhaps the idea of "excess" can be useful in understanding the way in which this figure operates in the text which Spivak theorizes as that which "marks the place of that other that can be neither excluded nor recuperated" and, in turn, engenders "moments of transgression" in the text (Spivak 1987, 180, 211).

The textual deployment of the no-name woman as a figure of "excess" allows Pooro/Hamida to define her own border positioning. The no-name woman's story is located at the limits of representation so that her traumatic experiences cannot be narrativized. It also points to the function of violence in collapsing meaning, annihilating language while testifying to a terror that cannot be brought into the realm of the utterable, as Veena Das contends (1995, 184). This paradoxically also allows a re-centering of the Hamida/Pooro narrative within the discursive limits of the text. As the beggar woman's story is both similar to and different from Hamida's, she represents both Pooro herself as well as an "other."

While still alive, the no-name woman is able to resist the efforts of the villagers to appropriate her body by clothing her. However, after she dies, the Hindus in the village testify that she was a Hindu, one of them having spied an *Om* (sacred symbol of Hinduism) inscribed upon her skin. Pooro/Hamida's own story serves as a counterpoint to the veracity of such absolute signifiers identifying and locating the female body within modalities of particular religious systems. Hamida's new name had also been forcibly inscribed upon her arm to signal the ownership of her body by a Muslim man, while she herself never loses an inner sense of allegiance with the Hindu community. Although her acceptance within the Muslim community endows her with a privileged vantage point, she mostly rescues and befriends Hindu women who had been abducted by Muslim men. She has no compunctions, moreover, about strategically displaying that violent branding of her body to accomplish the retrieval and restitution of her brother's abducted wife such that the violated body of the abducted woman itself emerges as the site of resistance in the text.

Pooro increasingly moves away from the rigid binaries of communalized identity, from identifying herself according to the dual imperatives of Hindu/ Muslim. Pooro/Hamida's fluid sense of identity constitutes a space in which these two contesting identities merge, and out of her own experiences is born an empathetic identification with women from both communities, and she remains sharply antagonistic to the official sanction of sexualized violence being perpetrated upon Hindu, Muslim, and Sikh women during Partition. *Pinjar* resists the construction of women both as collective victims of violence during the fury of Partition riots and also as passive "objects" of a violent history. *Pinjar* begins with the sexual violation of its female protagonist and then works out Pooro's survival and empowerment despite her traumatic experiences.[9] This in itself underwrites the "crisis of witnessing" which hegemonic, primarily male-authored Partition texts exemplify in fulfilling the ideological demand of nationalist literature that there be no survivors of sexual violence which posits the threat of "pollution" across ethnic and national borders. The "cage" is therefore a metaphor for the restricted lives of women, while alluding to the possibility of freedom outside the cage.

Partition had served to change the ideological constructions of "rape," as mass abductions of women acquired the magnitude of a national catastrophe. The violated female body had become the site of a bitterly contested political debate on both sides of the national divide. The government had issued edicts exhorting families to take back their recovered women.[10] Lajo, who had been abducted during the frenzy of the Partition riots, could legally claim the paternalistic protection of the state and is ultimately restituted within her family who are willing to take her back. As rape and other forms of sexual violence discursively move out of the privatized sphere of "home" into the public space of national politics, Hamida's words underline how the state defined along ethnic and religious lines and the family were working in conjunction while underlying how "violence" as a category is tied to larger power relations. Hamida is full of resentment: "When it had happened to her, religion had become an insurmountable obstacle; neither

her parents, nor her in-laws had been willing to accept her. And now, the same religion had become so accommodating!" (Pritam 1987, 39). The nation and the family in fact emerge as mirror images of each other – each supporting the authority of the other. Pooro's choice of opting to live with Rashida and their son despite her brother's desire to relocate her to her "proper" home may be read as an act of resistance to a forcible naming by the "official" mandates of the newly decolonized nation-states and the normative male citizen subject. This may also be read as a rejection of "home" and "nation" as sites which privilege only men with violence undergirding the female subject's experience of the post-colonial state, and the microcosmic space of the "home."

Similarly, Shauna Singh Baldwin's *What the Body Remembers* (1999) which depicts a bigamous relationship in colonial India stages the breakdown of the body politic against the background of ruptured familial and communitarian ties while interrogating the everyday and extraordinary instances of violence experienced by women.[11] Most of the novel deals with the power play between the younger wife Roop, and the older, childless Satya who demands the "gift" of Roop's children.[12] Both women are married to the same rich and influential man in pre-Partition Pakistan referred to only as *Sardaarji* and positioned as hostile social and sexual rivals.[13] Baldwin's text situates women's experience of violence in the private and public domains within a problematic of female consent. Female agency and victimhood do not emerge as antithetical categories but operate simultaneously in the novel.

The possibility of sexual violation exists prior to, during, and after Partition, the disciplinary fear of which powerfully influences the socialization of women in the text. The fear of male sexual aggression "is a dread Roop shares with other girls in Pari-Darvaza – Sikhs, Hindu or Muslim – fear of her own body, that lurer of lust from the eyes of unrelated men" (Baldwin 1999, 101). This disciplinary fear is what enables Hindu, Muslim, and Sikh fathers to retain a stranglehold upon their daughters' sexuality and autonomy, and leads to the constant policing and surveillance of young, unmarried daughters at home, often carried out by older women within the household. It consigns both Roop and her sister Madani to virtual *purdah* during the period when they acquire a very inadequate education and later after Roop is married to *Sardaarji*, who decides that there was "no need for … people to see even the color of his new wife's skin" (Baldwin 1999, 140). A form of symbolic violence, it underwrites Roop's mother's death. An extremely sick women, completely depleted by constant childbearing, she is not "allowed" to leave home to see a doctor at the Mayo Hospital in Lahore and dies trying to birth another male child at home.

What the Body Remembers constructs Roop's body as the object of the gaze – located at the interstices of collective social surveillance, the desiring male gaze, the critical gaze of other women which often coincides with the gaze of the omniscient third-person narrator. The omniscient narrator repeatedly uses Roop's body as a metaphor for the national imaginary: "Hindus, Sikhs, Muslims, they are like the three strands of her hair, a strong rope against the British, but separate nevertheless" (Baldwin 1999, 3) The metaphors of woman-as-nation and nation-as-woman lead to the territorialization of the female body as national space. Tropes of birthing and mothering structure the narrative, with Partition figured as a tortuous severing of a child from the womb. The female body is transformed into a site for the consolidation of religious orthodoxy and cultural nationalism among the various religious communities in pre-Partition India. A process which entails a violent appropriation of women's bodies, it marks an effort to reformulate female identity in terms of an "ideal" of ethnic authenticity. Homi Bhabha'a distinction between the strictly defined and demarcated realm of "pedagogic," as opposed to the fluid space of shared, "perfomative" nationalism, can be useful in understanding the transformation of ethnic and cultural identity in a condition of siege prior to Partition (Bhabha 1994, 139–170). Roop's father forbids the cutting of her hair as the first step towards his own religious restitution. Her husband, an orthodox Sikh, refuses to allow the wearing of vermillion powder, nose rings, and the *bindi* (dot on the forehead) because they were Hindu practices.[14] At a larger, national level, the female body becomes the site around which emerged both India and Pakistan's self-representations of themselves. The female body becomes a contestatory space, with familial, communal, and national discourses endeavoring to construct and contain it in mutually contradictory ways. As Jill Didur points out, the economy of meaning within the elitist, patriarchal, nationalist imaginaries circulating at the time of Partition conflated the sacredness of nation and woman, making women both an "object of protection and target of violence – both physical and discursive" (Didur 2006, 7).

Despite their upper-class positioning, none of the women in the novel are exempt from the performance of certain kinds of labor for the family and the state which underwrites the experience of everyday violence for both of the female protagonists. Both Roop and Satya are dispossessed – Satya from the locus of domestic power and fruits of her labor in safeguarding and managing her husband's economic assets. Sardarji's bestowal of Satya's jewels to Roop after he marries her draws attention to this, while underscoring Roop's symbolic usurpation of her former position. Roop, on the other hand, is unable to exercise any autonomy over her own body and the fruits of her reproductive labor. Roop's husband enjoins her to "give" both her children away to Satya with the words: "You will feel the joy of sacrifice, the happiness of giving. And don't worry, we will have another child" (Baldwin 1999, 166). Female identity is therefore constructed within a rhetoric of "sacrifice" which draws upon a readily available oral as well as textualized tradition. These derive from repeated references not only to female characters in Hindu mythology like Sita, but also to Sikh texts like Bhai Vir Singh novels popular at the time. The female heroine of these tales helped the Sikhs to fight Afghans, "and when the Sikh men didn't need her anymore ... the Sikh woman returned to being good-good, sweet-sweet, and dying undaunted, gave a rousing martyr's speech upon ever-smiling lips" (Baldwin 1999, 100). Female "sacrifice" in the interests of both the family and the state forms the core of a cultural mythology with honorable death being the only available script for female heroism.

Such forms of discursive and symbolic violence also engender acts of physical violence experienced by women as demonstrated in the reverent circulation
of the reports of the mass suicides of 90 women in the village of Thoa Khalsa to
save their "honor" which then engenders other, similar acts of female heroism
and "martyrdom" in the text. The novel draws attention to the mass suicides of
Sikh women during Partition to save the "honor" of the family and community,
and juxtaposes these "suicides" with men bragging about having "martyred"
their women. Partition was coded as a failure of the male nationalist to protect
the political integrity of the nation, as well as the inability of Hindu and Sikh
men to protect their women. This led to a very violent compensatory performance of (Sikh) masculinity. Women were accommodated within the disciplinary
parameters of a neo-nationalist discourse, only if they consented to be the objects
of violence. *What the Body Remembers* depicts two instances of female characters "consenting" to their own deaths to preserve the honor of the family and the
community, thereby problematizing the notion of female consent in certain contexts. The text makes visible culturally normalized and endorsed violence, to
which women "consent" as a consequence of having internalized the logic of
patriarchy. Women themselves are willing to perpetuate violence upon themselves and other women. During riots, "the women were ready to kill too ... old
women were giving opium to younger women ... preparing them for martyrdom"
(Baldwin 1999, 453).

Roop's sister-in-law Kusum is one such woman "martyred" by Roop's father
to "save" her from a rioting band of Muslim men. According to the version of
the incident offered by her father, Kusum "went to her death just as she was
offered it, baring her neck to Papaji's *kirpan*, willingly, Papaji says, for the *izzat*
of her *quom*" (Baldwin 1999, 456). Roop's father testifies that Kusum had
"consented" to be a "martyr," and willingly participated in the act. However,
according to Roop, Kusum had been trained never to say "no" to the wishes of
the men in her family and just could not find the requisite words when the need
arose for them. It is Kusum's sexual and maternal roles which spell her nemesis,
as Roop's father cannot bear the thought of the "seeds of that foreign religion
... planted in Sikh women's wombs" (Baldwin 1999, 455). She is "martyred" in
the same room in which Roop's mother died in childbirth, "martyred" to an
ambition to keep bearing sons, thereby tying extraordinary instances of violence
experienced by women during Partition with everyday violence experienced by
them as a consequence of their desire to be the ideal daughter, wife, and mother.
Hence Baldwin refuses to construct women's experience of violent history as
collective, political punishment perpetuated by "other" men, locating the
experience of violence firmly within the "home," perpetuated by fathers,
brothers, and husbands, sometimes even by other women. Ironically, it is
the sacrifice of a very different kind of an elderly aunt who faces the
rioting mob and converts to Islam which enables the rest of the family to escape
while emphasizing the gratuitous violence underwriting Kusum's ultimately
pointless "martyrdom" (even within the distorted logic which underwrites such
deaths).

Roop's brother Jeevan, who sets out "like Ram setting off to Sri Lanka to bring his Sita home," reaches her too late to prevent her death. Underneath a white sheet at his ancestral home he finds that "A woman's body lay beneath, each limb severed at the joint. This body was sliced into six parts, then arranged to look as if she were whole again" (Baldwin 1999, 446). Jeevan struggles to read the message inscribed upon his wife's body:

> She looked accepting ... Her hand was like this – unclenched. Her feet were like this – not poised to run. Her legs cut neatly at the thigh, why they must surely have used a sword or more than one! Why were her legs not bloody? To cut a woman apart without first raping – a waste surely. Rape is one man's message to another: "I took your pawn. Your move."

He scrutinizes and analyzes his dead wife's body to unravel the "mystery" of her death and dismemberment, and it is only after he discerns that her womb had been ripped out of her by her assailants that he finally "receives" the intended message. The body of the woman becomes a historical palimpsest on which Hindu, Sikh, and Muslim struggle to write their competing versions of the event. It is transformed into a transactional site upon which Sikh and Muslim men engage in a game of chess and communicate with one another. The violated female body itself becomes text, with words and the body doubling each other. Jeevan's first concern upon discovering his wife's dismembered body is to quickly immolate her, as the "message was one that should go no further. It must be ignored, so that no Sikh show weakness or fear" (Baldwin 1999, 448).

I want to end with a reading of the gendering of identity in conjunction with how ethnic identity marks the female subject in this text. While the text indicts hegemonic nationalist constructions of the "Sikh" as a deviant national subject, the discursive construction of Sikh identity occurs by locating the self with respect to an ethnic "other." Female, Sikh identity is premised upon notions of "difference," and not all instances of ethnic bias can be explained away as reflecting the attitudes of the characters in the novel. The text itself is complicit in perpetuating certain negative stereotypes about Muslims, emplacing its own knowledge-producing mechanisms within a larger, hegemonic representational grid.

Almost all the working-class women in the text are Muslim, which leads to a larger subalternalization of Muslim, female identity along class lines. The agency which Satya initially exercises in the text is demonstrated by her ability to control the labor of her Muslim servants, and her subsequent disempowerment is marked by her maid Mani Mai's refusal to extend her labor willingly and perform a socially subordinate role. Satya, though very resentful of her husband's appropriation of her labor, is eager to extract service out of women like Jorimon in order to raise her husband's children by Roop, assuming that "Jorimon will dress them, feed them, clothe them." Poor Muslim women remain the "others" against whom she defines her sense of autonomy: "Muslims in the Muslim quarter; she did not know them. They treat their own women so badly, so badly, they cover them up in *chadors* and *burquas*" (Baldwin 1999, 297).

Similarly, though Roop resents being cast in the role of the "gift giver who keeps on giving" by her husband, she herself demands such "gifts" of complete loyalty from Mani Mai and is distressed to discern Mai's divided professional fidelity to both herself and Satya (Baldwin 1999, 217). Despite a moment of shared solidarity as women, Jorimon, the Muslim nanny of Roop's children, is not cast as a savior figure or female hero. After an ineffectual attempt to pass Roop as a fellow Muslim during her hazardous border crossing into India with her children, Jorimon is almost raped by men of her own faith who wish to "teach her a lesson" (Baldwin 1999, 421). Ultimately divested of all agency, Jorimon has to be "saved" by Roop instead. Like Satya, Roop evolves a sense of self by constantly defining herself as the antithesis of her Muslim friend Huma: "I am not like Huma. Papaji doesn't make me learn Namaz prayers or cover my whole face with a chunni or burqa as Muslim girls do." Huma, who ardently defends the demand for Pakistan, is punished for her views. Roop "recognizes" her in one of the two "cringing burqua clad women" accosted by Sikh soldiers which she witnesses while crossing the border into India. Despite the women's cries for help, Roop does not stop her car, convinced that "compassion is weakness; disloyalty to Sikhs.... Every woman has her kismet" (Baldwin 1999, 398–399). Later, the narrator glosses over many such instances of Sikh violence against Muslims as a reaction to violence first perpetuated by Muslims.

The *purdah* functions as a signifier of the hyper-visibility of the ethnic otherness of Muslim women in the novel, though Sikh and Hindu women are often depicted as adopting the *purdah* as a signifier of their elite class identity. Others like Satya use the veil to symbolically appropriate the space of the "other" as convenient disguise. Sikh men like Roop's father virtually keep their daughters in *purdah* because of the fear of sexual aggression from "unrelated men." However, all such instances are prefaced by emphasizing that Sikh women autonomously choose to inhabit this site and can enter and leave it at will. The *purdah*, while it enables the mobility and safety of Sikh women within the public domain, remains symbolic of the oppression of Muslim women in the novel. Replicating the myopia that I have critiqued in hegemonic, male-authored Hindu versions of Partition, Baldwin's novel denies that Hindu and Sikh men also murdered Muslim men and abducted their women. Hence, while it is imperative to critique the version of "truth" that hegemonic Indian male-authored texts construct, it is also not possible to simplistically eulogize all women-authored texts as being unproblematically resistant.

Pritam's and Baldwin's novels interrupt hegemonic constructions of national identity and belonging and write women's bodies as contested spaces upon which contradictory domestic, national, and ethnic significatory processes operate simultaneously. They map strategies of resistance to its appropriation and forcible signification with rigid markers of identity. Both problematize the casting of women as national wombs inherent in the metaphoric connotations of "woman-as-nation," and "nation-as-woman" in nationalist literature. However, texts like Baldwin's, while representing women's experiences of Partition as violence, are also complicit with reproducing a form of discursive violence, which in its turn debunks the claim that all women writers write unambiguously subversive texts.

Women as social and historical agents often have mutually competing affiliations with race, class, caste, and religious collectives which complicate any such simplistic projects of feminist recuperation. It points to the difficulty of a neat cataloging of female authored texts as oppositional. While *Pinjar* resists the dichotomist fracturing of identity as Hindu/Muslim, the insertion of gender within other modalities of class and ethnicity makes visible the technologies of the self that produce the modern, Sikh female subject. Not only does this point to the historical revisionism inaugurated in the aftermath of the Partition crisis, but it also gestures towards the consolidation of ethnic identity in contemporary post-Partition South Asia within the logic of us vs. them. Public memory about Partition has constituted a kind of "social glue" that has defined ethnic/religious/national community, as well as demarcated its limits. Violence and community constitute each other and testify to the fact that the past is not the past, but is still being rewritten.

Notes

1 I have derived most of my statistical information from Urvashi Butalia's *The Other Side of Silence* (Butalia 2000). There is little consensus among Partition theorists and historiographers regarding the number of people who died and were displaced during the event. While Butalia contends that 12 million people were displaced, others like Sukeshi Kamra place the number of displaced much higher – at about 16 million (Kamra 2002; K. Singh 1956). According to historiographer Gyanendra Pandey, the numbers cited in official reports function as gestures which signal the enormity and sheer magnitude of the violence, and function within the realm of rumor and hearsay (Pandey 1994, 188).

2 See novels like Khushwant Singh's *Train to Pakistan* (Connecticut, CT: Greenwood Press, 1956), Bhisham Sahni's *Tamas* (New Delhi: Penguin, 2001, first published in Hindi in 1974), Chaman Nahal's *Azadi* (Boston, MA: Houghton Miffin, 1975), and Gurcharan Das' *A Fine Family* (New Delhi: Penguin, 1990).

3 Homi Bhabha theorizes upon the "third space" in his essay "Commitment to Theory" anthologized in *The Location of Culture*, London; New York: Routledge, 1994.

4 See Jill Didur's *Unsettling Partition: Literature, Gender, Memory* (Toronto: University of Toronto Press, 2006) for a further elaboration of this idea.

5 Amrita Pritam was born on August 31, 1919 in Gujranwala (Pakistan). Her mother died when she was 11. Born into an orthodox Sikh family, she was married at 16. She was 28 at the time of Partition and traveled from Gujranwala in Pakistan across the border as a refugee. She received the prestigious *Jnanpith* Award for her literary work in 1981. In addition to *Pinjar*, she has written another Partition novel *Dr. Dev* and a collection of poetry *Lamian Watan* on the subject – these works have not yet been translated into English so far as I was able to determine.

6 Communal riots between Hindus and Muslims had occurred in several towns and cities in the 1920s and 1930s. However, it was only after 1944 that the two communities clashed also in rural areas (Corrucini and Kaul 1990, 57).

7 See Debali Mookerjea-Leonard (2005, 142). Mookerjea-Leonard's analysis of Partition narratives further contests the cultural representations of home as a "safe space" and the family as being "unconditionally loving" to demonstrate how women who were sexually violated experienced "homelessness" within their homes and families.

"Divided Homelands, Hostile Homes: Partition, Women and Homelessness." *Journal of Commonwealth Literature* 40:2 (2005), 141–154.

8 At this point in the novella, Rashida had not yet raped Pooro. He scrupulously refuses to violate her until they are legally married.

9 In this context, see Rajeswari Sunder Rajan's analysis of feminist rape narratives in *Real and Imagined Women* (Sunder Rajan 1991). Sunder Rajan juxtaposes feminist narratives like Alice Walker's *The Color Purple*, Maya Angelou's *I Know Why the Caged Bird Sings*, and Malini Ramanan's "Prison" with Richardson's *Clarissa* and Forster's *A Passage to India*. According to Sunder Rajan, the feminist rape narratives locate rape at the beginning of their female protagonists' story; the rest of the narrative depicts survival after trauma and the development of the victim/woman's resistant subjectivity. The cost of rape for its victims is more complex than the extinction of the female self in death and silence. These texts also locate women within structures of oppression, rather than in heterosexual romantic relationships "gone wrong" (Sunder Rajan 1991, 150–167). In this context, I would also like to draw attention to the way in which abduction and rape marks the "end" of Ayah's story in Bapsi Sidhwa's celebrated Partition novel *Cracking India* (Sidhwa 1991).

10 Butalia draws attention to the numerous proclamations published by Gandhi and Nehru during the period testifying that abducted women still remained "pure" (Butalia 2000, 127).

11 Shauna Singh Baldwin was born in Montreal and grew up in India, and is now an e-commerce consultant living in Milwaukee. Her other books include *English Lessons and Other Stories* (Goose Lane Editions, 1999) and *A Foreign Visitor's Survival Guide in North America* (John Muir Publications, 1992). *What the Body Remembers* evolved out of a short story "Satya" which was awarded the Saturday Night/CBC Literary Prize and was nominated for a National Magazine Award in Canada. *What the Body Remembers* was the winner of the Commonwealth Writer's Prize for the best book in Canada and the Caribbean in 2000 (New York: Anchor Books, 1999).

12 The names of the two women are allegorical and point to the discursive function of these two characters. "Satya" means truth and "Roop" translates as beauty. The author intended the negotiation between the two women over the ownership of Roop's children as an allegory for India and Pakistan fighting over territory on the eve of Partition. See Baldwin's essay on www.randomhouse.com/boldtype/1199/baldwin/essay. html.

13 This is an epithet used for respectable Sikh gentlemen. In its refusal to name Sardarji, the text allies itself to narratives like Jean Rhys' *Wide Sargasso Sea* (Penguin Classics, 2007) which refers to the Rochester character only as "the man." Certainly, it has the effect of conferring anonymity upon the male protagonist who could literally be "any man" within that particular class. This refusal must be seen in the context of something which the narrative withholds from the figure of patriarchal authority in the text – the privilege of a name and an identity. The rationale that Sardarji repeatedly offers for his bigamy to his first wife who has been unable to produce heirs is that he must have a son to carry on "his name."

14 The rise in Sikh orthodoxy prior to Partition is presented as being a response to the increasingly fundamentalist Hindu *Arya Samajis*. Baldwin depicts fanatical Hindus violently recovering Sikh men "back" within the folds of Hinduism through purification ceremonies. The novel indicts the Congress Party as a Hindu-dominated party which had impelled Sikhs to organize their own party. Politicization had been marked by the rise of cultural nationalism within the Sikh community with detrimental effects upon the lives of actual Sikh women. Hindu fundamentalism is in turn seen as a response to Christian proselytizing initiatives and the numbers game introduced by the British through the system of representative legislation.

Bibliography

Baldwin, Shauna Singh. *A Foreign Visitor's Survival Guide in North America*. Santa Fe: John Muir, 1992.
——. *English Lessons and Other Stories*. New Brunswick, NJ: Goose Lane Editions, 1999.
——. *What the Body Remembers*. New York: Nan A. Talese, 1999.
Bhabha, Homi. *The Location of Culture*. London: Routledge, 1994.
Butalia, Urvashi. *The Other Side of Silence: Voices from the Partition of India*. Durham, NC: Duke University Press, 2000.
Corrucini, Robert S. and Samvit S Kaul. *Halla: Demographic Consequences of the Partition of the Punjab, 1947*. New York: University Press of America, 1990.
Das, Gurcharan. *A Fine Family*. New Delhi: Penguin, 1990.
Das, Veena. *Critical Events: An Anthropological Perspective on Contemporary India*. New Delhi: Oxford University Press, 1995.
——. *Life and Words: Violence and the Descent Into the Ordinary*. Berkeley: University of California Press, 2006.
Didur, Jill. *Unsettling Partition: Literature, Gender, Memory*. Toronto: University of Toronto Press, 2006.
Jeganathan, Pradeep. "A Space for Violence: Anthropology, Politics and the Location of a Singhala Practice of Masculinity," in *Community, Gender and Violence: Subaltern Studies XI*, edited by Partha Chatterjee and Pradeep Jeganathan, 37–65. New York: Columbia University Press, 2000.
Kamra, Sukeshi. *Bearing Witness: Partition, Independence, End of the Raj*. Calgary: University of Calgary Press, 2002.
Menon, Ritu and Kamla Bhasin. *Borders and Boundaries: Women in India's Partition*. New Brunswick, NJ: Rutgers University Press, 1998.
Mookerjea-Leonard, Debali. "Divided Homelands, Hostile Homes: Partition, Women, and Homelessness." *Journal of Commonwealth Literature* 40:2 (2005), 141–154.
Nahal, Chaman. *Azadi*. Boston, MA: Houghton Mifflin, 1975.
Pandey, Gyan. "The Prose of Otherness," in *Subaltern Studies VIII*, 188–221. New Delhi: Oxford University Press, 1994.
Pritam, Amrita. *The Skeleton; and That Man*. New Delhi: Sterling Publishers, 1987.
Sahni, Bhisham. *Tamas: Darkness*. New Delhi: Penguin, 2001.
Sidhwa, Bapsi. *Cracking India*. Minnesota, MN: Milkweed Editions, 1991.
Singh, Khushwant. *Train to Pakistan*. Connecticut, NH: Greenwood Press, 1956.
Singh, Sujala. "Nationalism's Brandings: Women's Bodies and Narratives of the Partition." *South Asian Review* 18:15 (December 1994), 54–68.
Spivak, Gayatri Chakravorty. *In Other Worlds: Essays in Cultural Politics*. New York: Methuen, 1987.
Sunder Rajan, Rajeswari. *Real and Imagined Women: Gender, Culture and Postcolonialism*. New York: Rutgers University Press, 1991.

Part II
Borders and belonging

3   Many Pakistans,[1] half a village[2]

Interrogating the discourse of identity through the Partition literatures of India

Ipshita Chanda

Beginning with the history of naming and its connection to the existence of a plural community, this chapter reiterates the dominant theme of Partition literature in India: the loss of plurality to divisive politics. But this, I submit, is the easy and obvious move. For, to an Indian writing within the Anglophone academia, the central question appears beyond this thematic reiteration. I ask whether – and how – academic reading can interrogate the discursive tropes of "identity" politics and retrieve the secular pluralism lost through freedom gained at midnight.

> Krishna Sobti's novel Zindaginama,[3] beginning in pre-partition Panjab and extending up to the point when division becomes inevitable, introduces us to the legendary friendship between Chajju Bhagat and Shah Miya Meer. One day Meer Sahib comes to Chajju's house, finds him cooking and stops at the threshold, asking permission to enter. Chajju replies, If only you had entered without asking, who could have refused you? But now, please remain outside. Meer Sahib, do peer-paikars, men of god, belong to different castes? … Why did you not come in and embrace me straightaway? My friend, it is my shame that you thought my cooking fire more important than me.
>
> (Sobti 1998, 391)

It is easy to be moved by the sentiments that unite the "Muslim" Meer and the "Hindu" Chajju until they are violently divided by devious colonial design. But what was the nature of their unity in the first place? Were they insistent upon their differences or did they forget them and embrace each other in a fit of humanism? How then did the cooking fire take precedence over the human being? With these questions we begin our search for "identities" established and destabilized by "borders" in the "partition" literature of the Asian subcontinent.

Rahi Masoom Raza describes Ghadipur, a village across the Ganges, in his novel *Adha Gaon*:

> It is said that on a dark night in the monsoon month of Ashadh, a sardar of Tughlaq's, named Syed Masud Ghazi crossed the flooded Ganges and

attacked Ghadipur. As a result, from Ghadipur, this town changed to Ghazipur. The roads remained the same, the alleys remained the same, the houses
and buildings remained the same, the name changed. The name might be
something like an outer skin, it can be changed. Perhaps the name has no
unbreakable bond with the person, because if there had been such a bond,
then the town should have changed too when it became Ghazipur from
Ghadipur, or at least this much was expected that the defeated Thakur,
Brahman,Kayasth, Ahir, Bhar and Chamar would say they belonged to
Ghadipur, and the victorious Syed, Sheikh and Pathan would claim they
were residents of Ghazipur.

(Raza 1998, 2007, 12)

In talking of his own home Ghazipur, Raza reminds the reader that the culture of
separate names, and of divisions posited ostensibly in keeping with the names,
was never the culture of Ghazipur. Rather, "when the taziya was lifted during
Muharram processions, someone would suddenly shout: 'Bol Muhammadi' and
the whole village would answer with one voice: 'Ya Hussain!'" (Raza 1998,
2007, 13). The alert reader will say: but that is a Shia festival. She will point out
that the name that survived was the name of the victor: Ghazipur remained while
Ghadipur became a page in history, and that history is amenable to being read
from the perspective of any reader as a certain sort of narrative, privileging one
group over the other or asserting the supremacy of some formation rather than
another. It is indisputable that the workings of power enable survival or oblitera-
tion, and that the struggle for this power will ultimately decide the contours and
ground of official history.

   But the sobering fact is that the contours of opposition to the official discourse seem already posited in the themes that occupy the academic mind in the
early twenty-first century. This is not to say that these themes are redundant: it is
only to point out that the way in which these oppositional themes are deemed to
be oppositional, and hence their relations to the praxis of emancipation, episte-
mological or ontological or phenomenological, often turn out to be variations of
the hegemonic theme itself. At its most strident, it is a wholesale negation,
taking an extremist – even fundamentalist – tone. At its most essentialist, it is a
wholesale acceptance of the mainstream, attempting to craft what has come to be
called a "counter"-discourse. The shades of the opposition in between these
extreme positions remain posited upon the variations of the hegemonic structure
of thought construction, discourse formation and affective response. The hegemonic theme itself is accepted as a given. This seems to be the irony in constructing an oppositional discourse founded on such a given theme. The
contradiction itself underpins the repertoire of practices that flow from it and
substantiate it as oppositional. Audre Lorde pointed out long ago that the
master's tools will never dismantle the master's house (Lorde 1984, 110–113). I
read this as a call for discursive responsibility for one's own action in positing
such a theme, founding such a discourse and then naming it as oppositional, in
respect to one's practices of living. The danger is in limiting the responsibility to

demarcating an identity as political and basing demands upon that identity as a means to some other end – what Figueira succinctly calls "academic activism" (Figueira 2008). These ends are rarely as transparent as one would claim: for in them, too, the operations of power and the strategies of control reveal themselves. The dispersed rhizomic idea of self-construction may be in opposition to the singular activity of tracing a single root upon which one's identity is constructed. But in the former case, what is the political manifestation of the rhizomic self? Is it a response on the phenomenological level alone? Can it be limited to the sphere of meaning only? A well-known example is of the difference that the proper name "Londres" evokes to the French-speaking person, a cognitive response different from that which is elicited by the proper name "London" from the English speaker, even if the latter is not an inhabitant of London. Here the difference is visible, and the translation of the proper noun (dis)covers that difference. But translation may not always be necessary. For example, the label "water" refers to a certain chemical composition of varying degrees of safety and purity when used by people from different parts of the world; one can even say that the very concept of purity does not exist in connection with water as a consumable, though its cleaning properties may not be held in doubt, even where health is not synonymous with purity. This is obvious enough if we differentiate between the material and the affective realms. But these realms cannot summarily be disjointed. The cognition of "water" and of "London/Londres" is similar if they are available to us as semantic elements: they will inevitably acquire difference when the affective and the material are conjoined in understanding them. Here I will attempt to conjoin both the affective and the material in understanding the field of play of a certain set of words that are crucial to current academic discourse. My argument is that these words, and the particular forms in which they are understood, used and deployed in particular discursive sites, and in the spaces opened up in opposition to those sites, may not be the only possible use for them. I embark upon this not-so-novel exercise with the words "identity" and "partition" and the attendant set of responses that it draws from those participating willingly and unwillingly in the discursive activity that is hinged upon it.

The exercise which follows stems from a consideration of terms in the general and not the particular sense, for it is from the general sense that theory is generated. In general terms, therefore, the preponderance of merely a geopolitical identity to the exclusion of everything else is enhanced by the drawing of a border, and the positioning of people on either side. The existence of difference may be made the subject of a number of varieties of exploitation, including a democratic exploitation of such differences as veritable vote banks. This may not be possible in a democracy in which difference seems to be screened by certain homogeneities, be they those of race or gender, or cultural practice and belief. Partition, in the two texts discussed in this chapter, does establish geopolitical and politicized borders without establishing anything else. The texts seek to understand the identity of the people forced to relocate or reinvent themselves in deference to those borders. The people in the texts in fact interrogate the identity of the borders rather than the identity of those who inhabit areas across or on either side of the borders. Who draws the borders and to what purpose? Who defines an aspect of the identity to the exclusion of everything else and to what end? These are the general questions that the texts address, though they finally provide particularized answers depending upon the characters who become involved in articulating these questions through their lives and emotions. Thus literature may be seen as a linguistic expression of these questions in the context in which they arise. Those who are trapped by the raising of these questions, whether hegemonic or oppositional, must negotiate with these questions as forms of living, located in time and space. Literature itself may be seen as an oppositional discourse, not because it takes this or that "side," but because it reveals the workings of the machinery that posits and legitimizes these issues through their effect upon human lives. It thus puts both sides into a living relation, problematizing and opening the foundational discourse to question. Further, it has the ability to suggest human answers to these questions and display human means for negotiating them, thereby undercutting the generalized limitations of theory.

Rahi Masoom Raza's *Adha Gaon* is set in the village of Gangauli, about which the author, a Gangauli dweller, comments: "These days the number of Gangauli-dwellers is decreasing in Gangauli, and the number of Sunni, Shia and Hindus is increasing" (Raza 1998, 2007, 13). This certainly does not mean that the Sunnis, Shias and Hindus did not exist earlier: it only means that a varied community accepted the single composite identity as "Gangauli-dwellers" once upon a time, when the idea of the locality seemed paramount in deciding one's own self-formation. Therefore, the writer writes a "Preface" on page 289 of the 344-page novel. That the Preface must occur at this point needs some explanation, and Raza does provide one:

It must be said without further ado that my grandfather was from Azamgarh, but I am Ghazipuri, I live in Gangauli. I belong to the maatam of grief on the fifth and the eighth days of Muharram, to Gaya Ahir, Haria Mistry and Komila Chamar. That Safirwahas gone to Pakistan does not grieve me – it seems that he has become a Syed there ... the Jan Sangh say the Muslims do not belong here. I do not have the ability to prove them wrong, but I can surely say that I belong to Ghazipur, my bond with Gangauli is unbreakable, this is not only my village, it is also my home. Home! This word exists in all the languages of the world, and it is the sweetest word in each of them. I belong to Gangauli because it is my home. Because: this word has such solid strength, and as long as this "because" is alive, I, Syed Masum Raza Abdi, will remain an inhabitant of Ghazipur, never mind where my grandfather came from. And I shall not give anyone the right to be able to say to me, "Rahi, you do not belong to Gangauli, so, leave Gangauli and go and live in, say, just for the sake of saying, go and live in Rae Bareilly." Why should I go sir? I absolutely will not.

(Raza 1998, 2007, 289)

The above quotation outlines the spatial and historical construction of an identity that transcends narrow limits related only to space, time, religion, language or other communal affinities. When each or any of these elements is taken in isolation from all others and made the basis of an identity, such an identity is unidimensional and amenable to being exploitatively politicized, however well meaning that exploitation may be. The paternalism that characterizes all attempts at programmatic identity formation is clearly problematized when Raza's family history is refused in favor of a lived experience of space and community. Wherever his grandfather arrived from, Raza remains a dweller of Gangauli, and can challenge all other attempts to redefine him with this certainty. This is compromised in a world that makes the identity an abstraction. It at once interpellates an individual as a discrete entity, and deprives her of all markers of specificity. And it appears, from Raza's depiction of his self, that these markers are existential and phenomenological simultaneously, especially for the purposes of literature.

At the start of the novel, the writer has acknowledged that he will be entering the text from time to time and he fulfills this promise continuously, innocuously as well as in pronounced ways. He has promised that the novel will be, generically, an amalgamation of an "aapbeeti" or what happened to the self, as well as a "jag beeti", what happened to the world. The reader must notice the generic nomenclature here (Raza 1998, 2007, 9–10). There is a fluidity in this generic name that will accommodate a process of becoming. It is not a fixed self that is posited here. If it were, the word "beeti" would lose its dynamism. "Aapbeeti" literally means what the self has lived through, and this endurance is the crux of a plot around which the narrative must be structured. The category that is chosen as distinct from the self is "jag", the world. What happens to the world is also a possible plot for a form of narrative. In both cases, there is a protagonist who may or may not act, but must endure the consequences of actions: the actions may be the protagonist's own, or that of others. This genre of "aapbeeti" may approximate the Bildungsroman, only if we agree that in the latter genre the mind in question does not have full control of the action. If, however, the mind is seen in the Bildungsroman as the sole, conscious and controlling agent of the action, then what or who may act upon the mind is not given any acknowledgment. Such a possibility is refused in the very name "aapbeeti". And that would signal a difference between the cultural horizons through which each of the genres is produced and received.

Similar concerns appear in the second text discussed in this chapter: Kamleswar's *Kitney Pakistan*, literally translated as "How Many Pakistans". The central character of this novel too is both a type and a person: there is scope here for both the "jag beeti", whose protagonist is the type, and the "aapbeeti", where it is the person who is the protagonist. This simultaneous yet unannounced double narrative is achieved by Kamleswar through an old maneuver: the central character is named Adib-e-Aliya, the respected poet, who has a constant and live relationship with history. The adib, the poets, have a supernatural power: they travel freely to any corner of history, and besides, "every writer's time is imprisoned in his own text. The power and solidity of each of these words has been proved to be more powerful even than the power of time" (Kamleshwar 2003). Thus it is easy for Adib to go to Ayodhya, where he meets Bahu Begum, the queen mother of Faizabad. Her grandson Wahid Ali Shah decided to shift the capital from Faizabad to Lucknow. The queen mother's response was: "Go! you're not the only son I have, I have many thousands and millions of sons, I cannot leave Faizabad" (Kamleshwar 1998, 8).

The trope of nation as mother, used by both critics and advocates of third world nationalism across history, must here be brought up against the "reality"[4] of legend, perhaps of history itself, since legends may represent history as fantasy, but cannot reject the existence of the structure of feeling which gave rise to legend in the first place. The queen mother is both mother and queen: and each of these identities adds a dimension to the other. She would have been a queen only in name and a mother in the limited literal sense if she had followed her son to Lucknow. But she is also a queen: the whole of Faizabad is, by virtue of this fact, under her maternal care. The construction of power through a familial relationship may be a mere trope, a political ploy of mythification, but it does fuse the separate identities of mother and queen for a definite purpose. The clarity with which this allegiance to both identities is acknowledged, explained and lived is often contradictory to abstractly and therefore exploitatively politicized identities upon which partitions are sought and maintained. This may be discerned in the idea of Partition and the process of formation of Pakistan itself in the minds of those "for" whom this step was deemed necessary, and for whose "benefit" it was carried out at such great human cost. In *Kitney Pakistan*, the central character, Adib-e-Aliya, is sitting in judgment on the past. History sends its witnesses and the poet hears their testimony and judges the age from which they come. A corpse comes before him and declares:

I have been killed.
Why?
Because I tried to create Pakistan within Pakistan
What does that mean? Was not Pakistan created in 1947?
Yes it was but that was a geographical thing. The map of Pakistan that was created in our hearts and minds is not completely drawn yet.
That will never be complete – yelled another corpse which carried a trident in its hand – now India will once more become whole, unfragmented. And he raised the slogan: Ram Krishna aur Vishwanath, Teenonlengey-saathsaath; we will take all three together.

(Kamleshwar 1998, 65)

Outraged and saddened too by the people from faraway coming to disrupt the lives of Gangauli which Tannu has treasured and still returns to, he ponders after the meeting with the sherwani-clad youth of Aligarh:

Are Hindustani Mussalman really not of this earth? But the Rajput Musalman of Dildarnagar and Gehmar are made of this very dust. So why is he voting for the Muslim League? Why does he feel the need for a watan, for a land whose culture time and space, is theirs? The Musalman who kissed Ram's wooden sandals as kadmey-rasool, the footsteps of Rasool wants to build Pakistan – why? Do all those people who will vote for the Muslim League know what Pakistan will be and how? Pakistan is certainly not god that it too must be surrendered to without one's having seen it.

(Raza 1998; 2007, 251)

The above reaction seems natural enough, as Islam was the plank upon which Jinnah based his demand for Pakistan. The religious identity of the Muslims in India, to the exclusion of everything else, is being evoked in the name of a new nation-state. Tannu has fought as an Allied soldier in World War II and returned to Gangauli as Major Hussain. Major Hussain tests the Aligarhi youth on the basis of the rationality of their position, and finds them wanting. Believing he can stem the tide of incomprehension, he offers an emotional reminder. Using his experience as an Asian, colonized soldier in a European battle, he explains to them the consequence of a battle fought on the basis of limited and well-defined cast-iron identities:

Look, I don't understand politics. But I have seen the battlefield.... There, the man who stands up to preserve himself from death is forced to hate the man who stands in front of him. It is possible that if I did not meet any one of them in the battlefield, but in Gangauli instead, I might have offered him a cigarette, or sugarcane juice ... we would have exchanged stories about our homelands, listened to each other's stories. But there, in the battlefield, if I did not kill him, he would have finished me. You people are giving birth to the fear of death. And we will be the ones to reap the harvest of this terror.

(Raza 1998; 2007, 249)

Major Hussain, or Tannu, tells the youth the story of Mosammat Kulsoom, whose son died in police firing at Kasimabad. When the boy realized that he had no hope of survival, he called upon a man who was running past him to escape the bullets and asked him to inform his mother that he lay here dying. This incident recurs in Kamleswar's novel. A number of incidents from Raza's novel become points of departure in Kamleswar's, because in the narratives of Partition it is history which is being judged and literature provides an important document of human realities which will testify to the consequences of the course that human beings choose to give to time itself. It is this human course that may be called history, and this gives Adib-e-Aliya, the cultured, learned poet, the power to call history as witness. So Kamleswar uses this same incident from Raza's novel to ground this singular definition of a self in the machinations of politics, exposing the latter by problematizing the very process of identity formation itself. Adib-e-Aliya recalls the incident of Kulsoom's son and echoes the words of Tannu to the black sherwani-clad youth who are naturally part of this episode in *Kitney Pakistan* as well:

The agony of the earth that is inherent in this message, you will not be able to understand ... your Jinnah sahib will leave a palace on Malabar Hill to go to Pakistan only to construct a bigger and better palace there, too. If he wants, he may even be able to relocate the grave of his wife Rati to Pakistan, because he has no bond with the earth whatsoever. But Kulsoom will not be able to do this ... she won't be able to take the grave of her beloved son Mumtaz who died in police firing at Kasimabad ... if all the graves are thus plucked out from the earth ... the Muslims will gain a broken down country, perhaps, but they will forever be deprived of home.

(Raza 2007, 248)

But Raza has yet another point to make through this same episode in his own novel. After the incident is narrated there, Tannu, Major Hussain, says to the Aligarh youths:

You will not understand (the language in which Mumtaz sent his last message), because you have made Urdu Muslim. But Khudakasam, I swear upon god, the language that I am even at this moment speaking is not my mother tongue. The language that Mumtaz used to send his message to his mother, that is my mother tongue, too. Because Hammad-da from our village speaks Urdu, he is mocked by everyone there. Tell me, when Pakistan is made, will you take Urdu along with you, or will you leave it here?

(Raza 1998; 2007, 249)

The issue of language is addressed in these words from various angles that are relevant to the formation and spread, and finally to the political use of Urdu in the quest for a homogeneous religio-political identity that led to partition. We may also notice the very use of the language itself as a cementing bond between people who are supposed to use Urdu by virtue of the fact that they belong to a specific religious community. The reality is that though some of the people of Gangauli are Muslims, Urdu is not the language they use: their mother tongue, despite their religious beliefs, is not Urdu but the "Hindi" that is spoken in the area in which they live, and which has no connection with religion at all. In fact, the practice of religion for the Muslims is carried out in another apparently "foreign" language, that of the Qur'an. Thus the logic of community formation based on religion is not automatically reinforced by using a common language with which the religion is identified. And if this is not the case, then one of the bonds insisted upon by the Aligrah youth, that of language, does not operate as a defining factor for the community they are addressing.

It seems that the very idea of Pakistan is spatially as well as conceptually remote from the understanding of the people who, by virtue of their religion, are designated as the natural inhabitants of this nascent country. So when Tannu hears Dullan saying, "Lekey rahengey Pakistan: we will not rest until we have wrested Pakistan," he asks the child: "'What will you do with Pakistan?' Dullan replies candidly: 'How do I know? All the boys back there were shouting this slogan, so I also joined in' " (Raza 1998; 2007, 246). But the slogan has invidious meaning for those who wish to use it as a weapon of division. We find the truth of this when Raza writes about the referendum for Pakistan, held on the eve of Pakistani and Indian Independence. This referendum rests on the consent of the people who are unable to grasp the mechanism itself because it is foreign to them to "choose" a country without bringing into the choice the considerations of their own past, their own lives and living practices so closely intertwined with the place in which they live and the history of their lives in that place. When Kulsoom is asked whom she will vote for, she says that she will "oat" for her dead son Mumtaz (Raza 1998; 2007, 244). The precious quality of the vote is respected fully by Kulsoom; and because it is so precious, she decides that it must go to the person who is most dear to her – her dead son. The spatial boundaries of the division are often unintelligible to the people of Gangauli: even when the Aligarh youths are not present, they discuss this problem among themselves:

> Tell me Bibi, where is this Pakistan being built?
> How do I know where it is being built?
> Isshh, if only it was somewhere near Ghazipur – then I would have been able to see it. I think Pakistan must be some sort of grand masjid.
>
> (Raza 1998; 2007, 244)

The looming reality of Pakistan is intertwined with the disruption of a way of life that is known, in all its loves and hatreds, its joys and pains, to those who have been Gangauli dwellers for as long as they have lived. Kammo and Sayeeda played together when they were children, though now, as they have grown up, the situation has changed somewhat. However, now, as Sayeeda folds her dupatta while Kammo holds an edge of the cloth in order to help her, they suddenly begin to talk of the future:

> If a city wants to go from one place to another, will that be possible? Kammo asked
> Ji? Sayeeda asks as she folds her dupatta.
> Friends are saying that Aligarh will go to Pakistan. I say that this is not possible.
> Why not?
> Arrey try and understand – are towns and cities people that they can go wherever they want?
> If the genie in the bottle can go anywhere it pleases, why can't Aligarh go to Pakistan?
> Kammo then went one day to Ghazipur with Jawaid Mian and asked Masum, Maddu, Shammu, Giggey and everyone else he knew – none of them could give a satisfactory answer. But at a function organized by the Muslim Students' Federation, this is what the Aligarh students had said. Kammo is taken aback: "Eybhai, this seems to be a problem then – what will happen to those who stay there already? Arrey if the city goes away

somewhere, where will the people who live in it go?" When he asks the Aligarh youths who have come to Ganaguli to canvas for votes this same question, they say by way of an answer: "If Pakistan is not separated, then the 8 crore Muslims will remain as untouchables in this country." Kammo is struck dumb. What are these college-educated boys saying? He says straightaway,

"Bhai, I think all your book-learning has gone to waste. I'll tell you why – you have not the least idea that it is the scavengers and the sweepers, the bhangi-chamar, who are untouchables. Are we bhangi or chamar? A person who was never an untouchable in his life cannot be made into one by any force, I tell you. Tell us how this can happen – we're listening."

In reply, the Aligarh-wallahs give an entire political speech. Kammo is unable to understand a single word of their speeches, because not a single word has any connection or relevance to the people of Gangauli or to Gangauli itself. He tries once more:

I don't understand this at all. Why will Gaya Ahir or Chikuriya or Lakhna Chamar become our enemies once Hindustan is made, without any rhyme or reason?Is this what they teach you in school where you come from?

You may not understand this now, but that is what is bound to happen. There will be cows chewing the cud in our masjids.

Arrey if the Muslims go away to Pakistan, then of what use are masjids – whether they become the homes for cattle or for horses, how does it matter? Hindus will surely not go there to read the namaz. We shall leave the land, and they will have to protect our masjids – that is nothing but an unfair imposition.

The Aligarhwallahs say: but when the Hindus drag your mothers and sisters out of the houses and abduct them, then don't come to us for help. A chamar was passing by just then, a bottle of kerosene in his hand. Kammo raised his voice and called out to him. He stopped upon being summoned.

Do you hear? Kammo says to him. What is it Mian? asks the chamar. These people have come from Aligarh to say that when Hindustan is azaad, free, then you folk will abduct our mothers and sisters.

Arrey Ram Ram! The chamar was dumbstruck. He turned to the people from Aligarh and said, "you are educated, thinking people. Just think about this a little – as long as we are alive, will anyone be able to even raise their eyes to look at the mothers and sisters of the Muslims here?"

(Raza 1998; 2007, 239–240)

Kammo then goes to school to find out where Aligarh is. He is told that Aligarh is in Hindustan, though he cannot believe this. Anyway, he is least concerned where Aligarh is: he is only afraid that Sayeeda may go away to Pakistan along with Aligarh (Raza 1998; 2007, 237).

All the arguments that were advanced by the proponents of a separate nation are addressed here – the condition of the Muslims in free India/Hindustan, the state of relations between the Hindus and the Muslims should the latter remain, the honor of what is dear to them, women or the mosque – and in each case, the response is a platitude that seems meaningless to the people of Gangauli. The relationships that exist, the connection to the land, the emotions that these arouse are the arguments that the advocates of Pakistan are unable to answer when they are posed as questions by the people of Gangauli. The land and its attendant life, the community and its history, memories and bonds, whether with Hindus or Muslims or even between them, make the very concept of partition an impossible one for people like those who live in Gangauli to understand, and, as history bears witness, difficult to implement except at great cost to all parties. The logic by which Kamleswar says that Jinnah is able to take his wife's grave with him is further illustrated by Migdad, a character in Raza's novel. When Migdad is asked whether he will go to Pakistan, he replies:

> I don't want to go anywhere. Let them go who are shy of the plough and the oxen. I am a kisaan, a farmer … where my field is, where my land is, there I shall remain.
>
> (Raza 1998; 2007, 216)

The apparently politically sophisticated arguments advanced by the advocates of separatism, whether Hindu or Muslim, are met with the same sort of puzzlement by all the people to whom they are addressed. When Chikuriya hears the Hindu schoolmaster advance a fundamentalist argument reinforced by the history of Aurangzeb's oppression of the Hindus in his kingdom, he wonders whether this is what this man teaches the youngsters entrusted to his care. His response is as direct as that of Kammo or Migdad:

> I don't know Aurangzeb. I know Zahir Mian, Kabir Mian, Fussu Mian and Anwarul Hussain Bari … those who have land must be oppressors. If they are not, they will be unable to make their zamindari function. And in this village, the Muslim Mians are the landlords, the zamindars.
>
> (Raza 1998; 2007, 173)

The landless Muslim and the landless Hindu are wary of what they will gain through Partition, as are the landed Muslim and the landed Hindu. It is a fear based on the understanding of the vagaries of class, where religion is an incidental in the eking out of livings. And even the religion through the evocation of which the subcontinent is being broken up into various nations is suspect for many of the people for whom, ostensibly, this separation is good and necessary. Anwarul Hussain Raki's son Farookh studies in Aligarh. When he is home for the holidays, Funnan Mian asks him for the latest news about Pakistan. His question initially is whether Gangauli will go to Pakistan. Farookh replies:

> No this will remain in Hindustan, Subah Sarhad, Panjab, Sindh and Bengal will go to Pakistan. And we are trying to see that Aligarh goes there as well.

Aren't you trying for Gangauli?

What about Gangauli?

If there is nothing about Gangauli, then what does it matter to us Gangauli dwellers whether Pakistan is built or not?

An Islamihukumat, a sovereign state where Islamic law prevails will be built.

Where is Islam left that an Islami hukumat can be built? The graves of my brothers, father and grandfathers are here, our chowk and imambara are here, our fields and pastures are here. Do you think we are stupid that we will be trapped by your Pakistan Zindabad, your Long Live Pakistan slogans?

When the English leave, this land will be ruled by Hindus.

Yes yes it will be. The way you are saying Hindu, it seems as if all the Hindus are hungry now, and they'll kill and eat us up as soon as they can. Arrey Thakur Kunwar Pal Singh is a Hindu isn't he? Jhiguriyais a Hindu as well. That Parshurao is also Hindu, when the Sunnis in the city were acting up and saying we shall not allow the banners of Hazrat Ali to be unfurled because Shias will read their prayers there, then it was he who made such a commotion that finally both banners were unfurled right there. Your Jinnah Saheb did not come to help us unfurl our banners.

Farookh starts to laugh.

Actually, we are doubtful about the sincerity of the Hindus.

About the what of the Hindus?

Sincerity, I mean that … what I want to say is that. …

What brother, you have forgotten the language of your forefathers?

Farookh starts to scratch his head in shame.

(Raza 1998; 2007, 154–155)

This exchange further underlines the nature of the problem that the advocates of separatism have not taken into account. It also underlines the source of these problems. That Farookh is unable to answer the question about the sincerity of the Hindus is no longer a surprise; but that he has to use a word foreign to any Indian language to assert this fact points to the root of the problem itself. The use of the English word in the text and Funnan Mian's reaction to it, as well as Farookh's own embarrassment, reveal the nature of the demands made for political expedience by the so-called leaders of the separatist movement on either side of the divide. It also points to the origin of the theory of separate nations and cultures for a people who have lived together for so long that they cannot any longer be easily separated into "local" people and outsiders – as we have seen thus far, the Muslims of Gangauli are inadequately defined without the spatial ties they a have with Gangauli and its life and history. The land is only a part of this life and history. There are the friendships of childhood tentatively maturing into love, the knowledge that the person one wants to see the most is within these houses somewhere, in the alleys, in the near corner, not across a border or beyond a partition.

The hellish reality of Partition occurred when one strand of the identity of all these people – real and imagined – was emphasized to the detriment of all the others. Many bombs blast off in the courtroom premises, one after the other: varieties of death come flooding in, the reason and method of each one etched upon its form in horrible detail. Yet each one is terrified of the penalty that this court, the seat of Adib-e-Aliya, the respected poet, can mete out. The functionary who attends the court asks them why they, so horrible in themselves, are afraid of the punishment of the court of the Adib-e-Aliya.

> I am afraid now because I am afraid, very afraid, of death. Because now I am human.
> So when you died, what were you?
> Then I was a Hindu.
> Are not Hindus humans too?
> They are. But when the poison of disgust and insult and dishonor begins to flow in my veins, I take off the bodily form of a human being and become a Hindu.
> Where does the poison of disgust and dishonor and insult come from?
> They are the harvest of the seeds sown in 47, hujoor. They have made the Hindu a bigger Hindu and the Muslim a bigger Muslim.
>
> (Kamleshwar 1998, 69)

Kamleswar may be faulted for some form of simplification, though in general, the policy of Divide and Rule is quite dramatically portrayed here. And he fuses this drama with the already inscribed reality of literature since, like all the witnesses from history who come to testify in the court of Adib-e-Aliya, there is literature too. The literature that enters Kamleswar's text as witness to history includes Rahi Masoom Raza's *Adha Gaon*, as we have seen. But Kamleswar also brings the writer Rahi into his own novel, and has him enter, distraught, on to the stage:

> Rahi stops briefly and catches his breath, and then, taking hold of himself, says:
> Listen, listen to what that eight–ten year old Dullan is saying!
> Lekey rahengey Pakistan! We shall not rest until we have wrested Pakistan.
> From whom will you wrest Pakistan? asks Funnan Mian with a grimace that should have scared the child.
>
> (Raza 1998; 2007, 246)

Funnan Mian is a formidable, tempestuous character in Raza's own book, a man who fights for the rights of the lower castes, whether Hindu or Muslim, and is thus ostracized by the upper castes in his own religious community as well as by the powers that be. Thus the characters of one text come to inhabit the other – they symbolize the "jag beeti" that is history, through the channels and alleys of which the self of the "aapbeeti" is formed and operates.

The partition of British India into Hindustan and Pakistan was achieved at the cost of not only the Hindus and the Muslims who were killed, raped or looted and left destitute, but the Pakhtuns, Pathans of the North Western Frontier Provinces, who were spread across the boundaries of Afghanistan and what became these two countries. The man who led the non-violent struggle among the Pakhtuns, Khan Abdul Ghaffar Khan, was asked by a foreign interviewer: Does this freedom you want have to be outside of Pakistan? Can you not be free within Pakistan? To this, Badshah Khan replied:

> This is a matter of no importance. What matters is that we be free to develop ourselves, to tear down our own Khans who have oppressed us, to make our own laws and to speak our own language.
>
> (Gandhi 2004, 10–11)

Let us take note that the aspirations of the Pakhtuns do not extend to geographical sovereignty, but to preserving a way of life that they identify as their own, not aligned to any named state which is already in existence or about to be formed. I am not suggesting that this is an ideal model which should have been followed by the leaders who felt that the coexistence of Hindus and Muslims as religious communities was politically impossible. The Pakhtuns themselves demanded Pakhtunistan after all their efforts at staying within India had failed. However, when they were amalgamated into Pakistan, Ghaffar Khan was opposed to the idea of "One Unit" floated by the Pakistani leaders who succeeded Jinnah. This was a proposal meant to weld all the diverse peoples who had arrived to live in the new state, and the diversities of the already existing inhabitants, into a homogeneous Pakistani identity. Ghaffar Khan was the staunchest of opponents to this homogenization. Rajmohan Gandhi reports:

> Still confined to the Rawalpindi Circuit house, though allowed to attend a session of the Constituent Assembly in the hill town of Murree, Badshah Khan asked in 1955, for a popular vote on One Unit and said that autonomy, not One Unit, would contain provincialism.
>
> (Gandhi 2004, 221)

It is not the purpose of this chapter to advocate a panacea for the past, an impossible task insulting to those who have lived through immense suffering. But an attempt to understand that such suffering was generated by dangerous attempts to turn human minds into permanent battlefields, a possibility that is still alive among us, is certainly within the scope of my concern. Hence, one might even suggest a possible way of engaging with this reality purely on the academic level. The sense that this reality is not our history but also our present will occur when we do engage with it thus. It is against the repetition of some part of that history that we attempt to invoke another part of what we must now reclaim as our history, too. The remainder of this chapter is a groping in that direction.

The discourse that can deconstruct the official oppositional discourse need not necessarily be structured as a binary of the hegemonic discourse to which any opposition is assumed to respond. The vagaries of modernity, in its theoretical and practical manifestations, is the crisis of limiting the number of discourses to two; one may even say that this limitation is a corollary of using the discourse of Orientalism as foundational in the understanding of several crucial elements of the postcolonial world, rather than reading it as a critique of such a construction. We are here once more visited with the possibility of another master discourse constructed in response to the same phenomenon: that of the proliferation of capital and its spread across the world. The varieties of responses to this phenomenon, when detached from one another, provide a repertoire of oppositional possibilities that have been flooding academia – liberal academia at least – in the past few years. This chapter has attempted to explore the nature of this detachment and its consequences. In its final stages, let us leave at least a series of questions. Olaf Caroe, one of the Raj's frontier-based officers and finally Governor of the North Western Frontier Provinces, described the Pakhtun society that Badshah Khan wanted to preserve and serve thus:

> The persistence of the Pathan tribal tradition has produced a society at all levels, starting from the nomad and the herdsman, through the articulated tribe and the sponsors of an Asian dynastic principle, to the modern lawyer, doctor engineer, administrator and politician. Standing over against the tribal village and the tents of the caravan are men for a century imbued with Western thought.... Anyone who cares to move in a twenty mile radius around Peshawar ... [can] daily enjoy a bodily translation into earlier phases of human society and life ... [and witness] a congeries of peoples engaged in a long march through the centuries from the fifth to the twentieth.
>
> (Caroe 1976, 63)

This excerpt is constructed along the very lines that the hegemonic discourse has laid out as the boundaries within which even an opposition to it must be constructed. Caroe's vision is expressed in a purely Darwinian metaphor of progress, the past being ranked lower than the present, progress being discerned along the axis of Western thought and Western professions; but he does articulate the simultaneous existence of many identities fused into a single person, of individual lives lived at the interstice of many overlapping spatial and temporal cultures. Does he remember the fact that doctors, engineers, etc., whom he uses as the markers of progress in Peshawar, have been walking those streets long before British intervention, with similar professions and similar responsibilities alluded to in a different language, with different tools, yet proportionate achievements? They were recognized and named differently because, in the past, they belonged to a different spatial and temporal culture, but their existence cannot be doubted. There was no capitalization in the culture of patronage which spawned these professions, and the economic and financial systems that fed them and were fed by them were differently positioned and differently oriented in the

cultures to which they belonged. Yet there is no way of arguing that the professions, the arts and the sciences they represented and contained, were in any way
invented or pioneered by the West. The contact with Western thought, too, went
back more than a century: the intermingling of worlds through routes of trade
provided opportunities for exchanging stories, at least, for which evidence exists.
The West may have pioneered a new system and a new culture where the position and function of these apparently modern engagements changed significantly,
but Western domination and its effects are the momentous changes which Caroe
may rightfully claim.

Caroe has displayed the vista on a vertical scale, but the scene he describes is
not merely or even grossly diachronic. Rather, for an Indian or a Pakistani who
has access to such milieus every waking hour of every day in the towns and villages across the subcontinent, at least, this is the very stuff of life. Yet why
should we follow even as perceptive a commentator as Caroe, who finally
resolves the scene into a hierarchy of temporal stages with progress/modernity/
Western thought/professions at the apex? If we are trained in simultaneity, in
multilinguality, from birth, it is because, as Edward Said said of the Pan-Arab or
Mediterranean society, there is "an extraordinary staying power despite mutilation by the nation-state" (Said 2002). Pointing out that "the genius" of Arab
culture was Catholicism, he puts Arab–Israeli relations in historical perspective:

> So what you are faced with is a kind of sublime grandeur of a series of trag-
> edies, of losses, of sacrifices, of pain.... But the people dealing with this
> gigantic painting are "quick-fix" Clinton, Arafat and Barak, who are like a
> group of single-minded janitors who can only sweep around it, who can
> only say let's move it a bit – let's put it in the corner.
>
> (Said 2002, 447)

The partition of the Indian subcontinent, despite its differences, can lay claim to
a similar history and a similar "quick-fix" solution which Said here criticizes.
Airing his doubts about the need for "secularism to be the necessary corner-stone
of any community that purports to be a part of the state," Said indicates that his
thinking about "nation," secularism and democracy does not merely invert the
master discourse that influences the practices of nation and community formation after the birth of nineteenth-century European nationalism. His response to
the Arab–Israeli conflict over political sovereignty is a particular kind of state:

> I would not necessarily call it secular-democratic. I would call it a binational
> state. I want to preserve for the Palestinians and the Israeli Jews a mech-
> anism or structure that would allow them to express their national identity. I
> understand that in the case of Palestine–Israel, a binational solution would
> have to address the differences between the two collectives.
>
> (Said 2002, 452)

Thus, we have more than the hegemonic model of the homogeneous nation-state
and the oppositional response of demanding an identity truncated from history

and space and pivoted on a single element that would, in its turn, demand a homogeneous nation-state of its own. The realities of Partition should have alerted us to the consequences of the insistence on difference, utilized for political gain. On the other hand, it should also have alerted us to our own rather heterogeneous plural identities. There is no disputing the fact that it is in this synchronic state that inequalities also exist; and the addressing of these inequalities, if done piecemeal, will yield the result that we have witnessed as the realities of Partition. The verities of life, social interaction, religious belief, faith and practice are continuities and breaks within this multiplicity of overlaps, and that is the life that the people of Gangauli, or the Pathans led by Badshah Khan, would want to preserve. Unconsciously, or perceptively, they are questioning the borders that force them to privilege any single one of these layers, one of these spaces, one of these times, material and affective, to take precedence over the others. The partition of India into Pakistan and Hindustan, by the very nomenclature itself, may have been an indicator of the loss that this exercise entailed; and a warning. The synchronic state of our being in the world, the place of religion and its practice in living this heterogeneity and the abstinence from easy "quick-fix" solutions that will overlook this heterogeneity in the name of expedience have all been revealed to us in greater or lesser degree through the history of the past 60-odd years. Perhaps the time has come now to take a vantage point at an intellectual distance from the man-made borders and redraw the terms of our engagement.

Notes

1 Kamleswar, *Kitney Pakistan* (New Delhi: Rajpal Prakashan, 2000). All references to the novel in this chapter are to the 2010 edition. Translation of all excerpts from this text is mine. The novel is henceforth cited in the text by the author's name.
2 Rahi Masoom Raza, *Adha Gaon* (New Delhi: Rajkamal Prakashan Private Ltd., 1998). The references to this novel used in this chapter are from the 2007 edition. Translation of excerpts from this text used in this chapter is mine. The novel is henceforth referred to by the author's name.
3 Krishna Sobti, *Zindaginama* (New Delhi: Rajkamal Prakashan Pvt Ltd., 1997). All references to this text in the chapter are to this edition. This text is henceforth referred to by the author's name; all translations are mine.
4 I have elsewhere discussed the nature of narrative "realism" in Indian-language texts (as distinguished from Indian English texts) (Chanda 2002).

Bibliography

Caroe, Olaf. *The Pathans: 550 BC–AD 1957*. Karachi: Oxford University Press, 1976.
Chanda, Ipshita. "'What is the Colour of Reality'? Dialogism and the Structure of 'Reality' in Two Indian Novels." *Critical Practice: A Journal of Critical and Literary Studies* 9 (June 2002).
Figueira, Dorothy. *Otherwise Occupied: Theories and Pedagogies of Alterity*. Stony Brook: State University of New York Press, 2008.
Gandhi, Rajmohan. *Ghaffar Khan, Nonviolent Badshah of the Pakhtuns*. New Delhi: Penguin Viking, 2004.

Kamleshwar. *Kitney Pakistan*. New Delhi: Rajpal Prakashan Private Ltd., 1998.
Lorde, Audre. *Sister Outsider*. Berkeley, CA: Crossing Press, 1984.
Raza, Rahi Masoom. *Adha Gaon*. New Delhi: Rajkamal Prakashan, 1998, 2007.
Said, Edward. *Power, Politics, and Culture*. New York: Vintage, 2002.
Sobti, Krishna. *Zindaginama*. New Delhi: Rajkamal Prakashan, 1998.

4 Fragments of familiarity

The Bengal Partition in Samaresh Basu's short stories

Sudipta Sen

Early on in the collective remembrance of the vivisection of the Indian subcontinent at the time of Independence, a distinctive literary imaginary of what is
known as the "Partition" had begun to surface even before historians gathered to
pick through the available evidence.[1] This much is now generally acknowledged
about Partition that it is made up of not one but many events. The same word
conjures up redrawn maps of the two Pakistans and India, the exodus and homelessness of millions, the mutual and retaliatory violence visited upon Sikhs,
Muslims and Hindus, the mass rapes and abduction of women and children, the
political travesty of the retreating Raj, and the hopeless squabbles between the
Indian National Congress and the All India Muslim League.[2] As a recent narrator of the period, Yasmin Khan, notes, the meaning of the term has been revis-
ited and reclaimed over the past 60 years along with diverging national
narratives, and it has now become "more than a sum of its considerable parts"
(Khan 2008, 9). Urvashi Butalia, in her path-breaking work on women's experiences during Partition, suggests that the term and its vulgate cognates render
little justice to the magnitude of the loss and survival at stake:

> How can these words take in the myriad meanings of this event? Not only
> were people separated overnight, and friends became enemies, homes
> became strange places, strange places now had to be claimed as home, a line
> was drawn to mark a border, and boundaries began to find reflection in
> people's lives and minds.
>
> (Butalia 2000, 285)

In a different sense, marking the creation of two nation-states as well as the division of one, "Partition" has always been an unstable, encumbered figure of
speech. Taken metonymically as the name of a fragment that characterizes the
whole, it signifies a diminution of the geopolitical whole, while read as synec-
doche it suggests, in retrospect, a relationship between two constituent parts
(India/Pakistan) (White 1973, 34–35). Thus the indeterminacy of its geographical referent persists, particularly so with the further secession of East Pakistan
and the subsequent birth of Bangladesh in a civil war of genocidal proportions
during 1971.

It is common knowledge that the events of Partition found their way into stories, memoirs, and films long before it became a topic of sustained historical inquiry. A historical perspective is often a function of temporal distance, but in this case the relationships between experience, memory, and history have remained particularly fraught and unclear. Butalia suggests that the neglect of history may simply be a result of deep-seated reticence in confronting the disturbing violence that engulfed the fateful year of 1947 (Butalia 2000, 75). I will argue here that the destabilizing effects of Partition are also manifest elsewhere, tied to narratives of home and belonging, whose temporalities are often at odds with those of received history.

This chapter traces certain fault lines in the historical memory of the splitting of Bengal in 1947 by looking at three short stories written by the illustrious Bengali author Samaresh Basu. Basu spent his early childhood years in Dhaka, Bikrampur, in a region that would later become part of East Pakistan, and today the nation-state of Bangladesh. His family migrated later to West Bengal. The events of Partition left, as it did on many of his contemporaries, a profound mark of his literary pursuits and his political beliefs; and many of his novels and stories are set in the context of 1947 and its immediate aftermath.

It has been argued that the deracination of inhabitants from the villages and cities fleeing the riots between Hindus and Muslims and the arrival of millions of refugees to the city of Kolkata (Calcutta), West Bengal, were events of a magnitude hard to fathom at the time.[3] Stories of such exodus do not conform to the linear historical narrative of Indian Independence, or the history of the emergence of the two neighboring nation-states. It points to an overwhelming sense of expulsion and loss, captured in the Bengali term (*udbastu*) for refugee: describing those forcibly uprooted from their ancestral homesteads. It is in this context that a lyrical, mnemonic figure of an "undivided Bengal" was reinscribed in the literary narratives that emerged out of Partition. The political failure to avert the division of Bengal and the breakdown of civil society along sectarian lines urged a particular view of the past tied to the imaginary of a bountiful and timeless, pre-Partition Bengal. In this refusal to accept the verdict of history, a bulk of the literature that emerged in response to the Partition registers a fundamental break with the narrative of national determination, especially in the context of Punjab and Bengal after 1947. There are early and important examples of such repudiation in the literature of both India and Pakistan, most memorably expressed in the poetry of Amrita Pritam or Faiz Ahmed Faiz.[4]

This counter-narrative was also based on the notion that the tragedy of the division of Punjab or Bengal should have been averted somehow, and also echoed in the lament that a society based on the neighborliness and trust between Sikhs, Hindus, and Muslims should not have been destroyed along the lines of religious conflict. For many, it was communal hatred that ultimately sullied the purity of the struggle for the nation, much more than the banal political machinations of the Indian National Congress, the Muslim League, or the Cabinet Mission set up by the British. Basu's stories, examined below, focus on the anteriority of the purportedly common inheritance of eastern and western Bengal.

They allude to a new, emotive, and sentient cartography subject to the memory of a shared landscape located in a particular form of the past.

After the divide: a context for Samaresh Basu's early fiction

Bengali literature around the theme of the great divide of 1947, read in its urban, middle-class (often Hindu) context, embraces a retro-national imaginary attempting to circumvent the stark reality of borders, boundaries, check posts, broken telegraph and railway lines, and the endless and terrifying facility of violence. Such a sensibility, at once nationalist, humanitarian, liberal, and at times doctrinaire Marxist, was largely shaped during the inter-war period in the urban milieu of middle-class Calcutta as the city witnessed periodic devastation and human suffering on a massive scale unfolding throughout the provinces of Bengal.

First came the Calcutta, Pabna, and Dacca riots of 1918 to 1926, and then the famine of 1943 caused by the wartime shortage of grain through army requisitions, speculation, and hoarding, which led, in a conservative estimate, to the loss of 500,000 lives in the city and countryside. Thousands of starving families filled the streets of Calcutta begging for leftover gruel from middle-class kitchens; the dead were heaped on the streets, spreading cholera, smallpox, and malaria. Third, the Great Calcutta Killing of August 1946, which in just three days time claimed about 4,000 lives (S. Das 1993, 171). Finally, the Boundary Commission set up by Viceroy Mountbatten's administration which awarded villages and towns with little regard to ties that bound Bengal across the riparian border of the river Padma beyond the confluence of the Ganga and the Brahmaputra. The exodus of millions left homeless, thousands struggling for shelter and work in Calcutta, filling up its slums and outskirts, further inscribed the image of this loss in popular imagination. They also left a deep impression on Samaresh Basu at the threshold of his writing career.

Like many of his contemporaries Basu began to write in the 1940s while actively involved in organized politics. The family left Dhaka between 1938 and 1939, and settled down in the township of Naihati on the Ganga river not far from Calcutta.[5] During this time Basu dropped out of school, became a street peddler, and also an active member of the Communist Party of India (CPI). In 1949 when the CPI was declared an illegal organization, he was arrested and held for interrogation in the Special Branch cell, and later transferred to the Presidency Jail in Calcutta. While he was in prison, Basu wrote the play *Preta* (Labor Officer) and the novel *Uttaranga*. Released from jail in 1951, he gave up his last realistic possibility of a steady job in the Ichapur gun factory for refusing to sign a bond stating that he would abstain from all political activity in future. Unemployed, he ventured into a full-time literary career the year after India was declared an independent republic, living in dire poverty, dependent on the meager support of literary magazines such as *Paricay*, *Prabaha*, and *Desh*.

The Communist Party of India at this time was facing an internal crisis of leadership and direction that would lead to a major split in the 1960s. A struggle was taking place between the more radical ideologues such as B.T. Ranadive (a follower of Stalin's confidant Andrei Zhdanov and the Yugoslavian Edvard Kardelj), advocating a rejection of Indian independence[6] and a return to armed struggle, and proponents such as P.C. Joshi who sought moderation and collaboration within the framework of national political parties. The "Ranadive Thesis," which along with the rejection of bourgeois values asked artists and performers to follow the prescribed and scientific path of socialist aesthetics, left many writers such as Basu uninspired and disillusioned (S. Bandopadhyay 1998, 5). He decided to leave the arena of active politics altogether in 1955. There is little space here to reflect on the breadth and impact of such experiences on his artistic sensibility, especially since his literary oeuvre is so extensive. However, as critics have noted, plots of his early novels such as *Saudagar* (*Merchant*, 1956–1957) – which narrates the story of a biscuit maker from East Bengal who left his home, his factory, and his business for an uncertain future in Calcutta during 1948 – were conceived when he lived near the Naihati railway station, and became familiar with the plight of the burgeoning refugee colony there.[7]

Threshold of history

Stories of survivors in refugee camps are easily digested within the singular historical narrative of the emergence of postcolonial Bengal or Punjab. Many historians of the Partition have had experiences similar to Urvashi Butalia's whose subjects' recollections never quite resembled what had been officially documented. Butalia writes of her own uncle's struggle with the memory of Partition with the caveat that "no historical document can approximate his pain and anguish; none can reflect his trauma or even begin to understand his confusion and ambivalence" (Butalia 2000, 74). An apophatic[8] reading of such retelling, focusing on vital questions that are not raised or answered, brings us one step closer to the muted utterances which are at the heart of the vexing problem of historical reconstruction. This problem has been brilliantly illustrated by Michel-Rolph Trouillot in his history of the Haitian Revolution, where he contends that silences are just as constitutive of history as are the more visible assemblage of facts and interpretations: "silences are inherent in the creation of sources, the first moment of historical production" (Trouillot 1995, 51). Disinterested, objective histories, which are merely invested in the production of historical facts as common currency of the past, rarely address such erasures.

This is particularly relevant to the subject of horror which is not faithfully or comfortably represented in the time and space of the typical historical account. For many contemporaries the scale and intensity of hatred between neighboring communities during Partition destroyed any sense of a shared history. The popular Bengali novelist Banaphul (Balaichand Mukhopadhyay) in his novel *Svapnasambhaba* ("Birth of a Dream") articulated the educated Bengali middle-class subject's futile search for an explanation for such violence in history through the figure of the confused protagonist Jatin:

Jatin had become strangely bewildered. He could not read the daily newspaper.... He wondered whether all human feelings had vanished forever!
What people were doing throughout the country in this twentieth century
would put ghouls to shame! During the Sepoy Mutiny Hindus and Muslims
had risen up as one. Azimulla Khan had been the right hand of Nanasahib.
Bahadur Khan of Bareilly had declared that he would stop ritual killing
(qurbani). The emperor of Delhi had forbidden the slaughter of cows.
Hindus and Muslims had fought side by side. Every rebel regiment had a
maulavi, a purohit ... And look what happened in the blink of an eye!

(Mukhopadhyay 1975, 3)

Communal butchery not only ravaged the lineaments of sociability in rural
Bengal but also took its toll in the middle-class and respectable neighborhoods
of the city of Calcutta. For the urban and the educated, it seemed to replace the
complex historic differences between Hindus and Muslims with a singular, ata-
vistic spectacle of dismemberment that defied the very logic of the struggle for
independence.

Although the question of class is not the main theme of this chapter, it is difficult to discuss Basu's take on communal conflict without considering his
Marxist views, which after all he held in common with a large section of the
Bengali intelligentsia. These constituted a common leitmotif of Bengali literature
produced during this decade, that communal hatred was a monstrosity created by
the British as part of a colonial conspiracy, or that Hindu–Muslim riots were
ultimately an outcome of failed class struggle.[9] Basu's stories, however, do not
easily conform to this kind of reduction. They do not seek fundamental causal
explanations for the failure of history, or relegate the murderous intent of religious mobs simply to communal "frenzy" capitulating human agency. Rather,
they capture a moment suspended at the margins of the familiar past, rendering
its protagonists as primal agents of violence and survival.

In the discussion of the two stories that follow in this section, *Adab* and
Jainal, I focus on Basu's treatment of the horror of miscognition during the
initial outbreak of communal violence. One dwells on the anonymity of death
and destruction during the Calcutta Killings of 1946 that reduces its victims to
their basic, instinctive appetites for survival; the other is a first-person narrative
of a friendship between a Hindu and a Muslim boy that is ravaged by bigotry
and intolerance.

Adab was Basu's first short story, published in *Paricay* in 1946.[10] Set in riot-
torn Calcutta under curfew, two men fleeing violent mobs discover each other as
they both try to hide behind a garbage can in a darkened alley. They desperately
seek to verify whether the other is a Hindu or a Muslim, but are terrified to ask.
As the wait becomes interminable they finally strike up a conversation. They
find that they have come from opposite shores of the River Ganga. One is a
worker in a thread mill, the other a boatman. They lie hidden behind heaps of
trash for hours, waiting, wondering whether they will ever see their families
again, asking the impossible question: why have the familiar streets and markets

turned into a river of blood? The factory worker offers the boatman a smoke, the boatman fumbles for a match, finds it in his pocket, and exclaims: "*subhanal-lah!*" – giving away that he is a Muslim. For a moment the two face each other in disbelief. Yet thrown together in this situation they try not to heed the murderous cries raging around them. They bid each other with the salutation "*adab*" after the din of rioting has finally died down, and it appears that the murderous mobs have retreated for the day. Soon after the boatman steps out of hiding he is shot down by the military police called out for the curfew. The mill worker creeps back to his hiding place wondering how the news of his acquaintance's death would befall on the family, turning the coming day of the Id festival into a day of mourning for his wife and little children.

Adab is a story about the humanity of poor, ordinary people whose lives are swept up in the tide of events beyond their grasp. In the story they are introduced simply as two "creatures" (*prani*) huddled by the side of a garbage can paralyzed with the fear of being lynched. They fight their fear and suspicion as they discover each other's identity in the brief flare of the match being struck. Cast into the margins of both history and society, these poor creatures who happen to be Hindu and Muslim, staring into each other's faces, realize the cruelty and heartlessness of human beings as a "species accursed" (*abhishapta jata*). Basu exploits this moment as a double, one of both cognition and horror, where communal identity is mirrored in both its absurdity and verisimilitude.

Jainal, Basu's other story set in the context of the outbreak of communal riots in the rural countryside of Bengal, is about the friendship between two adolescent boys from the two respective communities (Chaudhuri *et al*. 1994, 284). These two friends set out on a quiet fishing trip on the river. Their boat drifts into an adjoining lake, dangerously close to a place where a riot is taking place. People are fleeing in every direction. Another boat filled with rioters suddenly begins to gain upon them on the lake. While Jainal is trying to pull the boat into the weeds in order to save their lives, the narrator realizes, as if for the first time, that his friend is a Muslim. The story hinges on the truth of this intolerable moment:

> We blurted out in unison: Riot!… For a second my heart missed a few beats. In the gust of easterly wind, someone seemed to hiss … death! In an instant I remembered that I was a Hindu, and the people who were coming towards us, fishermen, were all Muslims … I glanced back at Jainal's face. His face appeared hard, his eyes transfixed toward me. Why? I recalled in a flash – Jainal, a Muslim? I could almost see the concealed amusement of a masked assassin playing on the corner of his lips.
>
> (Basu 1978, 118)

When this traumatic moment subsides, and they manage to escape together, the narrator finds refuge in Jainal's home with his family. He hides there for days waiting for the riot to subside. Jainal sets out to search for his elder brother Majid who has disappeared without a trace. News comes eventually in the form of Jainal's bloody clothes brought back to their parents by his missing brother for burial. It finally dawns on the protagonist of the story that he had failed to trust his best friend when his own life was at stake. His friend Jainal on the other hand did not hesitate to put his own family at risk to protect him. At the end of the story Jainal's death leaves the author utterly disconsolate.

Basu's use of the confrontal image, of the gaze alienated and returned signifying the instant of estrangement from the familiar, is key to his deliberation on the idea of fratricide. In *Jainal* he deploys the conventional ruse of a mask, where suddenly the visage of the killer appears on the face of his friend. The mask is a reminder of the externality of our everyday identities. Daniel McNeill writes that masks from time immemorial have functioned as emblems of the self, "donnable faces, instant personas, the most immediate and widespread kind of disguise" (McNeill 2000, 145). In *Adab*, the face that is briefly lit by the flare of the match is the face of a Muslim ("*Yes. I am a Muslim. So what?*"). Identity and difference are sublimated in such a specular encounter, precipitating a nightmarish, fragmented self. These are archaic images peering into the future that cannot be easily banished from the memory of a new political site conceived in the bloodshed of friends and brothers. They anticipate what Ashis Nandy would later call the "anxiety of self-confrontation" lurking in the selective memory of Indian nationalism (Nandy 2002, 214).

Basu's stories seem to drive towards an overwhelming impasse. If the imagined community of the nation is a *déchirement* at the very inception of its being, then what does it leave in its denial? Are certain images of Partition simply inassimilable as historical fragments that cannot be restored to a national history?[11] Rather than focusing on the vulnerability of nationalist historical discourse, it is tempting to resort to an explanation based on the idea of aggression as the source of a fundamentally anxious and neurotic modern subject. Basu's use of the violent encounter is a device that captures both the failure and resolution of the splintered national subject, where Hindu and Muslim figures are suddenly unable to behold each other in their old familiar faces.

René Girard in considering the relationship between desire and conflict argues that desire is essentially mimetic (Girard 1979, 145). As rivals share the same desire, the self beholds its own monstrosity in its exact double. Girard's provocation is suggestive in this context, because mimetic desire may be seen as a powerful response to the crisis inherent in the sacrificial economy of death. Genocide becomes thinkable only when the community is no longer able to restrict the death of its own members.[12] Similarly, the fatal desire for isomorphic nationalities inherent in the rise of rival, murderous communities in the disturbances of 1946/1947 provides a window into the murderous proximity of Hindus and Muslims that Basu's stories conjure up. Oppositional binaries such as Hindu/Muslim, East/West, brother/stranger, and enemy/friend seem to collapse here, confounding identity and distance. They recall, once again, the incredulous voices of contemporary witnesses such as the celebrated historian Jadunath Sarkar, who refused to accept two halves of Bengal as geopolitical reality, insisting that in terms of language, race and manner of life "people are exactly the same *except for religion*."[13]

Historians have long grappled with the link between personal trauma and aspects of collective behavior, evident in moments of crisis such as war and genocide.[14] It has been suggested that there may indeed be affinities between symptoms of individual psychosis and other neurotic aspects of modernity. Popular recollection of the violent events of the Partition suggests a breakdown of the basic foundations of social life, and a suspension of the everyday economy of event and experience. Individual memories of these events are often fragmented, episodic, inimical to the logic of historical sequence. Oral historians such as Butalia have encountered the force of this reticence during interviews with subjects, and they realize the power of silence where memories are too painful for words (Butalia 2000, 18). It is possible that the collective historical memory of such blighted pasts follows a similar pathology, where the initial moment of collective horror encapsulated in a particular set of events is never assimilated fully, and can only be revealed post datum and in fractions.[15] G.D. Khosla, both a witness and an early historian of Partition, writing soon after the events of 1947, could only offer a failure of reason as the cause for the detriment of human life, in lieu of history:

> History has not known a fratricidal war of such dimensions in which human hatred and bestial passions were to the levels witnessed during this dark epoch when religious frenzy, taking the shape of a hideous monster, stalked through the cities, towns and countryside, taking a toll of half a million innocent lives.
>
> (Khosla 1949, 3)

In the immediate aftermath of Partition, historical reason and the promise of future nations failed to provide a closure to the horrors of death and separation. During the following decade, as migrants began to repair their lives and reconcile their futures to new political realities, there was little space given to a meaningful avowal of this deeply troubled past.[16] It is possible to suggest that in such a context a migrant sensibility necessarily sought its object of attachment elsewhere, in the images of a shared time and place secure in their distance from the unbearable present. I examine one of Basu's most affecting short stories below to explore further such displacement and nostalgia.

Home, longing, and the artifice of memory

For the uprooted, pillaged, and the destitute streaming into camps in 1948 the historical significance of the birth of a new nation held little consolation. An exodus of such colossal proportions had irreparably ruptured the spatial and temporal integrity of the nation as an idea. At the same time, the nation also demanded a historical narrative that could transcend individual instances of death and loss, so that, one day, disparate fragments of individual experience could again be reconstituted into an acceptable sequence of events and causes. Wherever such events are assembled towards a preordained denouement,

historical meaning derives from what the philosopher of history Rienhart Kosel-
leck described as the minimal "threshold of fragmentation" below which the
assemblage falls apart. Historians of Indian Partition such as Gyanendra Pandey
and Ian Talbot suggest that conventional historiographical event-based accounts
of rape, murder, abduction, and flight – horrors that pervade popular memories
of Partition – fall short of just such a threshold.[17] Pandey points out that in the
context of communal riots in India, accounts of the experience of violence and
sexual assault remain impervious to the typical evidentiary paradigms of history
writing, and can only be represented as disjointed and fragmentary (Pandey
1991, 559–572). If the conventional register of history fails to connect the pages
of a diary or a police report, as Pandey argues, literature does not readily offer
any meaningful refuge for such experience either.[18]

Literary figures, nonetheless, provide clues to the sense of desolation resulting from the forcible expulsion of people from their known *habitus*. Alok Bhalla
has written evocatively about this pervasive sense of home and homelessness in
fiction of Partition, particularly poignant in the depiction of violence that shattered the shared life-worlds that once held together Sikhs, Muslims, and Hindus
as neighbors and members of a single community (Bhalla 2006, 14–16). Bhalla
points out, quite rightly, that characters in Partition stories are unable to put
behind them the memories of their abandoned homes (Bhalla 2006, 10–11) Their
recollections are often dissimulative in their very selectiveness, blurring the line
between history and reminiscence, eliding the painful experiences of conflict,
strife, and poverty. Here home, country, and provenance are often reinscribed in
shared memory, endowed with a transcendent temporality and renewed spatial
integrity.

Samaresh Basu's short story *"Binimay"* (Exchange) is a vivid re-creation
of the uneasy transposition of these spatial and temporal attributes in the
mnemonic re-creation of pre-Partition Bengal. Basu introduces a historical landscape in a series of bold strokes through the living memory of a schoolteacher
who has been forced to leave behind his native land in East Pakistan for a
miserable shelter in an immigrant slum of squalid industrial Calcutta (Basu
1978). *Mastermashai*, or the old Gandhian schoolteacher, is about to offer his
daughter Swarna's hand in marriage to an untrustworthy stranger – a feeble,
last-ditch attempt to protect her dignity in a hostile city and alien land. In such
a moment of crisis, stranded on a darkening street of this forbidding and heart-
less metropolis, fragments of his past life flash up before him like that of a
drowning man. He must give up his daughter, just as one would consign the
graven image of the Goddess Durga after her worship is over, after her seven
days of majesty are over, to be immersed as a lifeless frame in the waters of the
torrential river. Swarna is his daughter but is also the figurative Mother. She is in
her person the very land left behind. Not simply the whole, but also its constitu-
ents: the vast River Padma, the tumbling canal of Narayanganj, his birthplace in
Bikrampur; she becomes history, the 12 landlords who fought the Mughals,
Mansingh of Bikrampur; and cartograph – *pargana*, village, and ancestral home
– all at once.

Where is today that proud home of a hundred years – the unborn portrait of the country once visited in dreams? Nowhere. That dreamlike sleep has been shattered; the crude terror of a nightmare comes rushing to engulf his life built around Swarna, his daughter, and their only chance of being able to live on somehow as an inhabitant of a new Hindustan.

(Basu 1978, 104)

Here Basu hints at the ultimate futility of the schoolteacher's attachment to an ancestral home. Yet it is an obdurate illusion that refuses to admit the squalor and sprawl of the immense urban slum, the nauseous drain, the dirt, and the helpless plight of refugees huddled in street corners, public parks, and on railway platforms. Basu's forlorn figure is a subject without a future whose only refuge is a form of territorial longing. Such agonistic misplacement, which may very well refract Basu's own political voice, may seem like a desperate act of faith, an attempt to reclaim the fragile webs of normative social reality. This formulation is partly based on a reading of the Lacanian relationship between the unconscious and the real elaborated fruitfully in Slavoj Žižek (Žižek 1991, 17). Basu's rendition of the schoolteacher's moment of overwhelming crisis, I suggest, may also be read as a protest against the collective resignation of millions of unwelcome subjects of independent India.

"Binimay" is also about a father's futile, heroic attempt to defend the paternal responsibility of his generation. The giving away of Swarna amounts to a filial sacrifice: a daughter lost, a country left behind in exchange for a nation gained. The title "Binimay" or "exchange" is therefore a transaction replete with the terrible irony of a social contract that cannot be rewritten. The fact that women's bodies as targets of violence, abduction, and forcible recovery became the sites of national and communal honor and defilement has been well documented by oral historians of the partition such as Butalia, Menon, and Bhasin.[19] In Basu's "Binimaya", the offering of the daughter's hand becomes profoundly allegorical, a distillation of multiple separations: land, country, home, future.[20]

It is not only femininity – a very familiar trope in the literary depiction of the Bengal countryside – that seems to be at work here. Basu is clearly drawing upon the emotive landscape of Bengal as a founding national sentiment, dating back at least to the Swadeshi agitation against the partition of Bengal within British-India in 1905, if not earlier. Such gendered landscapes are strewn across the *locus classici* of Bengali literature on undivided Bengal, in Tagore, Jibanananda Das, Nazrul Islam, and Jasimuddin, to name just a few literary icons. Basu's empathy for the searing nostalgia in the "giving away" of the betrothed daughter does not soften his indictment of the old schoolmaster's abject helplessness. Basu suggests that the home and the world can only be reconciled in sterile retrospect. This is not the past perfect of history but the subjunctive past of remembrance, where home, country, and origin re-emerge endlessly as empty and consolatory gestures.

A dystopic imagination

All three stories discussed above provide a glimpse into elements familiar to students of the growing literature on narratives of Partition. In the three tragedies that strike – the shooting down of a chance acquaintance by the police in a curfew, the disappearance and murder of a friend, and the sacrifice of a daughter – Basu offers his own vision of the everyday human subject caught in the throes of a nation emerging and unraveling. There is nothing new or extraordinary in the fear of encounter between strangers in *Adab*, the loss of innocence in *Jainal*, or the loss of homeland in *Binimay*. These are in many ways archetypal stories of Partition. At the same time, reading them in retrospect, they still haunt, invoking a prelapsarian time-space when such events may have been shocking. They are surely meant to discomfit the reassuring, temporal distance of his Bengali middle-class readers and their sense of historical reason.[21] I would argue that they still disturb us in that way.

In doing so, they also take us back to the mythopoetic landscape of an undivided Bengal. Basu's stories are undoubtedly representative of this principal genre because of their location at a seismic moment of subcontinental rift. The rivers of East Bengal, for instance, Dhalesvari, Buri-Ganga, Padma, become emblematic of an indelible landscape, especially as they flow across the newly drawn lines of the colonial Boundary Commission. Landscapes, as Simon Schama reminds us, are artifacts of culture that are precursory to the idea of nature – constructs of the imagination projected on to land and water (Schama 1995, 61). The mnemonics of landscape as spatial orientation are elaborate and complex. As the geographer Yi-Fu Tuan has shown, mythic dimensions of space do not follow the logical relationship between part and whole. The fragment often mirrors a distinct totality.[22] Thus a host of elements signify domicile in unison: earth on which a house stands, ancestral foundations, village, city, river, or region. These scalar forms and their memories remain central to the techniques of relating the experience of diaspora. They mark points of detachment from an alternate, cognitive map of Bengal, separating the geopolitical from the experiential (Lefebvre 1991, 314–335).

The memory of an ancestral landscape hardly recompenses for the banishment from home. Nevertheless, the persistent allusion to an ancestral landscape of East Pakistan, not only in literature but also in post-Partition cinema, points to a kind of sublimation that takes place in the transition from eidetic to experiential memory.[23] The act of remembering, as Halbwachs once showed, forms a kinship with the past, and its impulse is always collective (Halbwachs 1992, 52–53). The past can never be entirely or voluntarily repossessed.[24] Basu's description of the loss of familiar and filiative space recalls the wrenching, melodramatic saga of banishment and separation memorably explored in the films of Ritwik Ghatak, who himself wrote about the Bengal of his boyhood days, a Bengal "whole and glorious" (Ghatak 2000, 49). Ghatak's films on partition are replete with reminders of the Bengal diaspora expressed through a characteristic cinematic landscape.[25] There is, for example, that memorable scene in his film

Komal Gandhar (*E-Flat*) where Bhrigu and Anasuya, brother and sister, are looking at a railway line that has been abruptly cut off at the border between two new nations. The camera comes to a stop at the end of the row of sleepers, where the road to East Bengal trails off. The sight, Ghatak wrote later, was meant to raise a "searing scream in Anasuya's heart" (Ghatak 2000, 50). In Ghatak's films the anxiety of separation without the promise of reunion or reconciliation lends a heightened significance to the themes of family, marriage, motherhood, and relationships between siblings (Biswas 2004; O'Donnell 2004). Critics such as Jyotika Virdi and Bhaskar Sarkar have pointed out that such themes of loss and reunion of families became an established genre in Hindi films in the decade after Indian independence.[26]

Basu's short stories invoke a similar *maladie du pays* but their signification lies elsewhere. Their brevity produces an effect quite different from similar subjects in films or novels. Novels, and to a degree films, are syncretic genres, while the fundamental characteristic of the short story is its abrupt suggestiveness (May 1994, 2, 118). The short story, as Georg Lukàcs observed, is a fictional form that deals with a fragment prised out of life's totality and deliberately violates the pattern of temporality by focusing on the discreteness of events (Lukàcs 1983, 21). A celebrated exponent of the genre, Julio Cortazar, saw in the short story the same paradox inherent in the photographic image that opens up the vision of something much larger than itself by purposely foreclosing the wider field of observation.[27] In this sense, the short story's aperture lends itself to the splintered experiences of the great divide in Bengal. Basu's craft here is similar to that of the great craftsman of the Urdu short story, Sadat Hasan Manto.[28] Returning their antagonists to the primary site of disenchantment, Basu takes us back to the indeterminate futures conjured up in 1947 and its immediate aftershock. Reading them today in the light of the capricious and resurgent forms of collective violence that still plagues the integrity of the national ideal in the Indian subcontinent one is reminded of Barthes' aphoristic statement that the task of dramatic art is not to express reality but to signify it (Barthes 1972, 74). True, Basu dwells, like many other writers of his generation who survived the ravages of the Partition did, on mourning, dislocation and the irredeemable passage of time. Nostalgia, often regarded as a determining pathology of the modern condition, however, is not an end in itself or indeed for the characters that inhabit these stories (Boym 2002, xvi). The Manichean histories of their disfigured homelands do not yield any such simple refuge.

Notes

1 On the emergence of the historiography from eyewitness accounts see Yong and Kudaisya (2000, 8–9).
2 Gyanendra Pandey distinguishes between at least three different aspects of Partition: the Muslim League's demand for Pakistan, the split-up of the Muslim majority provinces Punjab and Bengal, and the uprooting, massacre, and exodus of millions across the borders between India, West Pakistan, and East Pakistan (Pandey 2001, 25–39).

3 In the year 1948, at least 12,000 people migrated to West Bengal every day from across the newly drawn border demarcating East Pakistan. The refugee camps were utterly inadequate, and hundreds of thousands of refugees flooded the streets, railway stations, and outskirts of Calcutta (Khan 2008, 168).

4 See e.g., Faiz's commonly recited poem *Freedom's Dawn (August 1947)*, whose opening lines run famously as follows: "*Yeh dagh dagh ujala, yeh shab-gazida sahar/ Vo intezar tha jiska, ye voh sahar to nahin*" ("This leprous daybreak, this dawn mauled by the night/This dawn is not one we had waited for"). Amrita Pritam's haunting ballad, *Ajj Akhan Waris Shah Nun (I Say Unto Warish Shah)* (1949) implores: Arise O friend of the distressed/See the plight of your Punjab/Corpses lie strewn in the pastures/And the Chenab has turned crimson (George 1994, 946–947).

5 See "*Nijeke janar janye*", in *Galpasangraha*, Vol. 1 (Kolkata: Bisvabani, 1978), p. 5. For a biographical sketch see S. Chaudhuri, N. Sengupta, and B. Sarkar eds, *Samareśa Basu: Smaraṇa-Samīkṣaṇa* (Kolkata: Cayanika, 1994), pp. 567–570.

6 B.T. Ranadive, during the second congress of the CPI, stated that the independence declared in August 1947 was "a concession to the national bourgeoisie, and the national bourgeois leadership was striking a deal against the interests of the people." See *Review of the Second Congress of the Communist Part of India*, cited in Jean Curran, "Dissension among India's Communists," *Far Eastern Survey* 19:13 (July 12, 1950), 132–136. The Ranadive intervention was one of the catalysts that led to the split in Indian communism leading to the creation of the CPI and the CPI (M).

7 Ibid., 6–7. On the political significance of this novel see Parthapratim Bandyopadhyay, *Samareśa Basu: Samayera Cihna* (P. Bandopadhyay n.d., 46–54).

8 I have borrowed this phrase from Jean Baudrillard (Baudrillard 1997, 67–68). Apophasis simply denotes the act of "mentioning by not mentioning".

9 These ideas were expressed by major authors at the time such as Manik Bandyopadhyay, especially in the novel *Svādhīnatāra Svāda (Taste of Freedom)*.

10 For a discussion of the context in which Adab was written see the discussion by Parimal Bhattacharya in "*Samareśa Basura Chotogalpera Nirmāṇa: Kayekaṭi Kathā*" (Chaudhuri *et al.* 1994, 487–488).

11 As Ernst Renan pointed out in his much-quoted speech on the idea of the nation and its relationship to history, "lapses of memory" and historical error are crucial to the fabrication of the nation as an idea. Nationalist discourse is pernicious in that it admits deliberate and dangerous misunderstandings (*dangereux malentendus*) regarding the past (Renan 1947, 887–907). See Renan, "Qu'est-ce qu'une nation?" (Renan 1947).

12 Ibid., 162.

13 Sarkar, quoted in Yong and Kudaisya (2000, 143). Starker lost one of his sons during the Calcutta killings of 1946; emphasis added.

14 See Micale and Lerner (2001, 10). Much work has been done in this regard on the individual and collective experiences of the Jewish Holocaust in Nazi Germany, and on combatants who survived the two World Wars.

15 On some of the problems in studying collective and individual trauma in narratives of survival among women victims of Partition violence, see V. Das (2007, 102–103).

16 Yong and Kudaisya have discussed the protracted nature of this struggle in the fragmentation of families and identities, the plight of refugees, and their search (Pandey 1991) for basic rehabilitation and livelihood, subject to the fickleness of policy-makers (see Yong and Kudaisya 2000, 142–143). I am echoing here Freud's formulation of the *Nachtraglichkeit*; that is, a kind of *afterwardness* that is created to deal with psychological trauma. Freud implied that memory traces, experiences, and impressions effected a radical rethinking of the causality and temporality of memory, deferring the acknowledgment of something that is too troubling or critical. While the caveat remains that we should not extrapolate a collective psyche from individual episodes of trauma, some of these ideas of displacement remain crucial to historians of collective memory.

17 Pandey (2001, 49–50); see also Ian Talbot, "Literature and the Human Drama of the 1947 Partition," *South Asia* 18 (1995), 37–38.
18 On this point see Jill Didur's critique of the historiography of Partition and the deeply problematic relationship between historical objectivity and the category of the experiential in literary accounts (Didur 2006, 43–44).
19 See Ritu Menon and Kamla Bhasin, *Borders and Boundaries: Women in India's Partition* (New Brunswick, NJ: Rutgers University Press, 1998), 40–41, 122–123. For a study of the signification of women's bodies in Partition narratives as sites of domesticity, see Debali Mookerjea-Leonard, "Divided Homelands, Hostile Homes: Partition, Women and Homelessness," *Journal of Commonwealth Literature* 40:2 (2005), 141–154.
20 Shelley Feldman has pointed out how East Bengal even in contemporary discourse is constructed as the feminine other, rendering it different, invisible, and silent. Feldman argues that these images may be traced back to Partition (Feldman 1999, 169).
21 I am borrowing here from Roland Barthes' discussion of the shock value of photographs in *La Tour Eiffel*. "It is not enough for the photographer to *signify* the horrible for us to experience it," wrote Barthes. Referring to Geneviève Serreau's comment on a photo of the execution of Guatemalan communists, Barthes observed further that the horror of it resided precisely in the fact that "*we are looking at it* from inside our freedom" (Barthes 1997, 71).
22 Yi-Fu Tuan, *Space and Place: The Perspective of Experience* (Minneapolis: University of Minnesota Press), 99–100.
23 Eidetic memory is usually described as the retention of immediate sensory data. Some people are endowed with the ability to recall images with photographic detail in the short term. See the concept of *Anschaaungbilder* in Jaensch (1999).
24 On the involuntary character of memory, especially articulated by Walter Benjamin as a symptom of chronological disorder, see Franco Ferrarotti, *Time, Memory, and Society* (New York: Greenwood Press, 1990), 30–31. Part of the argument here recalls some of the most difficult passages in Edmund Husserl who questioned Kant's theory of universal, apodeitic time and the category of experience. See Husserl, *Ideas Pertaining to a Pure Phenomenology and to a Phenomenological Philosophy*, translated by Fred Kersten (New York: Springer, 1983), 244–245.
25 See Sarkar 2009, esp. ch. 5: "Ghatak, Melodrama and the Restitution of Experience."
26 Jyotika Virdi argues that the focus on the family in popular cinema relates to the unresolved questions regarding gender, community, and nationalism in the years subsequent to Partition (Virdi 2003, 12–13). Bhaskar Sarkar has argued that many of these plots are "sublimated tales of upheaval" that continue to haunt popular cinema (Sarkar 2009, 82–124).
27 Julio Cortazar, "Some Aspects of the Short Story," in May 1994, 246–247.
28 Aamir Mufti has shown how Manto in his stories questions the totality of the national experience and the normative idea of citizen-subject through the isolated fragment (Mufti 2001, 12–13).

Bibliography

Bandopadhyay, Parthapratim. *Samaresh Basu: Samayer Cihna*. Kolkata: Radical Impression, n.d.
Bandopadhyay, Saroj. *Samaesh Basu: Arjita Abhijnana*, Vol. 2, in *Samaresh Basu Racanavali* by Samaresh Basu, edited by Saroj Bandopadhyay. Kolkata: Ananda, 1998.
Barthes, Roland. *Critical Essays*. Evanston: Northwestern University Press, 1972.
———. *The Eiffel Tower and Other Mythologies*. Berkeley: University of California Press, 1997.

Basu, Samaresh. *Galpasangraha*, Vol. 1. Kolkata: Bisvabani, 1978.

Baudrillard, Jean. *Fragments*. New York: Verso, 1997.

Bhalla, Alok. *Partition Dialogues: Memories of a Lost Home*. New Delhi: Oxford University Press, 2006.

Biswas, Moinak. "Her Mother's Son: Kinship and History in Ritwik Ghatak." *Rouge* 3 (2004).

Boym, Svetlana. *The Future of Nostalgia*. New York: Basic Books, 2002.

Butalia, Urvashi. *The Other Side of Silence: Voices from the Partition of India*. Durham, NC: Duke University Press, 2000.

Chatterjee, Partha and P. Jegantahan. *Community, Gender and Violence: Subaltern Studies XI*. New York: Columbia University Press, 2001.

Chaudhuri, S., Sengupta, N., and Sarkar, B. *"Samaresa Basu" Smarana-Samiksana*. Kolkata: Chayanika, 1994.

Curran, Jean. "Dissension among Indian Communists." *Far Eastern Survey* 19:13 (July 1950), 132–136.

Das, Suranjan. *Communal Riots in Bengal, 1905–1947*. Delhi: Oxford University Press, 1993.

Das, Veena. *Life and Words: Violence and the Descent Into the Ordinary*. Berkeley: University of California Press, n.d.

Didur, Jill. *Unsettling Partition: Literature, Gender, Memory*. Toronto: University of Toronto Press, 2006.

Feldman, Shelley. "Feminist Interruptions: The Silence of East Bengal in the Story of Partition." *Interventions* 1:2 (1999), 169.

George, K.M. (ed.). *Modern Indian Literature: An Anthology: Surveys and Poems*. New Delhi: Sahitya Akademi, 1994.

Ghatak, Ritwik. *Rows and Rows of Fences: Ritwik Ghatak on Cinema*. Kolkata: Seagull Books, 2000.

Girard, René. *Violence and the* Sacred, translated by Patrick Gregory. Baltimore, MD: Johns Hopkins University Press, 1979.

Halbwachs, Maurice. *On Collective Memory*. Chicago, IL: University of Chicago Press, 1992.

Jaensch, E.R. *Eidetic Imagery and Typological Methods of Investigation*. London: Routledge, 1999.

Khan, Yasmin. *The Great Partition: The Making of India and Pakistan*. New Haven, CT: Yale University Press, 2008.

Khosla, Gopal Das. *Stern Reckoning: A Survey of the Events Leading up to and Following the Partition of India*. New Delhi: Oxford University Press, 1949.

Lefebvre, Henri. *The Production of Space*. Oxford: Blackwell, 1991.

Lukàcs, Georg. *The Historical* Novel, translated by Hannah Mitchell and Stanley Mitchell. Lincoln: University of Nebraska Press, 1983.

May, Charles. *New Short Story Theories*. Columbus: Ohio University Press, 1994.

——. *The Short Story: The Reality of Artifice*. Athens: Ohio University Press, 1994.

McNeill, Daniel. *The Face: A Natural History*. New York: Back Bay Books, 2000.

Menon, Ritu and Bhasin, Kamla. *Borders and Boundaries: Women in India's Partition*. New Brunswick, NJ: Rutgers University Press, 1998.

Micale, Mark and Lerner, Paul. *Traumatic Pasts: History, Psychiatry, and Trauma in the Modern Age, 1870–1930*. Cambridge: Cambridge University Press, 2001.

Mitra, K., Enskat, M., and Speiss, C. *Political Parties in South Asia*. New York: Praeger, 2004.

Mookerjea-Leonard, Debali. "Divided Homelands, Hostile Homes: Partition, Women, and Homelessness." *Journal of Commonwealth Literature* 40:2 (2005), 141–154.

Mufti, Aamir. "A Greater Story-writer than God: Genre, Gender and Minority in Late Colonial India," in *Community, Gender and Violence: Subaltern Studies XI*, edited by Partha Chatterjee and P Jeganathan, 12–13. New York: Columbia University Press, 2001.

Mukhopadhyay, Balaichand. *Banaphula Racanabali*, Vol. 7. Kolkata: Granthalaya, 1975.

Nandy, Ashis. *Time Warps: Silent and Evasive Pasts in Indian Politics and Religion.* New Brunswick, NJ: Rutgers University Press, 2002.

O'Donnell, Erin. "'Woman' and 'Homeland' in Ritwik Ghatak's Films: Constructing Post-Independence Bengali Cultural Identity." *Jump Cut: A Review of Contemporary Media* 47 (2004).

Pandey, Gyan. "In Defence of a Fragment: Writing about Hindu–Muslim Riots in India Today." *Economic and Political Weekly* March 1991, 559–572.

Pandey, Gyanendra. *Remembering Partition.* Cambridge: Cambridge University Press, 2001.

Renan, Ernst. *Oeuvres Completes*, Vol. 1. Paris: Calmann-Levy, 1947.

Sarkar, Bhaskar. *Mourning the Nation: Indian Cinema in the Wake of Partition.* Durham, NC: Duke University Press, 2009.

Schama, Simon. *Landscape and Memory.* New York: Vintage Books, 1995.

Trouillot, Michel-Rolph. *Silencing the Past: Power and the Production of History.* Boston, MA: Beacon Press, 1995.

Tuan, Yi-Fu. *Space and Place: The Perspective of Experience.* Minnesota, MN: University of Minnesota Press, 1977.

Virdi, Jyotika. *The Cinematic Imagination: Indian Popular Films as Social History.* New Brunswick, NJ: Rutgers University Press, 2003.

White, Hayden. *Metahistory: The Historical Imagination in Nineteenth Century Europe.* Baltimore, MD: Johns Hopkins University Press, 1973.

Yong, Tai and Kudaisya, Gyanesh. *The Afermath of Partition in South Asia.* New York: Routledge, 2000.

Žižek, Slavoj. *Looking Awry: An Introduction to Jacques Lacan Through Popular Culture.* Cambridge, MA: MIT Press, 1991.

5 Patriotic Pakistanis, exiled poets or unwelcome refugees?

Three Urdu poets write of Partition and its aftermath

Laurel Steele

This chapter looks at the literary and political complexities that Urdu poets faced owing to the 1947 Partition of the Indian subcontinent. The discussion focuses on three Urdu poets who came to live in Pakistan (or, at that time, West Pakistan). A poem by each of the poets that engages with Partition and its aftermath is examined. The poets are Faiz Ahmed Faiz (1911–1984), Josh Malihabadi (1898–1982) and Fahmida Riaz (b. 1946). Faiz, Josh and Riaz write in redrawn landscapes as they seek to relocate their creativity in different spaces, and engage with history, exile and memory. All three are Urdu poets who are considered Pakistani poets; yet they were all born in undivided India. Each had a different experience of Partition; those experiences are reflected in poetry and in reputation. Are they patriots, exiles or refugees – or were they all three at some time or another? These three poets' creative perceptions contribute to the cultural and political understanding of the division between Pakistan and India, and underline why that understanding is of the utmost importance and urgency today.

Before the discussion turns to the individual poets, it is worthwhile to think briefly about the genesis of the idea of dividing the Indian subcontinent, and about some of the initial consequences of the division. It was, in fact, a poet who first broached the idea of Pakistan in a public forum. Allama Muhammad Iqbal (1878–1938) spoke on December 30, 1931 at the annual session of the All India Muslim League in Allahabad. He was then the subcontinent's leading Muslim philosopher, and a poet in Persian and Urdu. Knighted by the British almost a decade earlier, his words carried both an immense political and poetic weight. In his presidential address to the Muslim League, Iqbal said:

> I would like to see the Punjab, North West Frontier province, Sind and Balochistan amalgamated into a single state. Self-Government within the British Empire or without the British Empire, the formation of a consolidated North-West Indian Muslim State appears to me to be the final destiny of the Muslims, at least of North-West India.
>
> (Sherwani 1995, 3–29)

Whether Iqbal was thinking in terms of settling on a geographic space that recognized Muslim predominance in that area or whether he was envisioning an imaginary homeland, his words were open to a multitude of constructions. By history's measure it was a very short time later that the idea of a Muslim space in the subcontinent was turned into a physical reality.

Iqbal lies buried today at the entrance to the mosque in Lahore Fort. He died in 1938, and did not live to see the Partition of India. He was from Sialkot, a town that was located in what became Pakistan. Even if he had lived, he would not have had to decide, like so many other Indian Muslims, whether to leave his home or to stay in a newly independent India. Nor did he live to see the psychological and political changes that the 1947 Partition wrought – changes for which no one was prepared, and which no one could have imagined. But his beautiful and venerated tomb in Lahore is a poetic and political locus for Pakistan. His verses punctuate Pakistan's official announcements and literary writings. The connection between Pakistan and its poet-imaginer emphasizes the role and importance of poets in Pakistan, and in Pakistan's view of itself.

After the dividing of India into India and the West and East wings of Pakistan, Muslim writers confronted a stark choice. Where did they belong? Specifically for those writing in Urdu, if they stayed in India, should they continue writing in what was now seen largely as a "Muslim" language? For the first time, given the new political landscape, writing in Urdu became linked to a particular space: Pakistan. After all, Urdu was the official language. Muslim writers in Bengali were not confronted with the same issues – Bengali was not associated with a Muslim cultural identity. Indeed, the insistence on Urdu as an official language for both wings of the new Pakistani nation was one of the seeds that led to the ultimate breaking away of East Pakistan into its own country. But for now, within the newly divided subcontinent, Urdu's political import in Pakistan, and the change of its status in India, was clear.[1]

In 1947, many Urdu writers and creative artists were allied with the Progressive Writers Movement. They were forward-looking, eschewing a politicized religion, and for the most part intellectually rejected the division of India. Would they now lose the link with the India of the past? Could they stay where they were, if that place was in the newly redrawn India? The Bombay cinema industry provided one such possible haven for Urdu writers within the new map of India. But if one were a Muslim, writing in Urdu, should he or she leave the old cultural and writerly wellsprings, and move to the "Muslim homeland"? Many Urdu writers ultimately relocated from all over India to the new country; some were already from the area that became Pakistan. To the surprise of all, once in Pakistan, travel back to where one had lived before was very rare. Easy passage across borders did not exist.

Not only did poets have to make personal choices about where to live after 1947; culture itself underwent a fundamental change. The milieu of what has been called "the composite culture" of undivided India – the culture of toleration and interrelationships of Hindu and Muslim – changed. Whether this culture existed in the form in which it was now so nostalgically remembered may be debated, but an undivided India had clearly embodied that ideal. Poets had all lived in one geographic space, whether British India or princely state – and no space was defined by religion.

After Independence and Partition, India's literary and political circles, including poets, were now without the focus provided by the struggle to oust the British, the struggle to which many of them had dedicated their lives. However, overriding the departure of the colonial rulers, poets confronted a new political map: India, as well as a separate country for the Muslims of India, called Pakistan. Poets' own experience of decolonization and their ability to think about the effect of the British departure were obscured by their experience of new boundaries and of a new country, with no historical precedent, carved from the old colonial and princely entities. And, for the three poets who are the subject of this chapter, the experiences of Partition, and the creation of Pakistan, with all its political instability and turmoil, are documented in poems that try to capture these feelings.[2]

The change engendered by Partition and Independence was unprecedented. Trying to imagine it, and trying to give it words, even a political leader like Jawarharlal Nehru framed the experience of the change in poetic terms. Nehru's speech as India gained independence with its ringing initial words "At the stroke of the midnight hour" served as a metaphor for thinking about what had happened. Faiz's poem took up these metaphors, and both Nehru's speech and Faiz's poem became iconic expressions of the experience of August 1947.

Later, critics and historians tried to explain the Partition experience. Aijaz Ahmad, in the context of his discussion of the Hindu right wing and of national literatures, has contributed to the debate in his *Lineages of the Present*, locating the politics of the divide in the mirror of the Urdu language (Ahmad 2000, xx). The historian Mushirul Hasan, writing 50 years after the event, enumerates the major issues that inform Partition and its aftermath for writers (Hasan 1997, 49–50). Hasan sees as significant, first, the sheer number involved in the massive dislocations, and second, the deaths as well as the question of who left India and who stayed and why. The third issue Hasan notes is the matter of writers' identities. Reflected in the bewilderment and confusion of those experiencing the events of Partition was the seeming inability of anyone to explain it or to figure out where writers belonged. Hasan writes:

> So, which country did poets like Faiz and writers like Manto [a prose writer] belong to? Manto, for one, tried in vain to separate India from Pakistan and Pakistan from India. He asked himself: "Will Pakistan literature be different – and if so, how? To whom will now belong what had been written in undivided India? Will that be partitioned too?" The uppermost question in his mind was: "Were we really free"?
>
> (Hasan 1997, 49–50)

India's partition cast its shadow over many aspects of state and society. Yet the literature on this major event is mostly inadequate, impressionistic and lacking in scholarly rigour. Even after 50 years of Independence and despite access to wide-ranging primary source materials, there are no convincing explanations of why and how M.A. Jinnah's "two-nation theory" emerged, and why Partition created millions of refugees and resulted in over a million deaths. Similarly, it is still not clear whether Partition allowed the fulfillment of legitimate aspirations or represents the mutilation of historic national entities. These were the issues that confronted both Faiz and Josh at the time, and later presented problems for Fahmida Riaz to resolve.

While the scholarly literature on Partition would be deemed deficient until recently, the fictional and poetic response was immediate and significant. Offering no grand explanations for what they had experienced, writers of fiction wrote particularly searing short stories in Hindi, Bengali, Urdu and Panjabi. Some of the most famous short stories about Partition were deemed obscene, the subjects so graphic, so hair-raising, about ethnic violence and societal break-down, that there was hardly a context for them. Only now do we know those stories when we hear them again, as stories of Serbia and Bosnia and Rwanda and Darfur are told, and they echo the (at the time) unknowable levels of ethnic violence of 1947. Sometimes the stories of India's Partition were masked. For years, Bollywood and Indian movies used themes of brothers separated at birth, lost children and reunited families to communicate the experience of national loss.

Poets, too, responded to the Partition of India in myriad ways. In the poems by Faiz, Josh and Riaz, we see different attempts to communicate Partition's effects. Other Pakistani Urdu poets tried other strategies – just like the fiction writers' attempts at new approaches to convey what could not be conceived. For example, rather than formulate new political identities when confronted with the aftermath of Independence and Partition, some poets took refuge in the older, traditional locations of the *ghazal*, a sonnet-like verse form. The relocation of the *ghazal* within Pakistan and its reinvigoration after decades of rejection by politically forward-looking writers contained its own unique significance. Instead of looking for a future, poets searched the past. And this new *ghazal*, using very short meters, seemed able to capture fragmentation and grief in a way to which a new generation of listeners could respond. As for Partition itself, what exactly had happened – how Independence was coupled with a dividing of the land into two countries – is still subject to fierce argument, and is still an event perceived very differently among those who experienced it at a personal level, let alone how historians or novelists or poets try to explain it.

Each of the three poets – Faiz, Josh and Riaz – had a different relationship with this border. Faiz Ahmed Faiz, the most well-known Urdu poet of the twentieth century, did not have to confront a physical relocation to a new homeland. He was from Sialkot, just as the poet-philosopher Iqbal was. Thus, his home was located geographically in what became Pakistan. Notwithstanding, this did not make Faiz an instant Pakistani nationalist, nor did it save him from political persecution. He was jailed twice by two Pakistani governments; towards the end of his life he left Pakistan, spending years in exile in Beirut.[3]

The second poet, older than Faiz and more established at the time of Partition, is Josh Malihabadi. He was known as the "Poet of the Revolution" during the Freedom movement. His name "Malihabadi" is from his birthplace in what was then the United Provinces of northeast India.[4] Josh spent a long time resisting relocation to Pakistan, and did not leave India until the end of the 1950s. There is a story that Jawaharlal Nehru himself begged him to stay.[5] The third poet, and the only woman of the group, Fahmida Riaz, was born the year before Partition near Delhi, and taken to Pakistan as an infant. Later, Riaz spent time in India as a political refugee during President General Muhammad Zia al-Haq's rule (1978–1988). All three poets have been seen as fighters against narrow-mindedness, or as transgressors – be it political, social or literary bounds they transgress. All three had or have a very complex response to Pakistan.

The poem about August 1947 that set the standard for responses to the granting of Independence was by the 36-year-old Faiz, already a recognized master of Urdu poetry. Faiz's poem was taken up by all, with the clarion cry *"Ye dāgh dāgh ujālā"* – "this scarred daybreak" – used as shorthand to capture the idea of the tattered freedom that had been obtained at the expense of the unity of India. The words spoke for those who had suffered the loss of their homes, the dashing of their fine hopes, and who had seen the map of India cut into pieces. Hundreds of thousands of Urdu and Hindi speakers can recite today:

> *Yeh dāgh dāgh ujālā, yeh shab gazidah saḥar*
> *Woh inṭizār thā jis kā yeh woh saḥar to nahīṅ*
> *Yeh woh saḥar to nahīṅ jis kī ārzu lekar*
> *Chale the yār kĕh mil jā'egī kahīṅ nah kahīṅ*

> This scarred, pitted daybreak, this night-bitten dawn
> That is not what we waited for, this is not that dawn
> This is not that dawn which we wished for
> Setting on our journey, thinking somewhere we would meet.[6]

The poem captures several different moods in its movement; it uses the standard images from the world of classical Urdu poetry to make its point. Lovers' meeting, night journeys, scars – all are used to tell a very different story than that of a night of love. For Faiz (just as for Nehru, with the Freedom at Midnight image in his speech given at Independence), it is a night journey that is invoked; but it is a journey with an ambivalent end:

> In the heaviness of night there is still no lessening
> The hour of the deliverance of eye and heart has not arrived

There are more echoes in the poem of Nehru's speech, delivered at the Red Fort in Delhi at midnight on August 14. Nehru's speech was in English, and in its organization and message it is a thoroughly English speech. Not a word of it was in Hindi, Urdu, nor any other local language of India, and its message was keyed to a moment in the political history of India of great import.

Yet, the allusions of Nehru's speech located the experience in a much older set of poetic allusions. He said on August 14, 1947:

Long years ago we made a tryst with destiny, and now the time comes when
we shall redeem our pledge, not wholly or in full measure, but very substantially. At the stroke of the midnight hour, when the world sleeps, India will
awake to life and freedom.

(MacAurthur 1992, 234–237)

Faiz's poem (this is Victor Kiernan's more literary translation) picks up some
of these metaphors:

Ye dāgh-dāgh ujālā, ye shab-gazīdā sahar
Wo intizār thā jiskā, ye wo sahar to nahīñ
Ye wo sahar to nahīñ jiskī ārzū lekar
Chale the yār ke: mil jāyegī kahīñ na kahīñ
Falak ke dasht meñ tāroñ kī ākhirī manzil
Kahīñ to hogā shab-e-sust mauj kā sāhil
Kahīñ to jake rukegā safīna-e-gham-e-dil
Jawāñ lahū kī pur asrār shahrāhoñ se
Chale jo yār to dāman pe kitne hāth paṛe
Diyār-e-husn kī be-sabr khwābgāhoñ se
Pukārtī rahīñ bāheñ, badan bulāte rahe
Bahut 'azīz thī lekin rukh-e-sahar kī lagan
Bahut qarīñ thā hasīnān-e nūr kā dāman
Subuk-subuk thī tamannā dabī-dabī thī thakan
Sunā hai ho bhī chukā hai firāq-e-zulmat-e-nūr
Sunā hai ho bhī chukā hai wisāl-e-manzil-o-gām
Badal chukā hai bahut ahal-e-dard kā dastūr
Nishāt-e-wasl halāl-o-azāb-e-hijr-e-harām
Jigar kī āg, nazar kī umañg, dil kī jalan
Kisī pe chār:e-hijrañ kā kuchch asar hī nahīñ
Kahāñ se āyī nigār-e-sabā kidhhar ko gaī
Abhī chirāG-e-sar-e-rah ko kuchch khabar hī nahīñ
Abhī garānī-e-shab meñ kamī nahīñ ā'ī
Najāt-e-dīda-o-dil kī ghaṛī nahīñ ā'ī
Chale chalo ki woh manzil abhī nahīñ ā'ī

This leprous daybreak, dawn night's fangs have mangled –
This is not that long-looked-for break of day,
Not that clear dawn in quest of which those comrades
Set out, believing that in heaven's wide void
Somewhere must be the stars' last halting-place
Somewhere the verge of night's slow-washing tide
Somewhere an anchorage for the ship of heartache.
When we set out, we friends, taking youth's secret
Pathways, how many hands plucked at our sleeves!
From beauty's dwellings and their panting casements

Soft arms invoked us, flesh cried out to us;
But dearer was the lure of dawn's bright cheek
Closer her shimmering robe of fairy rays
Light-winged that longing, feather-light that toil.
But now, word goes, the birth of day from darkness
Is finished, wandering feet stand at their goal;
Our leaders' ways are altering, festive looks
Are all the fashion, discontent reproved: –
And yet this physic still on usnslaked eye
Or heart fevered by severance works no cure
Where did that fine breeze, that the wayside lamp
Has not once felt, blow from – where has it fled?
Night's heaviness is unlessened still, the hour
Of mind and spirit's ransom has not struck;
Let us go on, our goal is not reached yet.

(Faiz 2000)

The first few lines draw from a series of interconnected symbols from the religious/erotic world of Urdu poetry – a tryst with destiny, a pledge to be redeemed, the midnight hour, the sleeping world, with India (the beloved) awake, the soul finding utterance, and the quest. Nehru, who moved so easily between the worlds of Kashmiri Brahmin and Oxford cosmopolitan, framed the experience of Independence and freedom with the old images of Urdu poetry. Deep within Nehru's images, the paradigms of Urdu poetry link annihilation with the devotion to an ideal – the tryst with destiny. Do these old paradigms somehow permit the many deaths of Partition? When sacrifice is made poetic, then moths rush to the flame.

Faiz's words are repeated in many fora, from history books to novels. For example, in Qurratulain Hyder's classic novel of India, and of Partition, *Āg ka Darya* (River of Fire) published in 1957, she inserts this poem into the English version. She adds a scene to her own translation of the work in which the participants – college age and a little older – are in a coffee house in Lucknow, just after Independence, discussing Faiz's poem. In the Urdu novel, this scene does not exist. Instead, Hyder gives a numbered chapter heading, and then leaves the chapter blank. I think she adds this fictional discussion of the poem because today nuanced recollections of Partition are not complete without Faiz's words. The addition of the scene underlines how recollectors now frame the event with this poem.

The young people hear the poem recited, and then translated, and later they talk about Nehru's speech. This is the fictional world:

"Have you read Faiz Ahmed Faiz's latest poem The Morning of Freedom? Yeh dag dag ujala, yeh shab-gazida sahar..." She went on to recite the poem. The audience became very still.

Pothan Abraham, the Malayali who worked for The Pioneer, broke the silence. "Now translate it into pidgin English, I couldn't understand a word."

"Translate Urdu poetry into English? How can you render *jigar ki aag* as the liver's fire?"

"Try," said Abraham, smoking his pipe dreamily.

Talat pondered awhile, then began, "Okay – The blighted dawn, this darkened sun. This is not the morn we waited for. We went forth in the desert of heaven, hoping to reach our destination of stars. We hoped that, somewhere, we would come ashore from the placid river of the night, that the barge of sorrow would end its cruise. Whence came the early morning breeze, where did it go? The wayside lamp does not know. The night's burden has not diminished, the hour of deliverance for eye and heart has not arrived. Face forward! For our destination is not yet in sight."[7]

The sobering and evocative effect that Faiz's words have on the fictional listeners in 1947 would persist in the non-fictional world. The poem will speak for the generation – yet one of the characters needs to have it translated in order to understand it. Its recitation is often used to underline the ambivalence of gaining freedom at the expense of Partition.

Nehru's speech and Faiz's poem contrasted significantly with Mohammad Ali Jinnah's relatively practical remarks concerning what he called the "cyclonic revolution" that had occurred. At the same time that Nehru could couch the changes in poetic metaphors, Pakistan's first Governor General tried to envision a more prosaic future – albeit an unlikely one of religions disappearing:

You know really that not only we ourselves are wondering but, I think, the whole world is wondering at this unprecedented cyclonic revolution which has brought about the plan of creating and establishing two independent sovereign Dominions ... [and ending with] Now, I think we should keep that in front of us as our ideal and you will find that in course of time Hindus would cease to be Hindus and Muslims would cease to be Muslims, not in the religious sense, because that is the personal faith of each individual, but in the political sense as citizens of the State.[8]

The way in which these two leaders framed the event also points to two contrasting realities. Nehru is seeing something visionary, on a large scale, while Jinnah's vision concerns how daily life will be lived, and how Hindus and Muslims will coexist.

The question of how one was to function in one's ordinary existence in the new geographic reality remained open. Daily life was one thing, but Jinnah's view of a future with disappearing differences between Hindu and Muslim went unrealized.

Faiz's image of something tattered also echoes Jinnah's much earlier complaints about "the moth-eaten" territories proposed in negotiations during the early 1940s with Gandhi and other Congress leaders.[9] But, for the new residents of the new Pakistan, there is no mention of their "new space" in Nehru's speech. He uses the name "India" to refer to the place in which his listeners now all find themselves.

There is, for him, no mention of the birth of the new entity of Pakistan, except in the regret of the redeeming of the pledge "not wholly or in full measure."

Josh Malihabadi, the second poet examined in this chapter, had already written many beloved poems by the time of Independence, earning him a special place in the struggle for freedom. His taunting and eloquent "To the Sons of the East India Company" was banned by the British censors. It had been on everyone's lips in the years before Independence. What Josh would write about Independence and Partition took on real importance because of his stature as a poetic commentator on history.[10] He wrote several poems directly about the events, among them *"Tarānah-e Āzādī-e Watan"* ("The Melody of the Freedom of the Country"), *"Istiqlāl-e Maikadah"* ("The Sovereignty of the Wine House") and *"Hind-o-Muslim kā Muttahidah Na'arah"* ("The United Slogan of Hindu and Muslim"). In the poem entitled *"Tāranah-e Āzādī-e Watan"* ("The Melody of the Freedom of the Country") he tries to capture the multiplicity of reactions to the event. The poem comprises several stanzas in each of three voices – I have chosen a representative stanza in each voice. Josh's first voice says:

> *Baṛho keh raqz-o-rang hai, uṭho keh bahār-i no hai*
> *Watan ke ru'e pāk par hai āb-o-rang-e sarwarī*
> *Qalandaroñ ke jām meñ hai badah-e to nagarī*
> *Samundaroñ kī ragnī, hamaliyah kī shā'arī*
> *Hujum dar hujum hai, qatar dar qatar hai.*

> Rise up, for there is dancing and color, rise for it is the beginning of spring
> The luster and color of sovereignty are on the pure face of the country
> In the sufi's cup is the wine of power
> The color of the ocean, the poetry of the Himalayas
> Is wave after wave, range upon range.

The second voice says something quite different:

> *Yeh baiwant aur yeh katar, yeh kāṭ chhānṭ, abtarī*
> *Shanāwaroñ kī ḍubkiyāñ, bahādaroñ kī thartharī*
> *Yeh kohkan kī bandagī, yeh pīr zan kī wawarī*
> *Qalandaroñ ke rūp meñ yeh rū siyah qaiṣarī*
> *Shaguftah-i barg-i tazah meñ nihuftah nok-i khār hai*
> *Khizāñ kaheñge phir kisse, agar yahī bahār rahe*

> This cutting up and clipping out, this pruning and hacking, deterioration
> The sinking of the strong, the shivers of the brave
> The slavery of the Mountain Digger (Farhad), the sovereignty of the old
>   woman[11]
> This black faced Caesar in the guise of Sufis
> In the fresh-branched blossom is the hidden sharp thorn
> What do they call autumn, if this is spring?

And the third voice:

Miyāñ yeh waqat-i jashan hai mubāḥissa se fā'idah
Mahal-i raqas o wajad hai kĕh rāstah to pā liā keh
Fizā se abur chat gayā, hawā kā rukh badal gayā
Jo dil meñ hai husainiyat to kyā balā hai karbalā
Wo kul banegā bustān jo ā khār zār hai.[12]

Sir what use arguing? This is the time of rejoicing
The road was found for the palace of dance and ecstasy
The cloud has scattered from the air, the direction of the wind
When Husain is in the heart then why fear Karbala?
What is a wasteland today will become a garden tomorrow.

Josh divides the reactions into their separate voices as a device to capture the stunned ambivalence of the speakers. He and others had devoted their lives to the fight for freedom, and now the fight was over. Josh had cast himself as both dissolute romantic and freedom fighter. In the first stanzas of his poem, the first voice celebrates Independence.

The second speaker sees the "cutting and hacking" that the subcontinent has experienced. Faiz's words and Josh echo each other here, where the third speaker chastises the second for expressing reservations. In Josh's poem, his spokesperson, asking about the "cutting and hacking," is shushed. In other words, the leaders' willingness to achieve Independence at the price of Partition is a *fait accompli*. No complaining now. With the third speaker, a resolution is seen in the future.

At the same time, Josh's speakers use the various features of the landscape as metaphors for the event. There are mountains of poetry and oceans of song. While the thorns hide in leaves a garden is predicted, though Karbala, the killing ground of Husain, looms. But "*husainiyat*" – imbibing the virtues of Husain – will carry them through.[13]

Josh also, in entitling the poem "*Taranah*," makes a reference to one of Iqbal's most beloved poems, "*Taranah-i Hindī*" ("The Melody of India").[14] That poem, written in 1908, was nearly made the national anthem of Independent India. It called up earlier emotions of unity and patriotism which Josh's poem is clearly trying to capture. Iqbal had written:

Sare jahān se achchhā Hindustān hamārā,
Hum bulbuleñ hain iski yeh gulistān hamārā!
Ghurbat meñ huñ agar ham rehtā hai dil watan meñ,
Samjho wahīñ hameñ bhī dil ho jahān hamārā!
...
Mazhab nahīñ sikhāta apas meñ bair rakhnā
Hindī haiñ ham watan hai Hindustān hamārā!
Yunān-o-misr-o-Roma sab miṭ gaye jahān se,
Ab tak magar hai bāqī nam-o-nishān hamārā!

Kuchh bāt hai kī hastī miṭṭhī nahīñ hamārī,
Sadiyoñ rahā hai dushmān daur-i-zamān hamārā
Iqbal! koī mehrām apna nahīñ jahān meñ
Ma'lūm kya kisī ko dard-i-nihān hamārā!

The best in the world
Our India!
In its gardens of delight
We are the nightingales.
Religion does not teach
Mutual discord.
Strung on a single strand
We are one
We are Indians.
Rome, Greece, Egypt have become reduced to relics
Of dead civilizations;
Only India remains.
Threatened for centuries
By world powers
Our civilization still flourishes.
Iqbal! you have no kindred soul.
Who will understand the pain concealed within your heart?

Iqbal's "*Taranah*" celebrated a unified patriotism; Partition's violence lay in mute rebuke to these elegiac words. Even Josh's "*Taranah*" cannot achieve the joyful note of strength in Iqbal's song. When Josh finally moved to Pakistan in 1958, he always said he did so because his family, who had already moved, had begged him to come. Nor was Pakistan a comfortable haven for Josh. Just as Faiz himself was jailed in the 1950s by two military governments, and was finally forced to take refuge in Beirut for some time in the 1980s, only returning to General Zia ul-Haq's Pakistan to die, Josh too died officially unmourned by the same government.

Fahmida Riaz, the third poet who addresses issues arising from the division of the subcontinent, was born in India and taken to Pakistan as an infant. Both a poet and a novelist, Riaz too has confronted the Pakistani authorities, taking refuge in India during the 1980s while Zia was in power. Just like Faiz and Josh, Fahmida Riaz's poems can be both shocking and familiar. The intention to shock by Urdu writers is not new. The tradition of transgressing runs from the long-ago anthology *Angare* (1931), quickly banned, with its inflammatory stories that seared religion and sex, to Manto's unforgettable "*Khol Do*," and onward throughout the work of Ismat Chughtai. When Josh boldly called on "the sons of the East India company" with such scorn that his poem was banned, Faiz shocked with his dismissal of Partition as tattered, and, in another famous poem, with his rejection of love. Josh arrested listeners with his transgressions into eroticism and his brutally and comically frank autobiography. That arc of electricity which is present in much of twentieth-century Urdu literature is in Fahmida Riaz's work as well.[15] Fahmida Riaz's work has the feel of the long "tradition of shock" and succeeds in shocking as she boldly asserts her connections to the syncretic soul of undivided India.

The power to shock in writing has diminished for some societies: writers in the old Soviet Union could rivet their audiences with banned political observations and garner underground followings, while English poets in the 1960s used obscenities to offend or startle audiences into a kind of transfixed attention. But now, for the most part, many words and ideas no longer shock. No one cares. In Riaz's literary universe, on the other hand, the power to shock has grown, if possible, stronger. When the publication of Salman Rushdie's *The Satanic Verses* forces the author to go into hiding, we can see some of the potential for extreme responses. Going outside the norm, transgressing boundaries and writing about certain subjects is to court physical danger, even death. This is the background against which Riaz works her themes of love and connection, of the experience of being female, of eroticism and of encounters with officialdom.

Riaz's work and the identity she asserts for herself is shocking to the "obscurantists" (Pakistanis' own codeword for the aggressively religious fundamentalists). Her identity is in question as well to those who see her as a *"mohajir,"* or "migrant from India," as not fully Pakistani, as fraught with the potential of an unpatriotic identification with India.[16] Just as with Josh, with Malihabad, an old locale of undivided India, embedded in his name, Fahmida Riaz's liberal sensibilities and open taboo breaking may be seen as vaguely unpatriotic. She has been dismissed as a "nymphomaniac," as Riaz herself comments(!) and/or as a traitor. Not only was she in self-imposed exile in India for much of General Zia's reign; in 2000 she had the dubious pleasure of being attacked by right-wing Hindus – verbally, and potentially physically (there was a gun waved) – at a presentation at Jawaharlal Nehru University in New Delhi. But her residence in India allowed her to produce poems where a Pakistani is looking at India through "Pakistani" eyes.[17]

So Riaz, and her poetry, have managed to enrage "them" for a long time. Even early poems like "The Soft Fragrance of My Jasmine" startle with their intimacy.

Merīchanbelī kī narm khushbū
Hawā ke dhare peh beh rahī hai
Hawa ke hāthon meñ khelthī hai
Terā badan ḍhuṇḍne chelī hai.

The soft fragrance of my jasmine
Floats on the breeze
Plays with the hand of the wind,
Is setting off in search of you.

In poems like "The Rain God" (*"Megh Dut"*), Riaz increases the intensity. "Eyes closed, arms outstretched, I run, I run, touching his blue body to mine"

("*Aur maiñ ānkh mund kar/hāth pasāre hu'e/dauRti chali ga'i/ang se lagār hi/ nil us ke ang kā*"). Full tilt, she runs into an embrace of a Hindu god, or of a lover, or both. It is how she confronts the reader; her words outstretched, her eyes closed, waiting for the reciprocal embrace (Riaz 2005, 110–112).

In the long tradition of Urdu poets writing about other poets, of eulogies and elegies, Riaz has written an elegy for Firaq Gorakhpuri. Just as Iqbal wrote a eulogy for Dagh, and Josh wrote one for Tagore, and, for that matter, so many wrote poems in praise of Faiz after his death, so Riaz writes for Firaq. An educated, older Urdu reader knows the long, illustrious career Firaq had as a professor of English at Allahabad University. Here was a *ghazal*-writing Hindu, notoriously homosexual, holding up the standard of classical Urdu poetry into the 1980s, and influencing generations of cosmopolitan Allahabadis.

The poem "In Memory of Firaq" concerns her place as a Pakistani when confronting India, as a poet, and shows how political divisions are now written into personal and artistic histories. In this poem she uses the confluence of the Ganga and the Yamuna to locate the speaker and the poet in space – the rivers that flow like time, and which do not recognize political boundaries. The location of the poem is the same city of Allahabad where Iqbal first located the outlines of the idea of Pakistan on the map of his imagination.

Riaz explains in English in her notes to *Four Walls and a Black Veil*:

> Firaq was a great poet of Urdu. He was a Hindu Brahman and embodied the secular tradition of India. (Urdu is the national language of Pakistan.) Firaq lived in Allahabad, in Uttar Pradesh, India. Triveni: The sacred confluence of the rivers Ganga and Yamuna. It is believed that a third river Saraswati also joining these two rivers at Allahabad … but has concealed itself from the human eye. Saraswati is also the goddess of the Arts. This attribute gives an added dimension to this stanza. This poem is an elegy for Firaq who died in 1983, when the poet (Riaz) lived in India in exile.
>
> (Riaz 2005)

"*Nazar-e Firaq*" ("Remembering Firaq") uses images from a sort of "eternal India," of sacred rivers and local vegetation, coconuts, sandalwood and idols, to remind the Pakistani reader that his or her roots are here. And Firaq himself, the Hindu, writing in Urdu, using traditional genres like the *ghazal* and the *ruba'i* – what of him?

Even within the set of images Riaz has used there lies another twist. *Ghazal*s and poems in other traditional genres, the kinds of poems that Firaq wrote, often made no use of observed landscapes like the ones in this poem. Firaq would have written just as easily about wine and roses. Where are his allegiances, with his dedication to the highest expressions of Urdu literary culture? Over the years, many had complained about the "non-Indian" landscapes of the *ghazal*. And yet here is a Pakistani Urdu poet, painstakingly invoking the observed landscape of India's sacred rivers. The context that Riaz's note gives will more likely help an Urdu speaker from Pakistan, unfamiliar with the river symbolism. The images do compel, even if not all their potent messages are accessible. The poet (Riaz) is in India, looking at the confluence of the Ganga and the Yamuna, at the city of Allahabad. The poem itself does not mention the city, nor Firaq's long association with it. So the beginning of the translated poem sets a very ancient scene:

> *Sangam ke panī par main ne dekhī thī kaisī taswīr*
> *Uṛā lahak kar ek jal panchhī khainch gayā pānī peh lekar*
> *Jamna kī nīlī gahra'i, bhid bhari chup se bojhal*
> *Gangā ke dhare kī janbash, ujli, tāqatwar, bekal*

> At Triveni, the place
> Of three waters, where Ganga
> And Yamuna flow together:
> A waterbird rising, its trailing feet
> Inscribe the surface.
> Yamuna: deep and blue,
> Languid, mysterious, silent
> Ganga: white, powerful, restless
> An onward pressing current that never ceases.

Later, the lines:

> *Pakistān se ā'e mohājir gende ki toti mālā*
> *Pānī meñ chāpu ki shab shab, bāton ke tote ṭukṛe.*

> Visitors from Pakistan to the land
> that was once their own. A garland
> of bruised marigolds floating by.

The Urdu lines contain the word "*mohajir*" so that the exact translation is in fact Pakistani "*mohajir*" rather than "Pakistani visitor." The "*mohajir*," now returned to India, is given a very political, rooted-in-the-past location in this Indian landscape. And, of course, *mohajir* is the name for those who came to Pakistan from India. Riaz has neatly turned the movement across borders inside out.

Marigolds floating in the river can have a number of symbolic significances – having been used as garlands for the exalted, as temple offerings to the gods. Or, the marigolds could have decorated a body that was burned at the ghat.

In another poem that uses this river symbolism, Riaz again locates the pain of Partition in the timelessness of rivers. Riaz calls to the River: "Ā, mare, ā – Come to me!" She says,

> *O, mahān miṭāle sāgar,*
> *Sun mare katha*
> *Maiñ baṛī abhāgan, bhāg mara*
> *Be dard hāth maiñ rahā sadā*

Tūta marā miṭi se natah
Kaise ṭūtā!
Ek āndhī barī bhaiyanak, lāl churail
Mujhe le Uṛī
Uṭhā kar paṭkā us ne kahāñ se kahāñ.

Magnificent River,
Hear the tale of my terrible fate.
My destiny was always in a cruel hand. My kinship
With the land was snapped – like that!
A fearsome whirlwind, witch-like, red-eyed,
Swept me away and dropped me
In unfamiliar lands.

Returning to the poem about Firaq, she says:

Jo samjhi, jo āge samjhon, jhalak rahā hai dil kā jām
Woh manzar jo khud se baṛā thā, is kā gher tumhāre nām.

Whatever I gathered from that view
Or later learnt in life, I know that vista
Was larger than what met
The eye. Its infinite outreaches
I dedicate to you, Firaq!

With its final wish for Firaq's reincarnation – "Life is not yet barren, they will surely reincarnate you" (*"Abhi to jiwān banjh nahin hai, phir tujh ko janmainge log"*) and its meditation on art flowing on, like the river – the poem is able to convey levels of regret, and a profound appreciation of the timelessness of nature and the river, along with the manifestations of culture and life on its banks.

But the poem has also woven the Hindu poet of Urdu poetry, Firaq, with the Pakistani poet in India who is writing his elegy, while it hails the triumph of their shared past over the political future. We are back to the images of Faiz and Josh as they search for "the anchorage for the ship of heartache" or the "song of the ocean." This is the vista that is larger than simple understanding.

Notes

1 Ralph Russell writes:

> Most readers of this article will be aware of what was happening to Urdu in the early years of independence. In the area which one might call the heartland of Urdu, UP and to a lesser extent Bihar, the state governments were doing everything possible to destroy it. This was achieved by an absurd interpretation of the "three language formula" devised by the government of India. This recommended that in every state three languages should be taught in the schools – (1) the language of the state (which would normally be the mother tongue of the

majority of its inhabitants), (2) another modern Indian language (Hindi would often be chosen where the first language was not Hindi), and (3) one other language. A good deal of elasticity was envisaged in the implementation of this formula, and in UP Urdu, the language of most inhabitants of UP after Hindi, could, and should, have been chosen. The UP government decided instead to declare Sanskrit a modern language, and the teaching of Urdu in the schools – it had been taught in all UP schools before independence – was discontinued. On the whole that situation has continued ever since, at any rate until fairly recent times, when I understand some minor changes have taken place in the situation.

From "Urdu in Independent India: History and Prospects" (Russell 1999, 95)

2 For a recent collection of writers from both Pakistan and India talking about their experiences of Partition, see *Partition Dialogues: Memories of a Lost Home*, edited by Alok Bhalla (New Delhi: Oxford University Press, 2006).

3 The "Pindi Conspiracy" is the name for the 1951 aborted coup attempt against the Pakistani military government, in which Faiz was involved. It would now certainly be barely remembered in the popular consciousness if it were not for the fact that Faiz Ahmed Faiz was arrested for his alleged part in the coup, tried and jailed. Thus, the new country's already famous poet was clearly marked as anti-government in the infancy of the country's existence.

4 Ayesha Jalal discusses city identifiers in poetic names. "The passion for one's city, encompassing as it did a range of cultural experiences and social relationships, was not one that could be easily submerged in the largely imagines identifications of the Muslims with India and Islam" (Jalal 2000, 14).

5 There are many discussions of Josh's eventual move to Pakistan. Khushwant Singh recently reminisced about it in a column "Remembering Josh," retrievable at http//blogs.outlookindia.con/default.aspx?ddm=10. The gist of most of the stories is that Nehru begged Josh to stay, and Josh moved for family reasons.

6 My translation; for another translation, see Victor Kiernan's version cited below.

7 Quratulain Hyder, *River of Fire* (*Āg kā Daryā*), "transcreated from the original Urdu" by the author (Hyder 1998), first published in 1959, in Urdu. I referred to this scene of the attempt to translate Faiz in the immediate aftermath of Independence and Partition in an essay of mine (Steele 2013).

8 This is the speech he delivered on his election as the first President of the Constituent Assembly of Pakistan, at Karachi in August 1947, and serves as his official remarks upon the Partition and Independence of India (Jinnah 1989).

9 When Gandhi endorsed a Rajagopalachari formula that called for a joint League–Congress demand for a national government tied to an understanding that "contiguous Muslim-majority districts" could secede following Independence, if the formula added, "mutual agreements shall be entered into for safeguarding defence, communications, etc." Jinnah called this "maimed, mutilated and moth-eaten." He disclosed that his Pakistan included all of the Punjab and Bengal, apart from Sind, NWFP and Baluchistan. This was significant, since it meant a Jinnah claim to eastern Punjab and western Bengal, large areas with a Hindu majority (Bose and Jalal 1997, 179).

10 Many other Urdu poets composed verses specifically about the granting of Independence – and many used the night journey as a metaphor. Not only Ahmed Faiz, and Josh Malihabadi, discussed in this essay, address the times, but Sahir Ludhianwi (1921–1980), Akhtar al-Iman (1915–1996), Jan Nisar Akhtar (1914–1976), Habib Jalib (1915?–1993), Himayat Ali Sha'ir (1926–) and Makhdum Muinuddin (1908–1969), and Mustafa Zaidi (1930–1970) are some of the major poets who wrote on this subject. Carlo Coppola includes a discussion of poems written about Independence in his dissertation (Coppola 1975).

11 This refers to one of the most loved stories in Persian; it is told throughout Iran and Central Asia. There are many versions, but the most well-known forms part of the

quintet (*Khamseh*) of Nizami Ganjavi (1140–1230). In his Khusrau and Shirin, he tells the story of the complicated romance between Farhad and Shirin, and the king's (Khusrau's) desire for Shirin. Farhad completes the task that the king has set him – he has dug the mountain canal in order to bring milk for Shirin's bath, and the king fears that now Shirin will choose Farhad as her consort. The "old woman" is the king's servant, and plays a crucial role in the killing of Farhad. The king wants Farhad dead, and is afraid to kill him, because he knows that he will never gain Shirin in that manner – there will be blood on his hands, and she will reject him. To help her master, the old woman says she can dispose of Farhad. She goes to Farhad and tells him that Shirin is dead. Farhad then kills himself. When Josh uses the image in his poem, he evokes a situation in which love becomes the instrument of death. The old woman's "sovereignty" – the old woman's triumph – is her knowledge of the sovereignty of love. Love destroys the lover and love can be used as a weapon of destruction. In Josh's political application of this poetic and romantic metaphor, within the love of freedom lay the destruction of the place known as India.

12 Josh Malīhabādī, *Intikhāb-i Josh* (Collected Works of Josh) (Malihabadi 1948, 52–56).

13 My gratitude to Muzaffar Alam who suggested this interpretation of husainiyat.

14 Discussed in Hafeez Malik, ed. Riffat Hassan, "The Development of a Political Philosophy" in *Iqbal Poet Philospher of Pakistan* (New York and London: Columbia University Press, 1971). Also appears in Kulliyāt-i Iqbāl (Urdu) (Centennial Edition. Aligarh: Educational Book House, 1976).

15 Sajjad Zaheer (ed.) *Angare,* first published in 1931, and reprinted as *Angare: An Anthology* (New Delhi: Educational Publishing House, 1995).

16 See also newspaper coverage of the time; for example, "'Muhajir' as a term will go by December 31, 'Azam's Stirring Call for Honest Hard Work'," *Dawn* (Karachi), December 5, 1959.

17 *Dawn* (Karachi newspaper) reports on August 11, 2003:

> It was in April 2000 that the two immensely admired poets from Pakistan, both votaries of peace, were visiting New Delhi to attend a mushaira. But suddenly on this evening something was to go horribly wrong. The tart verse [Riaz's], it seems, had provoked a man, later described as an army major, to whip out a pistol. "We cannot allow India-hating Pakistanis to be given this platform," the man screamed. He was overpowered and probably thrashed by the students.

Bibliography

Ahmad, Aijaz. *Lineages of the Present: Ideology and Politics in Contemporary South Asia.* London: Verso, 2000.

Bhalla, Alok. *Partition Dialogues: Memories of a Lost Home.* New Delhi: Oxford University Press, 2006.

Bose, Sugata and Ayesha Jalal. *Modern South Asia: History, Culture, Political Economy.* Delhi: Oxford University Press, 1997.

Coppola, Carlo. *Urdu Poetry, 1935–1970: The Progressive Episode.* PhD thesis. Chicago, IL: University of Chicago, 1975.

Faiz, Ahmed Faiz. *Poems by Faiz,* translated by V.G. Kiernan. New Delhi: Oxford University Press, 2000.

Hasan, Mushirul. "Partition, the Human Cost." *History Today* 1997, 49–50.

Hyder, Quratulain. *River of Fire.* New Delhi: Kali for Women, 1998.

Jalal, Ayesha. *Self and Sovereignty: Individual and Community in South Asian Islam Since 1850.* London: Routledge, 2000.

Jinnah, Mohammaed Ali. *Speeches and Statements as Governor General of Pakistan 1947–48*. Islamabad: Government of Pakistan, Ministry of Information and Broadcasting, 1989.

MacAurthur, Brian (ed.). *The Penguin Book of Twentieth Century Speeches*. London: Penguin, 1992.

Malihabadi, Josh. *Sh'olah*. Allahabad: Kitab Mahal, 1948.

Malik, Hafeez. *Iqbal: Poet Philospher of Pakistan*. New York: Columbia University Press, 1971.

Riaz, Fahmida. *Four Walls and a Black Veil: Poems by Fahmida Riaz*, translated by Patricia Sharpe. New Delhi: Oxford University Press, 2005.

Russell, Ralph. *How Not to Write the History of Urdu Literature*. New Delhi: Oxford University Press, 1999.

Sherwani, L.A. *Speeches Writings and Statements of Iqbal*. Lahore: Iqbal Academy, 1995.

Singh, Khushwant. "Remembering Josh." *Outlookindia.com*, February 22, 2012. http://blogs.outlookindia.com/default.aspx?ddm=10&eid=5&pid=2739.

Steele, Laurel. "Finding Faiz at Berkeley: Room for a Celebration." *Pakistaniaat*, spring (2013).

6 Nation (de)composed

Ritwik Ghatak, Guru Dutt, Saadat Hasan Manto, and the shifting shapes of national memory

Nandini Bhattacharya

What relates the political to the question of the aesthetic and to a sense of history in the work of Ritwik Ghatak, *enfant terrible* cinematic chronicler of post-colonial South Asia as wasteland?[1] I take up this question, certainly not for its originality but for its enduring relevance, particularly given the resurgence of histories of affect and intellect about Indian cinema of the 1950s. To engage the milieu more fully, moreover, I propose a consideration of these same questions as they emerge from the work of Guru Dutt, a filmmaker not usually linked with Ghatak. I also propose a linking of Ghatak and Dutt's work in cinema to that of yet another "alienated" wanderer in the wasteland of a decolonized South Asia: Saadat Hasan Manto, Urdu anti-"progressive" writer and sometime denizen of Bombay cinema. Why is the political in Dutt's aesthetic and sense of history deemed significantly different from that in Ghatak's, though both of them ostensibly proffer similar concerns about South Asian decolonization?[2] And how does Manto's vision of darkness over the land cast light on the questions of migrancy within both literature and the nation that it is said to compose? A comparison of the three is a better way to approach the question of an early aesthetic of alienation in postcolonial India, than to take these fellow travelers and strangers to each other as isolated *auteurs*.

In their anthology *Cosmopolitanism*, the editors depart from the stereotype of the Cosmopolitan as the savvy, debonair citizen of the world, locating the Cosmopolitan instead not in a poetics and politics of space but in homelessness and migrancy itself: "Refugees, peoples of the diaspora, and migrants and exiles represent the spirit of the cosmopolitan community" (Breckenridge 2002, 6). Current scholarship suggests an embalming of Ghatak as an iconic investigator of refugee experience in cinema. While the historical record indubitably points to Ghatak's obsession with the anguish of Partition, there may be unexplored implications of this equally obsessive critical chaining of Ghatak within the codex of the "displaced" individual chronicling the traumas of forced migration and homelessness.[3] Has Ghatak been too rigorously shackled to his artistic reputation?

For instance, consider the following. Ritwik Ghatak's iconicity as the narrator of rootlessness is indexed by a Worldcat database search with the keywords "Calcutta," "partition," and "refugee." It brings up citations of his two films – *Meghe Dhaka Tara* and *Subarnarekha* – and only those two citations.[4] Ghatak's

legacy is now squarely in the realm of the cinematographer of refugee experience. How does one grapple with the evidence, cinematic and print, and reassess
the record? Ghatak himself said many things at many times about being a
refugee. True, several of his comments tend to certify the record of Ghatak as
the alienated "glocal" soul, victim of the partition of Bengal and lifelong lover of
Mother Bengal thereafter.[5] But there are gaps and inconsistencies in the testimony too; at one time he is claimed to have said,

> You see, I was a refugee myself. I can never forget it. The Partition and
> everything that followed come to my mind most vividly. But I am not eager
> to take up this subject, because *I have not suffered myself. A person who has
> suffered can do better justice to it.*
>
> (Dasgupta and Bhattacharya 2003, 18; italics added)

Without question, apparent inconsistencies in Ghatak are not hard to find. No
hobgoblins of the small mind for him, he frequently suggests. Yet the interviews
conducted with him by Sibaditya Dasgupta and Sandipan Bhattacharya return
insistently to asking Ghatak to narrate his life in the context of the Bengal partition of 1947/1948, and he obliges, with said inconsistencies and occasional
flashes of temper and impatience. Yet his very evasions, and sometimes his very
insistences, recurrently evoke the question: is this mostly what there is? One
wants to ask: does his personal statement quoted above suggest a confusion or
denial in Ghatak, a mere capricious disavowal to drive home obliquely the point
about his own eccentricity and nonconformity, or is there an incoherent and
tangled truth about his statement on suffering? What alternative roles or niches
may be found for him, and how might we re-imagine him in the larger context of
filmmaking in the era of postcolonial devastation and rebuilding?

Undoubtedly, the indelible imprint of Manto and Ghatak's work must form
the basis of any examination of the liminal consciousness – say, that of "the
refugee" – inevitably undercutting the "homogeneous empty time"[6] – and I
would add the "empty inhabited space" – of South Asian decolonization and
nation-making.[7] An instance of "empty inhabited space" is the space that is the
non-space and the absence created by bodies spectralized by forced migration.
The spectral refugee, as she or he moves under the multiple blows of communal
violence, sexual violence, evacuation from home, the experience of shelters and
squatting shacks, and political brutality, creates an "empty space" which nevertheless contains a trace of the body that just vacated. This space, one might
argue, is also location of the "ambiguation" of lawfulness and lawlessness.
Dipesh Chakrabarty traces the transmutation of a politics of mass mobilization,
found to be an index of "popular sovereignty" during the Indian anti-colonial
struggle, into lawlessness and un-"political" activity during the Nehruvian 1950s
(Chakrabarty 2007, 31–54). In the course of an anatomization of the process
whereby anti-colonial and thereby "lawful" "lawbreaking" became politically
illegitimate disorderliness during the early years of Independence, Chakrabarty
cites the contestation by East Bengal refugees – Ghatak's people – of concepts

of lawfulness that denied them their basic humanity or sovereignty (Chakrabarty 2007, 48–49). A member of the West Bengal Legislative Assembly sympathetic to East Pakistan refugees once specifically invoked Gandhi's anti-colonial politics to turn the ideas of law and lawlessness upside down in favor of "illegal" refugee actions.

Law and lawlessness thus became stippled with each other's rhetoric and effects; this is one of the ambiguous spaces of political citizenship in postcoloniality that has particular relevance for Ghatak's personal life as well as his for his cinema. This ambiguated space wherein law becomes lawlessness, and vice versa, is analogous to the *habitus* of the spectral body of the forced migrant or refugee in Ghatak and Manto's work. Its stake in the "homogeneous empty time" of the nation is uncertain, as is its claim to citizenship. This "un"-citizen has had her claims to law and lawful recourse against violence entirely ignored; she or he then exists as a shadow or trace just exiting the frame still haunted by its recent, hurried departure. The architecture of this still-warm departure is the "empty inhabited space" that the nation signifies for some of its occupants. Since the space is empty as well as inhabited, it demonstrates the same predicament of ambiguation as the official law that is lawless by the anti-colonial logic, and the mass political mobilization that is now lawful by the refugee's logic. And for Ghatak as well as for Manto, clearly, to represent this ambiguated space and time of the spectral nation and the spectral citizen is to subpoena the notion of truth in art in impossible times of human suffering.

Ghatak's film *Nagarik* (The Citizen; made in 1953 and released posthumously in India in 1977) may be seen as the least developed mark of Ghatak's visual stylus; yet in some ways it is the starkest grapheme of his theories of the aesthetic versus the political, or, as he would put it, art versus truth. Ghatak stated repeatedly that he believed that art was unavoidably political and that truth superseded art. But what kind of truth of a displaced existence might be at the center of Ghatak's corpus? And what is the function of the aesthetic therein? He and his family are first seen living in a Calcutta tenement, with a sister at home to marry, and Ramu without a job. Ramu begins with youthful optimism and enthusiasm to re-establish himself and his family in West Bengal, but the status and stigma of refugeedom are too much for him to overcome. He finally realizes that he must remain in the ranks of the hordes of the unemployed and hungry in the new divided nation. In the penultimate scene he rips up a calendar image of a tranquil pastoral scene, emblem of his romantic quest for a lost home on the new horizon, when he moves on with his family to face "reality" as the Left saw it. In addition, the violin player, who alternately enticed and tortured Ramu by refusing to play unless paid, emerges from the shadows as Ramu leaves, and begins to play to compensate Ramu for an earlier unfulfilled promise, but Ramu must leave, and the violin breaks. At another point, the militant tones of the Communist "Internationale" sound to the marching footsteps of a street protest while the narrative converges on a final dissolution of romantic dreams of love and beauty.

As Ramu gains "true" consciousness, Ghatak implies, the beauty that he writhed for earlier in his dismal surroundings becomes incidental, materialized:

calendar art that rips and violin strings that break. Ramu, in other words, has successfully denaturalized his longings for a bourgeois art. But in *Jukti Takko Aar Gappo* (Reason, Argument, and Narrative, 1974) – Ghatak's last major feature film where the broken drunk and failed father and husband Neelkantha, played by Ghatak himself, tours the ravaged "New" Bengal in search of social justice and existential meaning, finding truth in a death that is also a "doing" something needful[8] – in a way Ramu has returned, a sadder and wiser man.[9] Neelkantha's wife has left him with their son, unable to tolerate his capitulation to failures and despair. Neelkantha befriends a young revolutionary and a young displaced woman, with whom he embarks on a quest for the lost soul of the Bengali motherland in rural Bengal, away from the cities. His rejection of everything urban and ideological at this point is signaled by his verbal duel with a maverick agitprop ideologue of an entrenched Marxist junta (played by the talented Utpal Dutt). Although the quest fails, with Neelkantha's death from the spray of police bullets meant for the Naxalite[10] youth hiding in the forests, Ghatak here seems to have written his qualified elegy for hope. This death is still a kind of doing of something meaningful, though for Bengal's youth it may be the end of dreams. It is also another comprehensive and ultimate statement on the possible balance between the aesthetic and the political in art. The aesthetic is not emptied out; indeed, in the middle sequence of *Jukti Takko Aar Gappo* Ghatak is clearly obsessed with the folk dance form *Chhau* which serves as a vehicle for the erotic and mystical energy of Bengal. However, art can only be realized through a politics of agitation – blooming in the tension between narration (*Gappo*), argument (*Takko*) and rational choices (*Jukti*) – not through recourse to a melodious poetic and aesthetic for a chaotic decolonization.

Guru Dutt, the Bombay filmmaker, on the other hand, also explored problems of an alienating decolonizaton: perpetual migrancy and homelessness as opposed to national self-constitution, the rampancy of capitalist exploitation, and the demeaning of women and of the sacred.[11] What makes Ghatak interesting but not compelling to many (as a friend said upon watching *Nagarik* recently) and obscure for many years, and Dutt one of the few directors in India considered to have one of the 100 best films ever made, according to *Time* magazine? Was the difference in the aesthetic and not in the mimetic, in that Dutt and Ghatak captured post-Independence fatigue, despair and melancholy in intrinsically different visual notations, the former through a mellifluent and lyrical camera, the latter through a Brechtian and alienated vision?[12] Was it that Dutt subordinated truth to art in the telling? His protagonist in *Mr. and Mrs. 55* (1956) seems to make such a claim about politics during an exchange: "Q. Are you a Communist? A. No, I am a cartoonist." Or is the difference to be located not in formal characteristics at all (or not alone in those), but in the different apperceptions of refugeedom in different structures of historical memory?

Let me define "historic memory." I coin this term to combine Gyan Pandey's influential definition of history as that which is a structure of the past, and memory as a living infrastructure of the present (Breckenridge 1995; Pandey 1999). Following Pandey's insightful distinction between history and memory, but diverging slightly from it, I suggest that the passage of postcolonial time alchemizes the line between history and memory and creates a sensibility that uneasily accommodates the two. An apperceptive category of history emerges that finds in cinema a critical nesting space; the cinema accommodates modalities of time remembered and experienced as both a past (history) and a present (memory).[13] In Ghatak's case this accommodation is a battle. In Dutt's case it is an acculturation.

Histories and aesthetics of space intersected in South Asia's traumatic decolonization. The contest for space has continued to be reflected in South Asian cinema from the 1950s to the present. Spatial politics and the aestheticization of spaces both reflect current politics and urban policies and also glance back at colonial and postcolonial histories of national fragmentation and nation formation. In this chapter the relationship of art and politics – of artistic and political truth questions – is examined. While Ghatak is generally seen as the testier, more radical oppositional chronicler of postcolonial South Asian national fragmentation and individual displacement, a lens such as Guru Dutt's commercial cinema offers an alternative reading of the exigencies of re-spatialization of a torn and decolonizing nation. Manto, as we will see later, provides an entirely more alienated third space, a dark margin, wherein the project of making meaning itself becomes overcast in total ambiguity.

Dutt's *Pyaasa* is the story of Vijay, a talented but penniless poet who cannot get his poetry recognized or published in a new India where the nationalist dream of egalitarianism has turned into a nightmare of rampant developmentalism and greed. His college girlfriend leaves him to marry a rich publisher, and Vijay's mercenary brothers throw him out as a useless mouth to feed. A prostitute named Gulabo finds his poems being sold as recyclables, and falls in love with him upon meeting him thereafter. In a nation without shame, Vijay continues to find himself walking among the degenerate and the desperate, until one day he switches his coat with a beggar who dies in a train accident and is identified as Vijay. Vijay's poetry is posthumously published by Gulabo's enterprise and becomes an overnight runaway hit. He then returns, as if from the dead, to reclaim his due, but, meeting with more corruption and greed, chooses to leave society with Gulabo.

In *Pyaasa*, Vijay – played by Dutt himself – interrogates the location of the national protagonist in a red light district. As the lyrics suggest, Vijay is looking for compatriots, not for the nation. The nation is "right here," as his taxonomy of the demos abundantly proves: there are the prostitutes, the pimps, the sick, the fraudulent, the fathers, the sons, the "public," the politicos, the mothers, the wives, and the sisters. And Vijay is right there too, his two feet planted on the ground. But where, Vijay asks, are those fellow nationals who speak of pride in their nation (one wherein the educated, unemployed youth have become coolies and "public sleepers")?[14] Where are the people who have this "pride" that Vijay, a new cadet of the unemployed corps of decolonized India, lacks? And how or why? Rushing out of the quarters of the prostitute who is a failed mother, Vijay's historic memory (available as a temporal modality within a cinema engrossed in encounters with illiberality, injustice, violence and exploitation) allows him to ask this question without becoming an actual refugee. Even at the end, though Vijay leaves "this world" in quest of something better with Gulabo the golden-hearted prostitute, there is not a sense of an "unworlding"; the quest is not for the past but for an unknown future.

In contrast, Ghatak's protagonist spends a life potentially arcing from the young Ramu's idealistic determination to the older Neelkantha's "encounter" with law and order wherein the crossfire is the only space that the homeless prot-agonist inhabits, the only piece of ground to which the refugee body can make a claim. This is evidence of that "empty space" of the historic nation which never-theless contains a trace of the body that just vacated it. This space is also the space of the ambiguation of the nation and its subjects. The difference between Ghatak and Dutt in this regard may thus be seen as a different capacity for his-toric memory in the sense that I have outlined before; the everyday reality of memory, the present plenitude of a consciousness of the past is an unbearable weight for Ghatak's protagonists from *Nagarik* to *Jukti Takko ar Gappo*. It is a weight they seek to lighten by pursuing history in search of a past; the quest tends to overtake and overshadow their capacity for living memory, a past lived in and through the present. Because historic memory in Ghatak looks only back-ward, truth in art for him becomes always an elsewhere, for the present is full of lies. An almost total renunciation of the present makes it an unbearable *locus habitus*.

Thus, finally, the matrix of historic memory, of a temporal consciousness of identity, is also a spatial one, as Gyan Pandey has pointed out. I use Pandey's ideas again to highlight the uses of space as what I call a "habitable locus" – a local address for life, dreams and memories – for historic memory in Ghatak and Dutt. Besides differentiating between history and memory as temporal modali-ties, Pandey also emphasizes an endemic distinction between community insiders and outsiders in postcolonial narratives about violence. The space of the community, the space of belonging and having common hopes and dreams, is fragile and coveted; boundaries are porous and dangerously indeterminate. Bad things – the community concludes – were done to "us," by quintessential "out-siders." Pandey documents the persistence of this trope of the spatial outsider in the "historic memory" of the survivors of violence, the legatees of the South Asian wasteland at Independence and Partition. Thus, as Pandey shows, in these survival narratives, habitable locus becomes critical; it is the space for remem-bering oneself in history. One is either an outsider or an insider, never both and neither. Here occurs a moment of absolute spatial thinking, something we also find in Ghatak's and Dutt's films.

In Dutt we find Vijay standing firm on his own ground; if need be, he takes the ground with him, but he never gives up the ground. Viewed from another angle, this is the take of the writers represented in Breckenridge's collection of essays: cosmopolitans are also refugees. The geopolitical displacement of the cosmopolitan is also their phenomenological emplacement. I suggest that the construction of this emplacement as displacement, and vice versa, is active in

Pyaasa and negatively realized in Ghatak. Trains in Ghatak signify not arrivals or departures, but liminal journeys that end up going to the proverbial nowhere, either for a person or for a people, as in a famous shot in *Komal Gandhar*. As Partha Chatterjee writes,

> [T]he shot of the camera moving forward rapidly on the railway track at Lalgola, to simulate a subjective angle, from the point of view of the engine, that comes to a halt abruptly to create a collision-like effect; and the screech of the brakes of the engine is again a cry of lament for the immediate past and the destruction of a more congenial way of life before politics and the blessings of modern civilization vitiated it.
>
> (Chatterjee 2002, 63)

The train in *Pyaasa*, in a very similar shot, appears to kill an old Vijay but brings to life a new one. I choose this one motif of transition and traversal deliberately: the relevance of this use of trains will not be lost on those familiar with the discourse of trains, life and death in the South Asian Partition.

The perpetually transitional in Ghatak's *Nagarik* and *Jukti Takko ar Gappo* appears as the transformed consciousness of refugee cosmopolitanism in Dutt's *Pyaasa*. Visually this is achieved partly as a powerful aesthetic effect: Dutt's mellifluent lens poses a strong contrast to Ghatak's jagged epic camera. But, more significantly, the visual signature corroborates or creates differing historical apperception whose signified is the refugee, the displaced/emplaced.

I now turn to Saadat Hasan Manto whose work in many ways complements that of Ghatak as another experimenter with an aesthetic of the South Asian crisis of decolonization. The Urdu-language author and Hindi film scriptwriter Sadaat Hasan Manto wrote stories about India's northwestern Partition at Independence (1947), while Ghatak focused on the concomitant eastern partition. The jagged cadence of the epic in Ghatak, his refusal of codified myth, as has been noted by film historian Ashish Raadhyaksha (Rajadhyaksha 1982), is also present in Manto's works such as *Siyah Hashiye (Black Margins)*, a collection of aphoristic short tales about senseless communal violence at partition.[15] An important critical view of a refusal of a mythic "aesthetic" in Manto – what I will hereafter call a mythopoesis of the nation – appears in Alok Bhalla's testy rejection of Khalid Hasan's translation of *Siyah Hashiyeh* which, Bhalla argues, softens the blow. In theories of refugee-ness, there is no place for such softening.[16]

Memory serves in Ghatak and Manto as conduit for an unfinished becoming, whose physical dispersal in pure refugee status creates new identities unmoored from habitable loci and habits of historic memory that form the bedrock of most forms of Indian anti-colonial nationalism. Whether or not Ashish Rajadhyaksha's description of Ghatak's cinema as a "return to the epic" is held to be the last word, Ghatak's (and Manto's) narratives approximate the epic in ways that superimpose jagged trajectories of terrain-shifting over calm historiographic cadences. The work of Sadaat Hasan Manto especially defies elegiac oeuvres that narrate and film South Asian decolonization as a process of creating a

singular migrant self in the face of threatened national and communal disinteg-
ration. His work would seem to exemplify Giorgio Agamben's identification of
the new identity of "Singularity" that is "freed from the false dilemma that
obliges knowledge to choose between the ineffability of the individual and the
intelligibility of the universal" (Agamben 1993, 1). It is in the detaching of
modern South Asian national identity from linear narratives of "habitable loci"
and "historic memory" that Manto's story-telling and Ghatak's filmmaking
capture the necrotic onset of modernization/modernity.

I have already outlined the ways in which Ghatak detaches his protagonist
from such narratives. Saadat Hasan Manto repeatedly uses similar tropes and
techniques in his stories. Manto wrote that these "were the times when philosophy, argumentation or logic had lost their meaning; they were nothing but an
exercise in futility" (Manto 1998, 103). As Alok Bhalla has written, and in such
stories as "1919 *ki Ek Baat*," "Toba Tek Singh" and "*Kali Shalwar*," for Manto,
history is not a culmination of events but

> of a regular and repeated series of actions ... "bloody tracks" – which
> invariably disfigure all the geographical and temporal sites of the nationalist
> struggle ... the calmer and more wonder-filled notion of "pilgrim tracks" in
> the Gandhian discourse on nationalism.
>
> (Bhalla 1997, 29)

Doubtless, the preponderance of a "refugee" consciousness in Manto is beyond
question. Take, for instance, Manto's incomparable "The Dog of Tetwal"
(Manto 2007, 80–87) where a stray dog that used to be the shared pet of the
Indian and Pakistani armies camped across the border between the two countries
suddenly becomes the target of attacks and dies in crossfire as communal hatred
mounts on either side. Manto writes:

> The dog jumped and flapped its ears violently. From his position, Subedar
> Himmat Khan fired his second shot, which buried itself near the front paws
> of the dog. Frightened out of its wits, it ran about sometimes in one direc-
> tion, sometimes the other.... Jamadar Harnam Singh, in a state of great fury,
> uttered a terrible oath, took careful aim, and fired. The bullet struck the dog
> in the leg, and its cry pierced the sky. The dog changed its direction and,
> limping, began running towards Subedar Himmat Khan's camp.
>
> (Manto 1998, 86–87)

The dog's terrible dilemma of belonging, at the point of the gun literally, is
performed in this story as an extended metaphor, of course, for the refugee
who is stateless and denationalized. The hatred visited upon it, Manto makes us
see, is spiked with the bitter taste of territorial loss and the burden of perpetual
vigilance, the burdens that the refugee carries as blame. In the empty space of
the border, like the dog, the stateless person is both trapped and constantly
attacked.

Still, in conclusion, I want to complicate somewhat the reception of Manto and Ghatak as poster-children of a literature of homelessness. I began this chapter by citing what results a certain kind of database search yields: Worldcat brings up Ghatak for a search on the keywords "refugee," "Calcutta" and "partition." Yet, when we place Ghatak and Manto in the milieu where Guru Dutt (and others in Bombay cinema) also worked, a milieu wherein the recent subcontinental trauma made displacement and upheaval for millions an inescapable historic memory for most Indians, we see a wider spectrum of consciousness of refugee-ness. Some who deal with the question about belonging in the postcolonial nation, such as Guru Dutt, wear a different set of cultural and political mantles. Others such as Ghatak and Manto receive – perhaps invite – critical attention as commonplaces that obsessively seek to recuperate histories and trajectories of nostalgic belonging. Critical discourse hints repeatedly that the obscurity of the two figures (until lately) is itself due to their treatment of the subject of the refugee – an uncanny history, no doubt. Here, critical discourse loops back again onto questions of art and truth. Moral detachment is more frequently noted to be Manto's signature; he wrote, it is iterated, that "we (the litterateurs) are not legislators, nor do we prescribe or proscribe anything" (Bhalla 1997, 132). Similarly for Ghatak; he is quoted as saying not only that politics is inevitable, but that the politics of truthful representation itself creates art.

No doubt, the fact that both were misunderstood, reviled and censored in their lives and careers would seem to require a compensatory, recuperative movement of enshrining and rememorializing. Rememorializing the artist of refugee-ness expresses itself in several crucial modalities. One is the critical emptying out of the aesthetic in Ghatak and Manto, in contrast with the aesthetic of, say, Guru Dutt, who deals with very similar contexts and denotations of a postcolonial wasteland in South Asia. Another is the attribution of an alienated ethics of truthfulness below the belt, an imagistic of exhausted and empty-eyed compassion resembling Benjamin's Angel of History who is swept up by the storm of progress.[17] A third is the foregrounding of the artist's personal revolt, the scandalous life and work, and mortiferous censorship. A fourth is the exaltation of the artist as icon of the refugee. These modalities are, of course, all interrelated.[18]

But it is in the final modality, the classification of Manto and Ghatak as icons of "refugee consciousness," that the true relationship between censorship, historic memory, truth and art in critical discourse begins to come into focus. As long as Manto and Ghatak remain outsiders to a history of the present and of the future, their work secures periodicity and the purity of a political concept. We can then remember Manto and Ghatak strategically and at critical moments as prophets of an apocalypse forever. What need not happen, then, is an engagement with their work as a particular type of intervention and engagement with a particular modality of refugee experience, one that does not thereby represent a totality of the significations of refugee-ness, even within the South Asian context.

Notes

1 *Enfant terrible* was the name coined for Ritwik Ghatak by Marie Seton (Dasgupta and Bhattacharya 2003, 139). Other perspectives include those in Banerjee (1985), Ghatak and Ray (2001) and Ghatak (2000).

2 See e.g., Cooper (2006); "Guru Dutt's 'Mr And Mrs 55' Is A Polished Musical Comedy," *Filmfare* (May 27, 1955), 21; also Virdi (2003).

3 "Latin cōdex, the source of our word, is a variant of caudex, a wooden stump to which petty criminals were tied in ancient Rome, rather like our stocks. This was also the word for a book made of thin wooden strips coated with wax upon which one wrote" (www.answers.com/topic/codex; accessed December 23, 2008).

4 Worldcat; accessed December 4, 2008.

5 Banerjee (1985). Drawing on the meaning of the "glocal" as the confluence of the global and the local here, I suggest hereby that Ghatak is someone with strong roots to the local (i.e. unpartitioned Bengal in his case) and powerful aspirations to the universal in his cinema.

6 This is the concept made current in scholarly discourse on nationalism by Benedict Anderson (Anderson 1991, 24). Anderson derives this concept from Walter Benjamin (Benjamin 1968, 263). On Manto and the liminal see Bhalla (1997, x, 33) and Chaudhuri (2001, 187).

7 See Partha Chatterjeee, "The Films of Ritwik Ghatak and the Partition," in Chatterjee (2002).

8 These are Neelkantha's dying words at the end of *Jukti Takko ar Gappo.*

9 Neelkantha's wife has left him with their child; her name is Durga, a variant of Uma, which was the name of Ramu's fiancée in *Nagarik.*

10 The Naxalite movement was the Marxist-Leninist Communist Party-led armed insurgency, supported by communist intellectuals and peasantry, crushed within a few months of its inception in West Bengal's Naxalbari region in 1967, but a political force to reckon with ever after in India. A brief but competent summary of the movement may be found in 'Naxalbari (1967), "The Naxalite Movement in India," http://venus.unive.it/asiamed/eventi/schede/naxalbari.html; accessed December 23, 2008). Ghatak himself said, "I have wanted to use the cinema as a weapon" (Banerjee 1985, 109).

11 These themes ring insistent notes in Dutt's *Pyaasa* (1957) and Ghatak's *Nagarik.* See Banerjee (1985, 85). One might easily say that they capture the zeitgeist of postcoloniality in India in the 1950s. I might call the aggregate of these themes a phenomenology of the decolonization of Mother India, though I am not advocating or illustrating a phenomenological approach here.

12 Dutt is reported to have said, "It is not difficult to make successful films ... which cater to the box-office alone. The difficulty arises when purposeful films have to be shaped to succeed at the box-office" (Banerjee 1985, 87).

13 On this question of cinematic image as accommodating several temporalities simultaneously, see "The Crystals of Time" (Deleuze 1989, 68–97).

14 I borrow here Arjun Appadurai's exquisite phrase about spectral demotic identity in postcolonial Bombay (Appadurai 2000, 54–81). These "public sleepers" (65), the "people" who sleep in public spaces and are gone before or because the police arrive, strongly resemble the spectral inhabitants of the empty national spaces, Ghatak's refugees.

15 Rajadhyksha's thesis on Ghatak is intriguing: "myth seals off a configuration of images from their material base, while the epic achieves a synthesis of form, a unity of perception that is the first step towards the overcoming of the fragmentation of our social sensibility" (Rajadhyaksha 1982, 11).

16 Most students of Manto's work insist upon this "texture" of Manto's writing; see Bhalla (1997, xii) and Bhalla (2002, 241–259).

17 Benjamin wrote in "Theses on the Philosophy of History" this now-famous meditation:

> A Klee painting named "Angelus Novus" shows an angel looking as though he is about to move away from something he is fixedly contemplating. His eyes are staring, his mouth is open, his wings are spread. This is how one pictures the angel of history. His faced is turned toward the past. Where we perceive a chain of events, he sees one single catastrophe which keeps piling wreckage upon wreckage and hurls it in front of his feet. The angel would like to stay, awaken the dead, and make whole what has been smashed. But a storm is blowing from Paradise; it has got caught in his wings with such violence that the angel can no longer close them. This storm irresistibly propels him into the future to which his back is turned, while the pile of debris before him grows skyward. This storm is what we call progress.
>
> (Benjamin 1968, 259–260)

18 Such modalities are found throughout the various critical sources on Manto and Ghatak that I have cited throughout this chapter; I therefore do not duplicate references to them here.

Bibliography

Agamben, Giorgio. *The Coming Community*. Minneapolis: University of Minnesota, 1993.

Anderson, Benedict. *Imagined Communities: The Origin and Spread of Nationalism*. London and New York: Verso, 1991.

Appadurai, Arjun. "Spectral Housing and Urban Cleansing: Notes on Millennial Mumbai." *Public Culture* 12:3 (2000), 627–651.

Banerjee, Haimanti. *Ritwik Kumar Ghatak: A Monograph*. Pune: National Film Archive of India, 1985.

Benjamin, Walter. *Illuminations*, edited by Hannah Arendt, translated by Harry Zohn. New York: Harcourt Brace Jovanovich, 1968.

Bhalla, Alok. *Life and Works of Saadat Hasan Manto*. Shimla: Indian Institute of Advanced Study, 1997.

——. "The Politics of Translation: Manto's Partition Stories and Khalid Hasan's English Version," in *Pangs of Partition, Vol. 2, The Human Dimension*, edited by S. Settar and Indira Baptista Gupta, 241–259. New Delhi: Manohar, 2002.

Breckenridge, Carol (ed.). *Consuming Modernity: Public Culture in a South Asian World*. Minneapolis: University of Minnestoa Press, 1995.

Chakrabarty, Dipesh. *Provincializing Europe: Postcolonial Thought and Historical Difference*. Princeton, NJ: Princeton University Press, 2007.

Chatterjee, Partha. "The Films of Ritwik Ghatak and the Partition," in *Pangs of Partition, Vol. 2, The Human Dimension*, edited by S. Settar and Indira Baptista, 59–68. New Delhi: Manohar, 2002.

Chaudhuri, Amit (ed.). *The Vintage Book of Modern Indian Literature*. New York: Random House, 2001.

Cooper, Darius. "The Mapping of Guru Dutt's Comedic Vision," in *Fingerprinting Popular Culture: The Mythic and the Iconic in Indian Cinema*, edited by Vinay Lal and Ashis Nandy, 156–185. New Delhi: Oxford University Press, 2006.

Dasgupta, Sibaditya and Sandipan Bhattacharya. *Ritwik Ghatak: Face to Face/ Conversations with the Master 1962–1977*. Kolkata: Cine Central & Manchasha, 2003.

Deleuze, Gilles. *Cinema 2: The Time-Image*, translated by Hugh Tomlinson and Robert Galeta. Minneapolis: University of Minnesota Press, 1989.

Filmfare. "Guru Dutt's 'Mr And Mrs 55' Is A Polished Musical Comedy." *Filmfare*, May 27, 1955.

Ghatak, Ritwik. *Rows and Rows of Fences: Ritwik Ghatak on Cinema*. Kolkata: Seagull Books, 2000.

Ghatak, Ritwik and Rani Ray. *Ritwik Ghatak Stories*. New Delhi: Srishti Publishers & Distributors, 2001.

Manto, Sadat Hasan. *The Best of Manto: A Collection of His Short Stories*, edited by Jai Ratan. Lahore: Vanguard Books, 1998.

——. "The Dog of Tetwal," in *Crossing Over: Partition Literature from India, Pakistan and Bangladesh*, edited by Frank Stewart and Sukrita Paul Kumar, 80–87. Honolulu: University of Hawaii Press, 2007.

Pandey, Gyanendra. *Memory History and the Question of Violence: Reflections on the Reconstruction*. Kolkata: K.P. Bagchi & Co., 1999.

Rajadhyaksha, Ashish. *Ritwik Ghatak: A Return to the Epic*. Bombay: Screen Unit, 1982.

Virdi, Jyotika. *The Cinematic Imagination: Indian Popular Films as Social History*. New Brunswick, NJ: Rutgers University Press, 2003.

Vohra, Ashok. "Manto's Philosophy: An Explication," in *Life and Works of Saadat Hasan Manto*, edited by Alok Bhalla. Shimla: Indian Institute of Advanced Study, 1997.

Part III

History, memory, and aesthetics

7 Toward a cognitive poetics of history

Pinjar, the *Ramayana*, and Partition

Patrick Hogan

Within the past few decades, the story of the *Ramayana* has almost certainly been the single most politically consequential narrative paradigm among Hindu nationalists in India.[1] In keeping with this, it has been an almost ubiquitous "substructure" for the emplotment of personal relations, social tensions, and, of course, history – including the history of the 1947 Partition of India. It is not difficult to imagine just what the default use of this paradigm is likely to be. Pakistan or, worse still, Muslims are Ravana, the demon who stole both land and women. India or, worse still, Hindus are Rama. The relation between India and Pakistan, Hindus and Muslims in this imagination is almost necessarily belligerent. Moreover, this emplotment places blame only on one side in communal violence generally, and Partition violence in particular. As a result, it emplots South Asian history in ways that contribute to antagonistic militarism and communalism.

In cases of this sort, it is clearly important to engage in ideological critique. Such a critique is likely to have two components. The first and more obvious component involves a focus on the history, an analysis of the degree to which the emplotment is accurate or inaccurate to the ascertainable facts. Often, inaccuracy will primarily be a matter of over-simplification – yes, the analogy of Ravana does fit some Pakistanis at some points; however, this cannot be generalized, since it would fit comparable numbers of Hindus or Sikhs. The second component of such ideological critique focuses on the paradigmatic model rather than the history. In some ways this is even more important, since the paradigm is commonly used to emplot many historical episodes. Its consequences are therefore more widespread. Such a critique may argue that the analogy is misleading, that it is not generally valid as a way of construing historical events. In this case, the contention would be that the *Ramayana* does not apply to history. It projects mythological backgrounds and consequences that do not fit the real world; it exaggerates the virtues and vices of the protagonists by analogizing them to gods and demons; indeed, it treats social forces and historical contingencies as if they were personal circumstances and individual motives.

In other words, in both cases, ideological critique often points us toward the (partial) restoration of the chaotic worldly complexity that had been filtered out through narrative encoding. In this way, we come to a third level. The problem is not only one of particular historical claims and particular models or analogies, but one of encoding and emplotment themselves. There is a sort of trade-off here. When dealing with complex phenomena, such as history, we often have to lose information in order to make any sense of those phenomena. But the more information we lose, the less accurate our understanding. Thus, at least frequently, the more sense we seem to make of history, the less accurate that sense is likely to be. We might refer to this as a sort of historical uncertainty principle.

In this context, *Pinjar* is a remarkable and daring work.[2] It does link Pakistan with Ravana and India with Rama.[3] At the same time, however, it engages in both types of ideological critique. First, it challenges the historical adequacy of this mythological emplotment of history.[4] One possible difficulty with such a challenge is that it may produce a sort of inverted over-simplification – perhaps a reductive story that celebrates Pakistan over India in order to counter a prior, reductive celebration of India over Pakistan. *Pinjar* does not present us with such a "reactive reduction." Rather, it explores the background to violence and the humanity of the people who engage in it – including their own combination of benevolent and malevolent impulses, admirable and objectionable traits. Indeed, the film indicates that admirable and objectionable traits are often inseparable from one another. In any case, it complicates our sense of the history. Perhaps more importantly, this work systematically revises the *Ramayana* as well, and it does so in the same complicating way. It leaves viewers with potential re-imaginations of both Partition and the *Ramayana* re-imaginations that restore some of the contradiction and chaos of the historical events, but without entirely surrendering comprehensibility. In the end, these re-imaginations repudiate violence while still celebrating the virtue of physical bravery and advocating a form of active political engagement based on both empathy and a respect for human autonomy.

In this chapter I would like to do three things, if in a necessarily somewhat brief and preliminary manner. First, drawing on recent research in cognitive science, I would like to consider some of the psychological complexity in our relation to history and politics, as these relate to such vast events as Partition. Specifically, I would like to consider some aspects of what may be called the cognitive poetics of history – "poetics" because it is at least in part a matter of emplotment (as Hayden White rightly emphasized). After outlining an account of this and relating it to ideological critique, I will very briefly consider the social and political conditions in which the story and movie of *Pinjar* were produced. Finally, I will go through the film in some detail, considering the ways in which the director tacitly relies on certain psychological processes in pursuing his political ends, particularly ideological critique.

Making sense of history: on the nature of events

One obvious way of thinking about history is by reference to events. History, in this approach, is first of all a series of partially interrelated and partially parallel events. Historiography involves describing and explaining these events.

The problem is that the notion of "event" is not at all clear. Crucially, it does not seem to make much sense to say that there are events in the world itself. The world is always a series of causes and effects, proceeding along its complex, inexorable way. In contrast with these apparently routine sequences we feel as if events are something special. But from the point of view of causality itself, there cannot be anything that does not arise out of causes, and no causes can be "special" (i.e., the general causal principles have to be the same all along). Why, then, do we count the Partition of India as an event while, in contrast, we do not count all the happenings in the same areas, say, five years earlier, as an event?

There are some obvious possibilities for answering this question. For example, one possible response is that the causes are more limited. The legal act of Partition caused massive violence, while ordinarily a day's activities proceed through local and particular causes. But, in fact, the Partition violence too proceeded through such local and particular causes, as people heard rumors of communal violence elsewhere and responded violently to those rumors, or took out old grudges in the context of riots, or responded pre-emptively to perceived threats. Yes, the legal act of Partition had bearing, but it had to work its way out through all the usual small causes as well. Moreover, even in ordinary times there are larger conditions that have broad consequences – for example, in ordinary times the system of law and the presence of police operate through all the usual small causes (individual people's interests, fears, expectations, etc.) to produce (the non-event of) routine activity.

Another possibility is the importance of components of the event considered collectively. For example, in the United States, the attacks of September 11, 2001 are universally considered to constitute a historical event. Why is that? Many people would probably say it is because the results were so horrible. But, in fact, people die in huge numbers from preventable disease, from hunger, from automobile accidents, all the time. Added up day after day, these deaths vastly outweigh those of September 11 – but we do not consider these deaths to be an event. Is this because September 11 was one day and these other deaths occur recurrently over many days? If that were the case the Partition violence would not count as an event, since it stretched out over an extended period. Moreover, it cannot be a matter of shared causes because it is not difficult to find shared causes for malnutrition or fatal illness throughout much of the world.

Yet most of us remain convinced that Partition was an event. Why?

In the first chapter of *Affective Narratology*, I argue that events – particularly events in our daily lives – are defined, not by causes or effects, nor by other properties bearing directly on the objective facts. Rather, events are defined by our emotion systems. Specifically, our emotion systems, in complex interaction with our systems for attention, inference, and so on, encode occurrences as events. (I use the word "occurrences" for *any* temporal sequence of causes and effects, including all those sequences that we would not consider events.) To say that we "encode" occurrences means that we *select* some causes and effects while leaving aside others, that we *segment* them into units that may be cognitively manipulated, and that we place them in *structural* relations with one another.

There are certain sorts of occurrence that we are cognitively predisposed to select, certain ways in which we are cognitively inclined to structure, and so on. Moreover, our emotion systems are more sensitive to some occurrences than to others. One of the most important features of our emotional and encoding sensitivities is that they tend to be activated by novelty. Like being an event, being novel is not an objective property of occurrences, but a feature of the relation between our cognition and occurrences. It is, in other words, a matter of our long-term or habitual expectations. Novelty is, indeed, bound up with why we tend to think of events as having a single cause. First, novelty inspires us to seek causes (Kahnemann and Miller 1986, 148). Second, when we seek causes, we tend to do so in a highly simplified way. Specifically, we tend to isolate any highly salient, temporally precedent occurrence as the cause of the event in question (Clore and Ortony 2002, 27; Zajonc 2000, 48). The saliency of any precedent occurrence is itself in part a matter of novelty or unexpectedness. Beyond this, we have a particular inclination to engage in causally reductive praise or blame – of individuals or of groups – in keeping with the proclivities of our emotion systems. For a discussion of this point, see *Understanding Nationalism* (Hogan 2009, ch. 4).

With events in our personal lives, this process is already excessively simplifying, as we often recognize. Thus, after our initial impulse to blame our boss or spouse or parents, we are likely to realize that there is something reductive about these attributions. The problem is obviously far worse in the case of historical events. These events commonly extend over much larger periods of time than personal events, involve many more agents, many and far more complex social relations, etc. Indeed, when responding to historical events, there may be too many or too few agents who are salient and thus open to praise or blame. Moreover, their entry into the unfolding event may be temporally staggered, such that it is difficult if not impossible to praise or blame them for fully instigating or sustaining the event. Indeed, historical events are unlikely to involve a single emotional response. They are likely to be ambivalent, to involve waves of emotion that are sometimes contradictory. As Ito and Caioppo point out, our emotion systems tend to avoid ambivalence. This is in part for evolutionary reasons (providing "clear ... action tendencies"). But, even in cases where the ambivalence is not strictly "maladaptive," we tend to find it aversive. Feelings of ambivalence do not constitute "harmonious and stable subjective experiences" (Ito and Caioppo 2001, 69).

The result of all this is that when we encode a complex event – most obviously a historical event – we often face a problem, or, rather, two related problems. First, the event is overly complex in its causal nature, not lending itself readily to praise and/or blame (or any other form of understanding). Second, our response to the event is aversively ambivalent. In response to these problems, we seek some comprehensible explanation of the event and some stabilization of our emotional response to the event.

A comprehensible explanation is something that we feel or experience as an explanation. This is related to, but distinct from a scientific explanation.

Something that we feel to be an explanation may not count as a scientific explanation. For example, we may feel that an ethnic stereotype explains behavior. However, it is not a scientific explanation of that behavior. Conversely, something that counts as a scientific explanation may not feel like an explanation to us (think of quantum mechanics). We tend to feel that something is an explanation to the extent that it has two properties. First, it should reduce the unexpected event to a familiar pattern. Second, it should make the event to some degree controllable. It should give us the sense that we could avoid or foster similar events in the future.

When faced with highly complex objects, such as historical events, we often pursue these goals by invoking models. Models are less complex cognitive structures that are both familiar and give a sense of control. Religious narratives are among the most common models that we invoke for understanding and responding to traumatic historical events in particular. For example, the cross-culturally recurring sacrificial narrative is often used to model communal devastation (e.g. in natural disasters, such as famines). This narrative involves a causal explanation of the event in terms of divine punishment for some collective sin, with the possibility of ending the devastation through collective sacrifice. For a discussion of this structure and its cross-cultural recurrence, see my *The Mind and Its Stories* (Hogan 2003, ch. 6). This sacrificial prototype is fairly general. On the other hand, some religious models are particular. For example, Israeli political discourse sometimes involves reference to the story of David and Goliath as a model for the relation between Israel and its Arab neighbors (Black 2002; Rothschild 2001).

There are also non-religious models, including other historical events. In one well-known study, researchers suggested (but did not explicitly invoke) either World War II or the Vietnam War in asking questions about a fictional political conflict. For instance, in the first case they had refugees leave by train and in the second case they had refugees leave by boat. Test subjects tended to understand and respond to the situations differently, depending on which model was suggested (and thereby "primed" or partially activated in memory). Thus, they were more likely to urge military intervention in the World War II-like case than in the Vietnam War-like case – even though the political conditions presented in the two cases were identical except in such irrelevant particulars as the vehicles used by refugees (Gilovich 1981).

Emotion stabilization also commonly relies on models which may simplify our emotional response to complex situations, in part by limiting attentional focus and fostering certain sorts of discounting or neglect. This occurs most clearly through the reduction of individual relations to group relations and the hierarchization of relations within and across such groups. In private life, emotionally consequential complexes of occurrences (i.e., events) typically have a direct impact on us individually. This is less often the case with historical events. Even when historical events do impact upon us individually, that impact is commonly chaotic and mixed up with non-egocentric or empathic feelings as well. These in particular may be modulated by in-group/out-group divisions.

For example, imagine someone simply dropping into the middle of a Partition riot. He or she would feel egocentric fear. But he or she would also feel a complex set of empathic responses to the suffering of others – as well as both egocentric and empathic horror, anger, and so forth. Of course, even limited familiarity with conditions surrounding the riot would provide some structure to this chaos. For example, one person would be killing another due to some communal identification. But, in itself, this still does not either fully explain or stabilize our emotional response. Our brains are set up to respond empathically to the pain of other people, not simply of other people who happen to be known as members of a particular group.[5] Models simplify this situation. For example, the cross-cultural heroic narrative places the origin of in-group/out-group conflict in the aggression of the out-group and characterizes in-group violence as defensive. This model simplifies the evaluation of the violence, biasing us toward construing violence from the out-group as aggression and violence from the in-group as defensive. This goes along with directing our expectations and attentional focus. When a member of the out-group is attacking a member of the in-group, my attention is on the aggression of the former and the threat to the latter. But when a member of the in-group is attacking a member of the out-group, my attention is on the well-being of the in-group member, whom I understand as responding to a prior threat (cf. Hamilton and Trolier (1986) on a study where test subjects interpreted the same action as more threatening if performed by a black person and more playful if performed by a white person).

Again, the models operating in these contexts may be prototypes or more concrete particulars, as when we model a current enemy on Hitler. Models here may be secular or religious as well, though there is often some level of religious association in any popular modeling of complex historical events. Moreover, in all of these cases, modeling may be recursive. We may model Hitler on Satan, then model Saddam Hussein on Hitler, implicitly carrying over the implications of the first (mythological) model to the second "target." (The "target" is the person, situation, or occurrence that we are trying to understand through the model. In this case, the first target would be Hitler and the second would be Hussein.)

Religious models tend to be particularly prominent because they are often widespread, salient, and emotionally consequential. They are likely to be even more prominent in cases where the crucial in-group/out-group division is itself religious. We find both situations in India, today and at the time of Partition.[6] Among religious narratives, several had great salience in the ordinary lives of Indian people. Among Muslims, these would include stories from the Qur'an, stories from the life of Muhammad, and so on. Sikhs, Parsis, and Christians had their own models and their own concrete relations to the occurrences that affected just how those models were developed and applied. I will focus, however, on Hindus. Among Hindus, there are almost countless models for social relations. Indeed, one of the most admirable aspects of Hinduism historically is that it encompasses such diversity of philosophical thought and, connected with this, such diversity of social models. Unfortunately, this diversity has been one target of much "Hindu" nationalism. Like other forms of reaction-ary traditionalism (i.e., the defensive affirmation of tradition in response to cul-tural threat, real or imagined [Hogan 2000, 10–14; 319]), Hindu nationalism tends to radically simplify, rigidify, and dogmatize – and thus profoundly distort – the tradition it pretends to promote. In the 1980s and 1990s, this reached a sort of climax in the elevation of the story of Rama – or, rather, one version of the story of Rama – to a place of central political importance.

The reference to Hindu nationalism leads us to a further complication here. Models may arise in the minds of ordinary people immersed in or learning about historical events. However, they may also be developed by political leaders in the service of political agendas. Thus we may distinguish between *spontaneous* and *ideological* models. At this point I wish to use the word "ideological" in an evaluatively neutral way. A model may be propagated by political leaders for political purposes. As a model, it will undoubtedly simplify our understanding of the event and our emotional response to it. However, this explanatory simplifica-tion may or may not count as a distortion, and the emotional simplification may or may not be objectionable. Of course, these things are difficult to judge. More-over, depending on our individual beliefs and goals, we may differ in our judg-ments. Nonetheless, most of us will probably agree that some ideological models are distortive and others are not, at least not in any consequential way. I take it that one constant of this division concerns dehumanization. When understanding historical events that involve conflict, we often invoke models that characterize some parties to the conflict in ways that are dehumanizing. Insofar as a model serves to dehumanize any group of humans – thus removing them entirely from our empathic response – I take it to be distortive. This is commonly (though not invariably) the case with the use of the story of Rama as a model for historical events, such as Partition.

Political leaders and analysts may not only seek to propagate popular models for events, they may also seek to criticize such models. In other words, a given writer may set out to change people's use of models. If this is directed toward distortive ideological models, then we refer to it as "ideological critique." While ideological critique is often explicit, it may be developed implicitly as well. More precisely, in any modeling relation, we may distinguish three components – the model itself or "source" (e.g., the story of Rama), the target event (e.g., Partition), and the mapping relations that link the source and the target (e.g., Muslims are raksasas; that is, demons). Moreover, we may distinguish two aspects of our relation to the source and the target: our understanding of each and our emotional response to each. Ideological critique may, then, involve chal-lenging our understanding of or emotional response to the target, the model, and/ or the mapping relations.

In connection with this, we might isolate, so to speak, two extreme forms of ideological critique. One is *positive historiography*. This focuses on restoring the complexity of the target; that is to say, the historical event. Such restoration involves seeking explanations for the event through empirical study rather than the application of popular models. For example, a positive historiographical treatment of Partition might examine the degree to which different groups engaged in violence at different times and with different provocations or motives. It may dispute even the communal character of some violence by isolating diverse motives. It may seek explanatory principles in factors such as proportions and situations of refugees in relation to group dynamics, the apparent availability of goods or property, the ability or willingness of police to stop riots, random features of network relations bearing on the spread of rumors, class or other non-religious factors, and so on. Ideological critique of this sort is more likely to be explicit and non-fictional, though certainly fictional works can move in this direction by trying to present more accurate and complex accounts of Partition.

The other extreme form is *remodeling*. This may involve altering any component of the ideological model. Thus it may change the source, the mapping relations, or the target. There are two ways in which the source may be altered. The most obvious and most common way is simply to choose a different model. To be effective, the model must usually be as widely accepted and emotionally forceful as the one it is replacing. Typically, the two models must be from the same "comparison set" or group of narratives that are understood as in some relevant way comparable to one another. In a Hindu context, one might reasonably argue that the *Ramayana* and the *Mahabharata* form such a comparison set, since they are the two main epics in Sanskrit. While the *Mahabharata* is not widely considered a sacred text as a whole, it does include the *Bhagavad Gita*, which has a religious status equal or superior to that of the *Ramayana* for many Hindus. Thus one way of responding to a *Ramayana*-based model of a historical event is by proposing an alternative *Mahabharata*-based model. Of course, this would not automatically change the outcome of the modeling. However, it would allow for at least the possibility of recognizing the kinship between Hindus and Muslims or Indians and Pakistanis (as the conflicting groups in the *Mahabharata* are cousins) and, depending on one's interpretation of the *Mahabharata*, it may suggest the futility of warfare.

The mention of one's interpretation of the source leads to the second way in which remodeling may affect the source – through changing our understanding of that source itself. As work by Romila Thapar, Paula Richman, and others has made abundantly clear, there are multiple traditions of revising the *Ramayana*, traditions that alter the virtues and vices of the characters, change our evaluation of them, transform the events. The revisions treated by Thapar and Richman are explicit retellings. But such transformations may occur implicitly as well. When this occurs, the revision of the source is commonly bound up with a revision of the target. Indeed, the revision of the target often reacts back on our understanding of the source. Suppose one establishes Rama as a model for a particular historical ruler. However, at the same time, one presents properties of this target character that are inconsistent with the way Rama is commonly understood. This may react back on our understanding of Rama, particularly insofar as the original epic gives some opening for this. For example, there are hints in the *Ramayana* that Rama has a tendency to excessive violence (see e.g., Valmiki II:

16–17). If Rama is used to model a character who exhibits excessive violence, then that character may make Rama's violence more salient.

This second form of source alteration – reunderstanding – is more complex, and more uncertain, than the first. For example, as to uncertainty, it is difficult to calculate when the alteration of the target may so to speak rebound on the source (e.g., on Rama). However, when such reunderstanding succeeds, it may be more ideologically consequential than the simple substitution of models. Specifically, it may foster a reinterpretation of the source narrative that carries over to other targets. For example, if our understanding of Rama and Ravana is altered by our account of Partition, that may carry over to other applications of that model (e.g. in relation to later communal conflicts or wars).

Finally, there are alterations in the mapping relations – also, in effect, a form of remodeling. These alterations simply shift what aspects of the source are connected to what aspects of the target. The simplest alteration of this sort is switching hero and villain – for example, mapping Rama on to Muslims and Ravana on to Hindus. Of course, the problem with this sort of reversal is that it is unlikely to be any less ideologically distortive than the original. Another possibility involves mixing the characters and events in ways that are not emotionally or causally consistent, ways that operate to return some of the ambivalence to the complex historical event.

Remodeling is perhaps most effective when it is developed in emotionally provocative detail, thus in fiction or in highly literary historiography. Moreover, insofar as it sets out to revise the source along with the target, it may be more effective insofar is it is partially implicit. At least, when a given story is sacred, significant explicit revisions of that story may be perceived as sacrilegious by believers. However, implicit revisions may subtly affect one's understanding of the story without provoking antagonistic responses. This too makes remodeling a particularly apt task for fiction.

The *Ramayana* in 1947 and 2003

As already noted, the story of Rama has been particularly important in the rise of Hindu nationalism. As Hansen explains, "Ram was made into a metaphor of the essential Hinduness of Indian culture" (Hansen 1999, 174). Indeed, Hindu nationalism became prominent with the campaign to restore a temple putatively marking the site of Rama's birth. In connection with this, Jan Platvoet points out that Hindu nationalist groups promulgated "The equation of the secular government and the Muslim community with Ravana," characterizing "Muslims as the demonic enemy" (Platvoet 1995, 218). The modeling was general, and not confined to Partition. However, Partition served as a primary case of Muslim demonic evil. Indeed, the time of Partition involved not only murder and displacement of millions of people; it also involved the abduction of women. Of course, women were abducted on both sides. However, the abduction of women by an enemy is usually much more salient than the abduction of women from the enemy. Moreover, in a Hindu context, such abduction was almost certain to recall the story of Ravana – thus rendering the demonic evil of "the Muslims" still more salient. Note that, even if all the abductions had been by Muslims, it would still be the case that the overwhelming majority of Muslims did not abduct anyone; thus blaming the entire community for the abductions would still be wrong. It would still be a matter of distortive ideology. That ideology is clearly fostered by a model that identifies Muslims as raksasas in general and as Ravana in particular.

On the other hand, even in its standard political usage, the *Ramayana* model was more complex than it may at first seem. It operated not only to condemn the abductors (quite rightly, of course), and to condemn Muslims generally (again, wrongly). It also served to exonerate the abducted women, to remove the taint of the abduction by modeling them on Sita. As Urvashi Butalia points out, "A number of pamphlets were published which used the story of Sita's abduction by Ravana, showing how she remained pure despite her time away from her husband" (Butalia 2000, 127).

In many ways, Pritam's 1950 novella follows out this modeling of Partion-related abductions on the abduction of Sita. Pritam's novella forcefully condemns the injustice of repudiating abducted wives and daughters. However, Pritam was also clearly aware of the risks that arise from this model – the degree to which it fosters the dehumanization of Muslims and encourages belligerence. Thus she also engages in remodeling by seeking to alter our cognitive and affective orientation toward the source (the *Ramayana*), the target (Partition), and the relations linking the two. The 2003 film largely follows the novella, and maintains Pritam's positive feminist concerns as well as her ideological critique. However, it does so in a new context, a context where the dangers posed by the Rama model have become an imposing reality through the growing political power of Hindu nationalism. The screenwriter and director, Chandraprakash Dwivedi, makes a number of alterations in the original story both in order to intensify the emotional impact of the film and, more importantly for our purposes, to make the remodeling more salient and more emotionally consequential.[7] These revisions undoubtedly bear on the change in political conditions between the time when the novella was written and the time when the film was made.

In India, understanding and responding to contemporary political events is closely bound up with understanding and responding to Partition. As Kaul puts it, "Though Partition had a very different impact on different parts of" India, "its consequences have in fact defined our nation and our nationalism" (Kaul 2001, 9). Similarly, Jain writes that "the aftermath" of Partition "seems to be an ongoing one and every communal riot, every border skirmish, every war takes us back to it" (Jain 2007, 1). Due to its enhanced relevance to contemporary political developments, the following analysis will concentrate on the film version, making reference to the novella primarily to note contrasts between the two.

Pinjar: story, myth, and history

The word *pinjar* – or *pījar* – may be translated as "skeleton" or "cage" (see McGregor 1993). In her novella, Pritam tends to stress the former meaning. Perhaps in part because it relates more directly to the *Ramayana* story, Dwivedi tends to stress the second meaning. In any case, the image is evocative of Partition in both senses. As "skeleton," it alludes to the hundreds of thousands of deaths that occurred at the time. As "cage," it refers to the people who were now trapped in either India or Pakistan, unable to reach family and home on the other side. It also refers to the imprisonment of women – perhaps 75,000 of them (Butalia 2000, 3) – who were abducted at this time. Again, this was one element of the historical event that particularly fostered the use of the *Ramayana* model.

The film begins with an invocation of Waris Shah, the eighteenth-century Sufi poet and author of a famous work on the lovers Heer and Ranjha. Sufism is important to the general concerns of the film, since Sufism has sometimes been seen as offering a solution to the Hindu/Muslim conflict; for example, Engineer has maintained that "If the national integration is to be achieved, we need to revive the spirit of Sufism" (Engineer 1991, 123). Drawing as it does upon aspects of both Islam and Hinduism, this tradition of spiritual mysticism is associated with tolerance and intercommunal harmony.[8]

Following this opening song, the film takes us to an apparently unprovoked attack on Sikhs by a group of Muslims in 1946. This serves to locate the personal story of Puro, Ramchand, Rashid, and the others more firmly in the historical context leading up to the great historical event of Partition. It may also seem to suggest that violence is initiated by Muslims. Indeed, this is an obvious objection to the film. Due to its central ideological importance, it is worth briefly addressing this issue before continuing.

Although the film does portray Muslim violence more directly than Hindu or Sikh violence, the case is not entirely straightforward. For example, in the key event of the film the Sheikh family kidnaps Puro. But we learn of an earlier abduction from the Sheikh household by Puro's family. On the other hand, despite such qualifications, the film does seem to convey a general sense that Muslims are more proactive. This leads to problems when the action involves violence. But it can also lead to good. Thus Rashid not only kidnaps Puro, he also saves Lajo, showing the same daring in both cases – the same "*himmat*" or courage, as Puro puts it. Hindus and Sikhs are not always clearly differentiated in the film. Some (more clearly Sikhs) tend to be brave, but not proactive. Others (perhaps more often Hindu) appear to be relatively passive, perhaps committed more to a sort of contemplative withdrawal than to social action. These tendencies are valuable in that they are unlikely to provoke or even sustain violence. But they are also unlikely to do active good.

There are obviously problems with any such stereotypical representation of the Muslim, Sikh, and Hindu communities. This is to some degree mitigated by the fact that, within the film, communal differences in part reflect the location of the action. Insofar as the action occurs in a Muslim majority area, one may reasonably expect Muslims to be more self-confident and secure, and thus more prone to act. Thus Puro's family avoids helping her due to fear. But, in a Hindu-dominated area, Rashid is similarly helpless to oppose what is in effect an abduction of his and Puro's/Hamida's adopted child.

Moreover, when considered solely within Hinduism, in the context of a militant Hindu nationalism that elevates Rama as a martial hero, one might argue that there is a salutary aspect to Dwivedi's portrayal here. As we will see, the most extreme case of contemplative withdrawal is Ramchand. In this way, Dwivedi may be seen as subtly revising the *Ramayana* and its rather violent ideals through the character of Ramchand.

In any case, the result of the attack by Muslims – and the defense by Sikhs – is a street littered with corpses of people from different communities. This suggests the rather commonplace idea that violence is destructive to all sides, and thus both pointless and tragic. But, as the film develops, we see that the suggestions are more controversial. Later on, during another riot, Ramchand simply runs away. In the context of martial valor this may seem objectionable, but the result is that Ramchand saves himself and his family. Although unheroic, Ramchand's rational and largely non-violent behavior is no less successful in saving lives than Rashid's rescue of Lajo. The point is all the more important insofar as it reacts back on our understanding of and response to Rama, Ramchand's model.

The next scene brings us to Puro's brother, Trilok. He is a nationalist activist, and is spoken of as a follower of "Bapu," "father," or Gandhi. However, there is no evidence in the film that he is in fact a Gandhian. Over his desk, Dwivedi has placed a very prominent photograph of Lenin. This suggests that his affiliations are more with revolutionary Marxism than with Gandhism. In keeping with this, he is the one proactive non-Muslim character in the film – or, rather, the one proactive non-Muslim character among men. However, his activism is problematic. First, it is almost inhuman in its narrow focus – a focus that leads Trilok to ignore his young wife in favor of his missing sister. More importantly, his activism manages to cause suffering without producing any good. Finally, it is not really brave either. He engages in destruction when no one will be able to oppose him.

As the film makes clear subsequently, Trilok is linked with Hanuman. The relative activism of Hanuman and relative passivity of Rama are properties already present in the *Ramayana*. Specifically, when separated from Sita, Rama to a great extent bemoans his state while Hanuman seeks her out – eventually finding her in Lanka and engaging in a destructive confrontation with the raksasas there. This is, then, a difference taken over from the source. However, in producing these particular fictional characters, Pritam and Dwivedi have greatly reduced the activity and violence of both characters, virtually eliminating it in the case of Rama. Moreover, they have rendered the remaining violence ineffective.[9] Again, this is a point at which remodeling may go in both directions; it specifies the target in certain ways that then may react back upon the source, tacitly reorienting our response to the *Ramayana*, by changing our associations with that work, our ways of thinking about its characters, our implicit imagination of the "facts" underlying what the epic tells us.[10]

Of course, up until this point a first-time viewer of the film is unlikely to have any sense that the *Ramayana* is operating as a model in this story. The first real clue comes when Puro's marriage is being arranged with *Ramchand* – though this is only a small clue, since the name itself is common enough. Perhaps more significantly, when he actually appears, Ramchand is singing a devotional song about Sita's fire ordeal, which served to prove her purity after being abducted. Even first-time viewers are likely to know that the film treats a woman's abduction and are thus likely to link the song with the story at least implicitly. However, at this point, the function of the allusion is not clear. The filmmaker could be accepting the fire ordeal as a legitimate part of the *Ramayana* model. Alternatively, he may be bringing up the topic in order to contrast it with what happens later in the film. In other words, this may be part of straightforward modeling or it may be part of remodeling and tacit revision of the *Ramayana*. Unsurprisingly, perhaps, it ultimately turns out to be the latter, when Ramchand offers to take back Puro without any conditions. Although the fire ordeal is not mentioned at that point, it is clear that this new Rama (Ramchand) is specifically *not* demanding any such proof of purity.

The connections with the *Ramayana* are further reinforced when we learn that Ramchand is translating Valmiki's *Ramayana* into Urdu (a language spoken and read primarily by Muslims). To show that this is not communalist proselytizing, we are told that Ramchand also plans to translate the Muslim poet, Ghalib, into Sanskrit, the sacred language of Hinduism. Later, over his desk, we see two pictures. One is Shakespeare. The other appears to be Rabindranath Tagore. Again, Trilok/Hanuman, the activist, is linked with Lenin. In contrast, Ramchand is a poet, associated with Shakespeare and, perhaps, Tagore. His approach to conflict is not to engage in violence but to share literature. It is difficult to tell just what the attitude of the film is toward this. On the one hand, this tacitly revises the belligerent Rama into the non-violent Ramchand, who is also spoken of as Gandhian (in this case plausibly). On the other hand, it is not obvious that translating anything into an ancient language such as Sanskrit has much practical value – though one may argue that doing any work of Islam into Sanskrit has effects simply by sharing the sacred language with Islam. In any case, up until this point it is not entirely clear just what our attitude should be toward Ramchand. Given this, most viewers probably do not yet have a strong inclination either to revise the ideals of the *Ramayana* in the direction of Ramchand's non-violence, or to evaluate Ramchand harshly by contrast with those ideals.

The balance begins to tip in the following scene. Puro is with some of her friends waiting to glimpse Ramchand as he cycles by. One of the friends calls out to Ramchand, then begins to flirt with him. Ramchand makes a joke about having his brother cut off her nose. She insists that she is not Surpanakha as he cycles off. I take it that its purpose here is two-fold. First, it calls to mind the rather brutal scene from the *Ramayana* in which Surpanakha flirts with Rama, then threatens Sita, before being brutally disfigured by Rama's brother

Laksmana. This is possible in the *Ramayana* in part because Surpanakha is entirely dehumanized by her identification as a raksasi (female demon). Here, the young woman is fully human and entirely sympathetic. It is perfectly fine for Ramchand to joke with her in this way, matching her own boldness, but harming her would clearly be a terrible thing to do. In this way, the ideal of Rama is slightly altered. Second, and perhaps more importantly, reference to this incident recalls to us that Ravana was not simply acting out of evil motives. His sister had been brutalized by Rama and Laksmana. His attack on Sita was driven in part by his own lust. But it was initiated by Rama's and Laksmana's treatment of his sister.

In keeping with the *Ramayana* story, the film now turns to Rashid's abduction of Puro. The abduction of Sita by Ravana is, again, one of the most prominent stories in Hindu tradition. In consequence, Indian viewers are almost certain to connect it, implicitly or explicitly, with any story in which the heroine is kidnapped from her beloved by a villain. Like Ravana with Sita, Rashid does not force himself on Puro sexually. Their sexual relations begin only after they are married. This in part reacts back on the epic model, to some extent humanizing Ravana. At the very least, it makes salient the fact that Ravana did not violate Sita, that he insisted "I will not lay my hands on you so long as you do not want me" (II: 388) and proposed marriage to her (canto 55 of the "*Aranya Kanda*"). In addition, Rashid has two motives in abducting Sita. The initial motive is revenge for crimes committed against his family by Puro's family, including the mistreatment of his father's sister. Puro rightly objects that she should not be punished for those crimes, but they remain crimes nonetheless. For our purposes, there are two important consequences of this. First, this partially reorients our response to the *Ramayana* story by making still more salient the fact that Ravana was avenging his sister's mistreatment. Second, it takes us back to the larger historical event that is examined in the film – Partition. It suggests that seemingly unprovoked violence, particularly that of Muslims (e.g., that presented at the outset of the film), is almost always a response to a sense of prior victimization.

This is not all there is to Rashid's abduction of Puro. He also explains that he fell in love with her when he first saw her. Thus his motives are a mix of vengeance and desire. This is true of Ravana as well, as he was entranced by Sita's beauty. More importantly, this serves to model Partition violence. That violence was a complex mixture of revenge and greed – as indicated more literally by the occupation of houses and the theft of goods from fleeing Hindus and Sikhs later in the film. At one level, this is a fairly commonsensical view of Partition violence, but it is rendered more forceful by its connection with the paradigmatic model of the *Ramayana*. Moreover, it helps to make both motives visible – not denying the greed, while at the same time stressing the larger history of injustice that lies behind violence.

Of course, it remains the case that the violence we actually witness is largely or entirely perpetrated by Muslims, even if we do sometimes hear about violence from Sikhs or Hindus. This is not to say that the film is without criticisms of the other religions. However, these criticisms tend to be different, and, again, stereo-typical in parallel with the stereotypical criticisms of Muslims. For example, Rashid explains to Puro that her parents will never accept her back. Not believing him, she escapes one night and returns home, only to be rejected. Her father explains, "Teri qismat ab hamare pas kuch nahī" – roughly translated, your fate has nothing to do with us now. The reason is two-fold. First, they fear the consequences of accepting her back – physical harm from the Sheikh family and ostracisim from the community. Second, they see her as impure. Her father explains, "*Tera dharm gaya*" – Your dharma [approximately, ethical and religious role in society] is gone. Again, one main purpose of the original novella was to oppose the view that abducted women were polluted. For Dwivedi, however, this was not such a pressing issue and the point appears to involve a broader criticism. That criticism may have to do with notions of impurity, or with the rather shallow way in which dharma is often understood in actual social practice. The point is not developed in the course of the film and is therefore difficult to specify. Nonetheless, there is clearly a criticism of the non-Muslim family's ethical limitations.

Upon learning of Puro's abduction, the families of Puro and Ramchand conclude that Ramchand should marry Puro's sister. (Puro's brother had also been engaged to Ramchand's sister. That relationship is unaffected.) In the novella, this marriage is followed through. However, in the film, Ramchand remains loyal to Puro and refuses the marriage, urging his cousin as a replacement. This is a very nice touch on Dwivedi's part. Standard invocations of the *Ramayana* stress Sita's fidelity to Rama as the ideal of female chastity. The film presents a revised version of gender ideals, stressing Ramchand's/Rama's fidelity to Puro/Sita. That fidelity is there in the canonical versions of the epic. However, it is not commonly taken up ideologically. Ramchand's chastity also has consequences for the emotional force and thematic consequences of the conclusion.

After her marriage to Rashid, Puro (now Hamida) becomes pregnant. She violates the midwife's orders, in effect inducing a miscarriage. In the film, this leaves her childless, a point with significant consequences for the ending. For our purposes, perhaps the most important aspect of this sequence is that Puro's pregnancy gives Rashid a profound sense of his own sinfulness. He engages in repentance specifically by visiting a Sufi shrine. Here, as in so many other works, we see the suggestion that Sufism is an anti-communal devotional practice and religious philosophy. It is presumably no accident that Rashid becomes increasingly admirable after this visit to a Sufi shrine.[11]

Subsequently, Hamida accompanies a relative to a holy man in Rathoval, Ramchand's village. This allows her to have a brief glimpse of Ramchand. This is in effect an instance of "*darshan*" (seeing) in its devotional sense of receiving the spiritual benefit that comes from even a glimpse of the form of a deity. Hamida's *darshan* of Ramchand has this resonance due, of course, to the *Ramayana* model, which links Ramchand with Rama, and thus God. This has at least the possible effect of valorizing Ramchand's character and actions, particularly his fidelity and non-violence. There are two other relevant aspects of this scene.

First, it places Hamida in the active role. Unlike the relatively passive Ramchand, she is the one who seeks out and finds her beloved. This has general consequences for our understanding of the possibilities for women's activity in social and personal life. As such, it is in keeping with some explicit revisions of the *Ramayana* (Thapar 1991, 154; 156) – though *Pinjar* implicitly repudiates the violence of revisions in which Sita is often not merely active, but destructive. It is also in keeping with certain aspects of Sita's portrayal in Valmiki's canonical version, aspects that are largely ignored in the common (patriarchal) ideological understanding of that work – such as her challenging of Rama's violence (Valmiki II: 16–17). Indeed, one could see *Pinjar* as combining the activism of Sita in certain revisions with her non-violence in parts of Valmiki.

At this point we are reminded once again of the *Ramayana* model, so that we do not lose sight of it in what follows. Specifically, Ramchand's sister alludes directly to Rama's exile, asking Ramchand when he will end his "*vanvas*" or forest exile. Ramchand replies that it will end only when "Janaki" is found. "Janaki" is another name for Sita. This recalls for the viewer that Rama was able to end his exile from Ayodhya only after he found Sita and defeated Ravana. However, Ramchand does not say anything about avenging Sita. He mentions only finding her. This has important consequences later on, since Ramchand does not participate in the (otherwise apparently beginningless and endless) cycle of retributive violence that marked the Partition and its aftermath – and arguably extends even to the present day. His statement about the end of his exile already begins to suggest this.

Of course, there remains the problem that Ramchand does not appear to be doing much – or anything – to find Puro/Hamida. Dwivedi is good at showing how virtues and vices tend to be intertwined, sometimes even inseparable from one another. In this case, Ramchand's virtue of non-violence seems to be paired with a vice of passivity. Trilok is more active, in keeping with his *Ramayana* precursor (Hanuman) and his political affiliations (indicated by the picture of Lenin). But, again, his activism seems to be nothing more than unproductive, vengeful violence – if violence that is relatively minor in comparison with that of the rioters seen elsewhere in the film. Specifically, Trilok investigates Puro's disappearance and concludes that Rashid was responsible. Rather than trying to find Rashid and his sister, however, he goes out when no one is around and burns Rashid's crops. This is parallel to Hanuman's burning of Lanka. However, both the novella and the film stress that this destruction harms innocents, including Puro herself. Puro is pleased that her brother remembers her and has done *something* in response to her abduction. Indeed, this sense of support given to victims is generally one benefit of activism – including violent activism – in response to injustice, but it remains clear that the violence does Puro no good. Indeed, it creates potential hardships for her. Here too the point affects both the mythical source and the larger historical target of Partition. It renders Hanuman's devastation of Lanka more ambivalent and it suggests once again the counterproductive character of even retributive violence. Of course, here as elsewhere, the target could not react back on the source if they were entirely incompatible in this regard, but they are far from incompatible. In fact, this understanding of Hanuman's action is available from the original story, even if it is not the usual interpretation. Thus Kuruvachira represents the events in the following way: Hanuman is "a symbol of irrational destruction," having "charged through the city and the surrounding countryside causing untold havoc and burning all the crops with his fiery tail" (Kuruvachira 2006, 98). Kuruvachira does not overstate the case. The scene in Valmiki is brutal. For example, when the fire engulfs houses, "Women carrying babies suckling at the breast, fell screaming. Some, their bodies enveloped in flames … fell from the top floors" (Valmiki 1981, 474). Here again, the connection is not politically inconsequential. As Kuruvachira explains, "Today, Hanuman is the model for the Bajrang Dal activists – the Indian [i.e., Hindu Nationalist] version of the Nazi Stormtroopers" (Kuruvachira 2006, 98). Finally, as already noted, the act is not only pointlessly destructive, it is also cowardly. Trilok does not face his antagonist visibly and directly. Rather, he attacks covertly, when he cannot be seen, opposed, or blamed.

Just as the great war between Rama and Ravana follows Hanuman's burning of Lanka, so too does the Partition violence follow Trilok's burning of Rashid's fields. Once again, the violence here seems to be initiated by Muslims – in part due to the location in a Muslim-majority area. Ramchand's response to the fighting is not that of the militant Rama. Rather, he runs away from the fight. Moreover, he does so with obvious fear. On the other hand, his escape is not presented negatively. In running away, he manages to save himself and his family. Had he tried to fight, he almost certainly would have been killed and his family may have been lost as well.

The exodus of non-Muslims from Rathoval provides an occasion for a third instance of unprovoked Muslim aggression, in this case an attack on the refugees which leads to the abduction of Ramchand's sister.[12] Once again, Hamida is the active agent who finds her way to the relatively passive Ramchand. In this case, Ramchand pitifully tells Hamida of his sister's capture. Hamida shows a commitment to active social engagement, great bravery, and great intelligence in devising a plan to find Ramchand's sister.[13] The sister, Lajo, also shows bravery and intelligence. Neither behaves violently. In effect, these women combine the virtues of the stereotypical Muslim and Hindu man. This has at least two consequences. First, it gives depth to the character of Sita. Second, it serves to differentiate women's roles in Partition from the roles of men (a point suggested at the outset of the film with its dedication to a long list of anti-communal women activists).

There are several aspects of this rescue that are important for the present study. First, Lajo escapes only because Rashid carries her away in an act that is directly parallel to his earlier abduction of Puro (a point made explicitly by Puro). In this way, we see a concrete instance of his active nature leading to a (rough) balancing of evil and good actions. This is part of the pairing and paralleling of virtues and vices that we have seen already. (In contrast, Ramchand, while doing no active harm, is also incapable of doing this sort of active good.)

One of the most significant aspects of Hamida's plan involves giving Rashid a ring that he will use to identify himself to Lajo when he comes to rescue her. This is directly parallel to a well-known scene in the *Ramayana* where Rama gives Hanuman a ring by which he can identify himself to Sita (see Canto 36 of the "*Sundara Kanda*"). This involves a remodeling that shifts the mapping from source to target. In this case, Rashid, and thus a certain group of Muslims, is connected with Hanuman; moreover, Puro is linked with Rama. This works against a tendency to identify Hindus with the side of Rama and Muslims with the side of Ravana. In addition, it confuses gender identifications. It may at first seem odd to identify Puro with Rama, but that is only because we see sex as such a fundamental defining category. Puro takes on the role of directing Rashid/ Hanuman and more generally stands as a model of good action, which is to say, the fulfillment of dharma (despite her father's earlier comment). Thus there is no reason why her sex should make her less appropriately identified with Rama than, say, Ramchand. Indeed, in most crucial ways, she is far more like Rama than Ramchand is. In order to make the link clearer, Lajo refers to her abductor as a raksasa.

Once Lajo is taken by Rashid, she can be returned to India. It is noteworthy that Ramchand takes the lead in this, not Trilok. While Ramchand is active in this recovery, it is not the sort of "muscular" and "masculine" activism that we found in Trilok. Rather, it is the sort of activism we saw in Puro when she managed to meet Ramchandra. In this way, Ramchand's activism is "feminine." I put the word in scare quotes because it is a culturally marked property shared by some men and some women. Thus it is not simply a trait of women (though Pritam and Dwivedi do seem to see it as more common among women than among men). This further nuances the valuing of women in the film, somewhat shifting the film's portrayal away from a sex-based dichotomy in which men are violent and women are victimized, resistant, or complicitous. Rather it indicates that a more proper axis of opposition is between a largely fruitless, "masculine" violence and a productive, "feminine," non-violent action.[14] The idea contrasts perfectly with the current political use of the *Ramayana*. As Bhattacharya points out, Hindu nationalist politicians seek "to forge a combative unity amongst Hindus ... to reconstitute Hindu identity as an aggressive, masculine identity" (Bhattacharya 1991, 131).

The culmination of the film comes in 1948. It is the end of Partition violence, the aftermath of this great historical event. On the one hand, the film represents an actual historical situation, part of this event – the return of abducted women. On the other hand, it idealizes this resolution, presenting a possibility for the future, thus a revision not only of the historical event (Partition), but of the present and the mythical past as well. Specifically, Ramchand and Rashid meet. Ramchand thanks Rashid for saving his sister. Rashid begs forgiveness from Ramchand for abducting his fiancée. In effect, they acknowledge their paired virtues and vices. Rashid is thanked for the active good he has done, good that could never be achieved by Ramchand. At the same time, Rashid pleads for absolution for the active evil he has done, active evil that would be impossible for Ramchand. They embrace in reconciliation. It is an exquisite moment for viewers who have followed not only the story, but the *Ramayana* model. This is Rama and Ravana, Hindus or Sikhs and Muslims, with their arms around each other, reconciled in combined gratitude and forgiveness. This too is an utter transformation of the source, a transformation that presents a hopeful possibility for future intercommunal and international (India/Pakistan) relations – a non-violent alternative to Rama's beheading of Ravana in the original version.

Finally, in the film, Trilok explains that Ramchand would still accept Puro as his wife. This is not possible in the original novella, as Ramchand is married. In the novella, Trilok does say that Puro/Hamida could return home, but it is not really much of a choice because – like so many abducted women in 1948 (see Butalia 2000, 128) – she would have had to abandon her children. The film makes the choice much more real – and the offer itself much more consequential.

First, the offer bears on our understanding of and response to Rama once again. The ideal man is not the epic character who had his wife pass through fire, then abandoned her anyway. Rather, the ideal man is a different version of Rama, one who accepts his fiancée as a wife even though she has lived with another man as her husband, one who does not force tests on her, or exile, or anything else. Indeed, this is a Rama who accepts his wife's autonomy, even when she chooses to be Pakistani. Subsequently, Ramchand says that they should not force Puro to be deprived of her home a second time. The comment is important. In the aftermath of Partition, women were often forced to leave their husbands even when they insisted that they wanted to remain with them. In these cases, putative communal identity took precedence over the actual emotional ties of the people involved (Patel 2006, 114–118; Butalia 2000, 101ff., 117ff.). This once again may affect our view of Rama, as his avatara, Ramchand, values non-violence and respects his wife's autonomy, even with regard to communal identity.

The second main consequence of the ending derives from the fact that Puro chooses Rashid. She has now formed a bond with him that should not be broken and cannot be replaced. The choice is not forced on her by fear of separation from a child. It is a choice of this person – and, in consequence, a choice of the associated religion and nation. Rashid has left the area so that she can make her decision without feeling any pressure from his side. Realizing that he has gone, she searches for him desperately. It is a great relief, for her and for the audience, when she finds him. This has perhaps the most powerful emotional consequences for the film's project of remodeling. It encourages the viewer to feel compassion and even a sort of affection for Rashid, a desire for his well-being and for his continued life with Puro. This potentially revises the viewer's sense of the *Ramayana* story radically, by leading him or her to wish for the union of Sita and Ravana – an outcome that may seem almost unimaginable, but which appears quite natural by the end of *Pinjar*. At the same time, this ending may revise the sense of Partition and of intercommunal relations held by many viewers, at least non-Muslim viewers. Rather than dehumanizing Muslims and

Pakistanis as raksasas, it extends the viewer's sympathies and even affection to them, encouraging him or her to sympathize with the heroine's choice of Pakistan as her nation.

Conclusion

Large historical events present us with unthinkably vast complexes of causes and effects that are deeply emotionally consequential, but also deeply emotionally contradictory. As a result, we draw upon models to simplify those events both cognitively and emotionally. As models become simpler, their comprehensibility increases, but their accuracy decreases. Thus historical comprehension is, in general, inversely correlated with historical veracity. At a certain point, for a given purpose, we may begin to view a model's simplifications as distortive. In other cases, we may consider a particular model or set of mapping relations as false from the outset. Models come in different forms and operate at different levels of generality. Some are broad, prototypical structures. Others are individual stories. Some are religious or mythic. Others are themselves historical.

The 1947 Partition of India was in some ways an extreme case of a historical event in that it was profoundly emotionally conflicted and incomprehensibly chaotic. Thus it has been a prime target for emotional and cognitive simplification through modeling. Given the importance of religion, or rather religious affiliation, in the Partition, it is no surprise that a major religious paradigm – the *Ramayana* – has served as a recurring model for this terrible event. Moreover, given the centrality of religious affiliation in subsequent South Asian history, it is unsurprising that Partition and the *Ramayana* should both figure in understanding the subsequent events of riots and wars as well.

As commonly used, the model of the *Ramayana* tends to distort Partition. The effect of that (simplifying) distortion has commonly been communally divisive, and conducive to senseless violence. One obvious response to this is to reject the model itself. But this is probably futile, given the fact that the *Ramayana* is so important to many Hindus and so central to the way many people in India think about a range of personal and political events. The other options are as follows: (1) change our interpretation of the target (Partition); (2) alter the mapping relations between the model (the *Ramayana*) and the target, and (3) revise our understanding of and emotional response to the model itself (following a long tradition of *Ramayana* revision within Hinduism). *Pinjar* takes up these possibilities. The story focuses on one aspect of Partition, the aspect that relates most closely and most obviously to the *Ramayana* – the abduction of women. It begins equivocally, introducing the model in ways that could be consistent with the distortive ideologies of Hindu nationalism. But it soon begins to complicate our understanding of Partition, of abduction, of the mapping relations between the *Ramayana* and Partition – and even of the characters, situations, and actions depicted in the *Ramayana* itself.

More exactly, though it is somewhat marred by its stereotypical characterization of Hindus and Muslims, the film nonetheless presents a vision of intercommunal relations that is mutually appreciative, even mutually admiring. It also

challenges patriarchal ideologies of male courage and female passivity in relation to such historical events as Partition. Without diminishing the horrors of
Partition violence, it presents an account that may help to shift some viewers'
understanding and emotional response away from dehumanization and belligerence. Again, it develops this alternative vision by implicitly altering the source,
target, and mapping relations in what is almost certainly the most common and
consequential Hindu model of Partition in particular as well as Hindu/Muslim
and India/Pakistan relations in general – the *Ramayana*. Insofar as those alterations endure beyond the end of the film, they have at least some potential to
produce beneficial changes in the understanding of and emotional response to
other historical events as well.

Notes

1 The *Ramayana* is one of the two main Sanskrit epics and has the status of a – or even
   the – central religious text for many Hindus. Although the original is quite long, a
   summary of some major events would run something like this. Rama is the incarna-
   tion of the god Visnu, who takes human form to save the world in times of danger.
   One such danger comes from the raksasa or demon, Ravana, king of Lanka. Rama is
   born as a prince in Ayodhya. However, when he is set to inherit the throne, the machinations of his stepmother result instead in his exile. He goes into the forest with his
   brother Laksmana and his wife Sita, who is the goddess Laksmi, incarnated by being
   born from the earth. Among their various adventures they are accosted by Ravana's
   sister Surpanakha. She propositions Rama and threatens Sita, whereupon Laksmana
   disfigures and mutilates her on Ramas orders (Valmiki II, 39). She returns to Ravana
   and bewails her mistreatment. Ravana is not only angered by the offense to his sister,
   he conceives a great passion for Sita. From vengeance and desire he determines to
   kidnap her, which he succeeds in doing. However, he does not molest her. Sita lives
   forlorn but chaste in Ravana's kingdom. Rama laments the loss, then forms an alliance with the monkeys to find Sita. Ultimately, the monkey god, Hanuman, seeks and
   locates Sita in Lanka, which he partially burns in a sort of rampage. As a sign that he
   comes from Rama, he shows Sita a ring. Hanuman informs Rama of what he has dis-
   covered. Rama then travels to Lanka, ultimately defeating and beheading Ravana.
   Rather than accepting Sita back initially, he has her pass through fire to prove her
   fidelity. Sita makes it through the fire unharmed. Unfortunately, the citizens of
   Rama's kingdom do not witness this. When Rama returns to Ayodhya to become king
   at last, there is dissatisfaction that he has accepted back this erring wife. Compelled
   by public opinion, Rama abandons Sita – now pregnant with Rama's sons – in the
   forest. She is given shelter in a hermitage. Many years later, Rama meets Sita again
   and offers to accept her back if she passes through a second fire ordeal. She refuses
   and instead calls on the earth, her mother, to receive her. A chariot arises from the
   earth and descends again with her. There are different versions and interpretations of
   the story. The summary given above is probably the most mainstream. But it is far
   from unchallenged, as we will see.
2 The story of *Pinjar* is slightly different in the novella and in the film. I will be focusing on the film, with only occasional reference to the novella. The central character is
   Puro, a young woman who has just reached marriageable age at the beginning of the
   story. Her family arranges for her marriage to Ramchand and for the marriage of her
   brother, Trilok, to Ramchands sister, Lajo. However, Puro is kidnapped by Rashid.
   This act is in part revenge against Puro's family for the abduction (and subsequent
   abandonment) of Rashid's aunt. Puro's parents do not do anything to help her, fearing

both scandal and violence from Rashid's family. Indeed, when Puro escapes, she is rejected by her father. Puro's brother takes a few small steps to try to help his sister, but these are vigorously opposed by his father. Rashid does not molest Puro after abducting her, but marries her. They move to another village, where Rashid changes Puro's name to Hamida. Puro becomes pregnant and has a miscarriage, leaving her childless. (In the novella, she and Rashid have a son). In the interim, Trilok marries Ramchand's sister, but Ramchand remains unmarried. (In the novella, Ramchand marries Puro's sister.) At the time of Partition, Puro's and Rashid's village is in Pakistan. Puro helps an abducted Hindu girl to escape. In the course of this, she meets Ramchand, whose sister has been abducted. She and Rashid manage to find Lajo and help her escape from her captors. At the end of the film, Puro, Rashid, Lajo, Ramchand, and Trilok all meet in Lahore. Lajo returns to her family. Trilok explains to Puro that she too can come to India and that, indeed, Ramchand is still willing to marry her. Puro, however, opts to remain with Rashid in Pakistan.

3 Surprisingly, this connection, clearly present in both the novella and the film, has been almost entirely ignored by critics. For some representative discussions of the novel, see J. Singh (2006), More (2006), Varma (2006b), and in particular Matringe (2004). One exception to this is Rao, who for some reason sees the presence of the parallel as confined to the film, and interprets it as, possibly, "a subtle indication of the director's sympathy for the Hindutva cause" (Rao 2004, 117). As the following analysis should make clear, I believe that Rao has entirely misunderstood the film. Rao also overstates the genuine problems with the film in claiming the "total absence of any sympathetic Muslim character other than the anti-hero Rashid" (Rao 2004, 117). First, Puro is Muslim at the end of the film, and she is entirely sympathetic. Second, many of the Muslim women are sympathetic. Third, most of the Hindus and Sikhs are no less problematic than the Muslims, though in a different way (as we will see). In fact, the main axis of moral difference in the film seems to be between men and women, not between Muslims and Hindus – though this too is not absolute. In this context, it is perhaps worth connecting *Pinjar* with Sumar's *Khamosh Pani*, as some other critics have done (see e.g., Joshi 2004). Rao sets up the two films as polar opposites – *Pinjar* as covert Hindutva propaganda versus *Khamosh Pani* as a truly progressive work treating the abduction of women during Partition. *Khamosh Pani* is indeed a fine film that powerfully explores the rise of fundamentalism in Pakistan. However, its treatment of the abduction of women is, I believe, far more problematic than that of *Pinjar*. *Khamosh Pani* takes place 30 years after Partition and the story of the main character is told in brief flashbacks. As it turns out, the woman was a Sikh and, during Partition, her father ordered the women of the family to commit suicide. She refused, ran away, and was given shelter and food by a Muslim man, who eventually married her. This film, then, suggests that Sikhs were cruel child-killers and that Muslim "abductors" were in fact benevolent saviors.

4 The following analysis focuses on emplotment and its ideological consequences. Due to this focus, it will be concerned with story and story-world elements of *Pinjar*. Certainly, stylistic features may be recruited toward thematic purposes, including ideological critique. For a discussion of style and theme in Indian film, see for example, my *Understanding Indian Movies* (Hogan 2008, ch. 5). However, the style of *Pinjar* would be the topic of another essay.

5 The point is bound up with the operation of mirror neurons (Iacoboni 2008).

6 There are specifiable reasons why one identity category becomes important in a given society and another does not. It is not possible to outline these reasons here. For a discussion, see my *Understanding Nationalism* (Hogan 2009, ch. 1).

7 Of course, I am not saying that Dwivedi thought of his project in these terms. However, he does seem to have been self-conscious about the revisions of the *Ramayana* undertaken by the novella and to have enhanced these revisions in the film.

8 On the other hand, it remains a version of Islam. It is not a distinct, third religion. In this way it is not perfectly suited to resolving Hindu/Muslim conflicts.

9 I am leaving aside the very limited moment of self-defense when Ramchand throws a piece of debris at his pursuers, impeding their progress.

10 Even when reading a work of fiction, we automatically reconstruct what we take to be the "real story" from the more fragmentary evidence we are given in the text itself.

11 The use of Sufism may suggest that the film is aiming at revising Muslim models for thinking about personal and political action as well. However, this revision is not developed anywhere near as extensively or with anything like the same degree of narrative particularity as the revision of the *Ramayana*.

12 Another ideologically problematic aspect of the film is its apparent over-representation of Muslim abductions of Hindu women. At the end of the film, Dwivedi does indicate that there are Muslim women being returned to Pakistan. Moreover, since the action of the film takes place in Pakistan, it makes sense that there should be a focus on abductions by Muslims. Nonetheless, it is easy to imagine viewers coming away from the film with the sense that the abductions were perpetrated almost entirely by Muslims. In fact, over 20,000 abducted women were returned from India (Patel 2006), and there were undoubtedly many women abducted in India but never found.

13 As this suggests, I believe Sujala Singh is quite mistaken in asserting that the film presents two options – men protect women and men threaten women. In fact, it seems clear that the film presents women as more likely to engage in action that is just, brave, and rational. In contrast, men tend to be overly passive or unjustly and imprudently active. Thus it is true that men threaten women. But women protect themselves and save one another – perhaps with the help of a man.

14 Indeed, Rashid's later physical bravery in saving Lajo is not marked by the same stereotypically masculine violence as the initial abduction. It is, in this respect, more in keeping with the action of women in the film.

Bibliography

Bhattacharya, Neeladri. "Myth, History and the Politics of Ramjanmabhumi," in *Anatomy of a Confrontation: The Babri Masjid-Ramjanmabhumi Issue*, edited by Gopal Sarvepalli, 122–40. New Delhi: Viking, 1991.

Black, Eric. J. www.pbs.org/wgbh/pages/frontline/shows/oslo/parallel/8.html. June 2002 (accessed November 22, 2007).

Butalia, Urvashi. *The Other Side of Silence: Voices from the Partition of India*. Durham, NC: Duke University Press, 2000.

Clore, Gerald L. and Andrew Ortony. "Cognition in Emotion: Always, Sometimes, or Never?", in *Cognitive Neuroscience of Emotion*, edited by Richard D. Land and Lynn Nadel, 24–61. Oxford: Oxford University Press, 2002.

Dwivedi. *Pinjar*. Directed by Chandra Prakash Dwivedi, 2003.

Engineer, Asgar Ali. "Sufism and Communal Harmony," in *Sufism and Communal Harmony*, edited by Asgar Ali Engineer, 160–171. Jaipur, India: Printwell, 1991.

Gilovich, T. "Seeing the Past in the Present: The Effect of Associations to Familiar Events on Judgments and Decisions." *Journal of Personality and Social Psychology* 40 (1981), 797–808.

Gopal, Sarvepalli. *Anatomy of a Confrontation: The Babri Masjid-Ramjanmabhumi Issue*. New Delhi: Viking, 1991.

Hamilton, David and Tina Trolier. "Stereotypes and Stereotyping: An Overview of the Cognitive Approach," in *Prejudice, Discrimination, and Racism*, edited by John Dovidio and Samuel Gaertner, 127–163. New York: Academic Press, 1986.

Hansen, Thomas Blom. *The Saffron Wave: Democracy and Hindu Nationalism in Modern India*. Princeton, NJ: Princeton University Press, 1999.

Hogan, Patrick C. *Colonialism and Cultural Identity: Crises of Tradition in the Anglophone Literatures of India, Africa, and the Caribbean*. Albany: State University of New York Press, 2000.

——. *The Mind and Its Stories: Narrative Universals and Human Emotion*. Cambridge: Cambridge University Press, 2003.

——. *Understanding Indian Movies: Culture, Cognition, and Cinematic Imagination*. Austin: University of Texas Press, 2008.

——. *Understanding Nationalism: On Narrative, Cognitive Science and Identity*. Columbus: Ohio University Press, 2009.

——. *Affective Narratology: The Emotional Structure of Stories*. Lincoln: University of Nebraska Press, 2011.

Iacoboni, Marco. *Mirroring People: The New Science of How We Connect with Others*. New York: Farra, Straus & Giroux, 2008.

Ito, Tiffany and John Caioppo. "Affect and Attitudes: A Social Neuroscience Approach," in *Handbook of Affect and Social Cognition*, edited by Joseph Forgas, 50–74. Mahwah, NJ: Lawrence Erlbaum, 2001.

Jain, Jasbir. "Introduction: Creativity and Narratability," in *Reading Partition/Living Partition*, edited by Jasbir Jain, 1–9. Jaipur: Rawat Publications, 2007.

Joshi, Pant Kumar. "Pinjar." *South Asian Cinema* 5–6 (2004), 112–113.

Kahnemann, Daniel and Dale T. Miller. "Norm Theory: Comparing Reality to Its Alternatives." *Psychological Review* 93:2 (1986), 136–153.

Kaul, Suvir (ed.). *The Partitions of Memory: The Afterlife of the Division of India*. New Delhi: Permanent Black, 2001.

Kuruvachira, J. *Hindu Nationalists of Modern India: A Critical Study of the Intellectual Genealogy of Hindutva*. Jaipur: Rawat Publications, 2006.

Matringe, Denis. "Nomen omen: partition intime et accomplissement dans Pinjar d'Amrita Pritam (1950)," in *Littérature et representations culturelles en Asie du Sud*, edited by Annie Montaut, 89–111. Paris, Ehess, 2004.

McGregor, R.S. *The Oxford Hindi–English Dictionary*. New Delhi: Oxford University Press, 1993.

More, D.R. "Amrita Pritam's Pinjar (The Skeleton): An Apology for Woman's Emancipation," in *Amrita Pritam: Life as Literature*, edited by Bhagyashree Varma, 102–112. New Delhi: Prestige, 2006.

Patel, Kamla. *Torn from the Roots (Mool Sotan Ukhdelan): A Partition Memoir*, translated by Uma Randeria. New Delhi: Women Unlimited, 2006.

Platvoet, Jan. "Ritual as Confrontation: The Ayodhya Conflict," in *Anatomy of a Confrontation: The Other Side of Silence*, edited by Jan Platvoet and Karel van der Toorn, 187–226. Leiden: E.J. Brill, 1995.

Pritam, Amrita. *The Skeleton and That Man*. New Delhi: Sterling Publishers, 1987.

Rao, Maithili. "Pinjar and Khamosh Pani: The Bitter Harvest of Untold Stories." *South Asian Cinema* 5–6 (2004), 114–122.

Richman, Paula (trans.). *Many Ramayanas: The Diversity of a Narrative Tradition in South Asia*. Berkeley: University of California Press, 1991.

Rothschild, Matthew. "'Israel Isn't David … It's Goliath.' (Interview with Irena Klepfisz.)." *The Progressive* (July 2001), 27–29.

Russell, Ralph. *The Pursuit of Urdu Literature: A Select History*. London: Zed Books, 1992.

Singh, Jagdev. "Amrita Pritam's Magnum Opus: Pinjar (The Skeleton)," in *Amrita Pritam: Life as Literature*, edited by Bhagyashree Varma, 94–101. New Delhi: Prestige, 2006.

Singh, Sujala. "Nationalism's Brandings: Women's Bodies and Narratives of the Partition." *South Asian Review* 18:15 (1994), 54–68.

Sumar, Sabiha and Paromita Vohra. *Khamosh Pani*. Directed by Sabiha Sumar. Produced by Vidhi Films, Unlimited, Arte, and Flying Mook Filmproduktion, 2003.

Thapar, Romila. "A Historical Perspective on the Story of Rama," in *Anatomy of a Confrontation: The Babri Masjid-Ramajanmabhumi Issue*, edited by Sarvepalli Gopal, 141–163. New Delhi: Viking, 1991.

Valmiki. *Srimad Valmiki Ramayana*, translated by N Raghunathan, 3 vols. Madras: Vighnewara Publishing, 1981.

Varma, Bhagyashree. *Amrita Pritam: Life as Literature*. New Delhi: Prestige Publishing, 2006a.

——. "Amrita Pritam's Pinjar (The Skeleton): A Chronicle of Conflicting Loyalties," in *Amrita Pritam: Life as Literature*, edited by Bhagyashree Varma, 113–119. New Delhi: Prestige, 2006b.

White, Hayden. *Metahistory: The Historical Imagination in Nineteenth Century Europe*. Baltimore, MD: Johns Hopkins University Press, 1973.

Zajonc, Robert B. "Feeling and Thinking: Closing the Debate Over the Independence of Affect," in *Feeling and Thinking: The Role of Affect in Social Cognition*, edited by Joseph P. Forgas, 31–58. Cambridge: Cambridge University Press, 2000.

8 Representing Partition

Poetics of emotion in *Pinjar*

Lalita Pandit Hogan

> An airy crowd came rushing where he stood,
> Which fill'd the margin of the fatal flood:
> Husbands and wives, boys and unmarried maids,
> And mighty heroes' more majestic shades.
> And youths, intomb'd before their fathers' eyes,
> And hollow groans, and shrieks, and feeble cries.
> Thick as leaves in autumn strow the woods,
> Or fowls, by winter forc'd, forsake the floods
> And wing their hasty flight to happier lands;
> Such, and so thick, the shiv'ring army stands,
> And press for passage with extended hands.
> Now these, now those, the surly boatman bore:
> The rest he drove to distance from the shore.
> The hero, who beheld with wond'ring eyes
> The tumult mix'd with shrieks, laments, and cries,
> Ask'd of his guide, what the rude concourse meant.
>
> (Virgil 1697)

In Virgil's epic, Aeneas makes a journey to the underworld where he will meet the father he had carried on his back from the burning city of ancient Troy. Accompanied by the Sibyl, Aeneas is confronted by a "an airy crowd" of the dead and wonders about the meaning of this "rude concourse." To him the ghosts seem "thick" as autumn leaves scattering in the woods, or fowls forced by winter to flee. Virgil's anthropomorphism that likens humans to autumn leaves is, at the start of this discussion, intended to draw attention to a global poetics of forced exile, of people becoming unmoored like the autumn leaf and the migratory bird, and the *rude concourse* this displacement creates. The ghosts of Aeneas' dead, who "press for passage with extended hands," are dealt with with indifference by the "surly boatman"; some are borne to the other shore, others driven to a distance from the shore. Aeneas' own destiny, of becoming the founder of a new empire in Italy, is foretold by the spirit of his wife whom he could not save from being engulfed by flames. The lines cited above constitute a micro *chronotope* of historical trauma, not of heroes but of ordinary people that include "boys and unwed maids" as well as "Youths, intomb'd before their fathers' eyes." As a central term in Bakhtin's theory of how meanings are constructed in literature, *chronotope* in Russian simply means time-space, whereby time becomes space detached from historical specificities. Bakhtin reminds us that in an artistic chronotope, spatial and temporal indicators are fused, because "[t]ime, as it were, thickens, takes on flesh, becomes artistically visible; likewise, space [is] charged with and responsive to movement of time, plot and *history*" (Bakhtin 1981, 84–85; emphasis added). This intersection of axes of and fusion of indicators characterizes the artistic chronotope. Taking this further, Bakhtin says that "The chronotope as a formally constitutive category determines to a significant degree the image of man in literature" and that "the image of man is always intrinsically chronotopic." In a note to the English translation of *Dialogic Imagination*, Michael Holquist draws attention to, and differentiates between the Kantian idea of space-time aesthetics and Bakhtin's. While Kant's notion is "transcendental," Bakhtin's artistic chronotope, though anchored to the cognitive process, is grounded in "immediate reality" (Bakhtin 1981, 84–85). Across literary and film texts separated by time, language and cultural tradition, it is a carry-over of the affective nature of immediate reality that is of consequence. In the context of time-space as it is configured in Virgil's descriptions, the equivalent of birds and autumn leaves in the Partition film, *Pinjar*, are not only the dead, but also the undead refugees. Just as a leaf *has to* part from the tree, they have to part from their homes. It has been decreed as if by nature, and they have as little agency as a leaf. These images, though very ordinary, underscore the extraordinary inevitability of historical time that forces certain journeys on certain populations. The following discussion of poetics of emotion in *Pinjar* (with specific focus on palliative appraisal and anaesthetization of emotion) will be approached with Bakhtin's artistic chronotope in mind, his notion that image of man (or woman) in history is *intrinsically chronotopic*.

Palliative appraisal, artistic chronotope and the poetics of emotion in *Pinjar*

The heroine of *Pinjar*, Puro is not an epic hero like Aeneas; her destiny is not to found an empire; but her *will to power* enables her to make a choice in a situation in which most people have no choice. The film begins with many characters believing that the *batwaara* (the partition) of the Punjab can never happen. Such things do not happen. In part characters in this film, like thousands of real people in the Punjab, Kashmir, and other regions did at that time, seek a *palliative appraisal* of impending disaster of a very great magnitude. Evolutionary history has created built-in mechanisms in the brain through which the organism can protect itself from pain that may otherwise inhibit the ability to survive. Unlike *The Aeneid* and *The Ramayana*, the object of special concern in the Hindi film as well as the Punjabi novel by Amrita Pritam, on which the film is based, are not continents, countries, nations, and empires, but a specific geographical region, the Punjab, during its partition in 1947. Most characters in the story world of the film are primarily concerned with survival (of bodies) and that motivates their choices and decisions. As an artifact, the film is organized by anxieties regarding survival of the spirit, about the ability of humans to salvage some residual piety and the sanity of the human heart. It is no wonder, then, that Amrita Pritam also begins with an apostrophe to the lyric poet, Waris Shah, who penned the immortal story of star-crossed lovers, Heer and Ranjha. Pritam assumes that only Waris Shah could tell the story of Partition as it ought to be told. In Virgil's *The Aeneid*, being a heroic epic of 19 BCE, palliation is in general sought through mystification when the ghosts are seen in the midst of a sad underworld journey. Story-telling relies on transcendent emotion and spectacle because the heroic genre typically gives meaning to suffering and trauma by designating tasks for future heroes, as happens in *The Aeneid*. The elegiac lyric, however, exemplified in Virgil's passage cited in John Dryden's translation above, stands apart from the narration of heroic tasks, and bears similarly to the mournfulness of the film, *Pinjar*, where people are depicted in their generic humanity, not group identity. Virgil's "surly boatman" of the other world bears an unmistakable likeness to members of this-worldly border police, who were indifferently taking people from this side to that, in the aftermath of partition violence in the autumn of 1947. Also in Virgil's evocative elegiac lines, individuating distinctions are made among "hollow groans," of the ghosts, their "shrieks" and "feeble cries." In *Pinjar* too such individuating distinctions are cinematically depicted throughout.

Chandrprakash Diwedi's film *Pinjar* (2003), though it alludes to and revises the epic story of *Ramayaṇa*, portrays Partition as a combined human catastrophe, something the imagination can give meaning to only through the act of mourning. The only heroic action proposed by the film is the ability of people in modern democracies to separate categorial identities (that label them on the basis of the abstractions of religion, race and gender) from their practical identities that focus on what their concerns, skills, habits, abilities, vulnerabilities, potentialities, and even faults may be. While the question for a realist is how can one find peace in the midst of horror, the question for a moralist or an ideologue would be who is wrong and who is right or who is evil and who is good? The question the makers of this film have chosen to focus on is: *for whom should we sorrow?* To this, the poetic answer is: *for everyone*. In the two Punjabs language is the same, habits are similar, arts, crafts and cultural practices meld well, colors are similar, people dress in a more or less similar fashion, seasonal festivals and fairs collate in interesting ways, crops are similar, vegetation is the same; animals, birds, cartwheels cannot tell one from the other. Only the rioting crowds, soldiers and the newly formed Border Force are in charge of partitioning people and spaces. Few of the agents causing destruction and managing the crisis are diegetically included in the song sequences, however. In an essentially elegiac form, a great deal of artistic effort in *Pinjar* is invested in anesthetizing fear, hate, anger, disgust, alienation, and associated social emotions, such as condemnation. Amrita Pritam's novel gives graphic descriptions, for instance, of Puro's disgust at sexual violation. She perceives the growing fetus "as an insect in the peapod" or a "slimy slug" (Pritam 1987, 11). In the film, there is only minimal focus on Puro's disgust and it is instantly juxtaposed, through quick cuts, to Rashid's care and concern as husband and prospective father. In his exploration of the "Anaesthetics of Emotion," David Novitz talks about how some works of art, in place of using "rational persuasion" to invite viewers/ readers to change their deeply rooted beliefs and values, do something different. They "anesthetize emotions" by not making an "attempt to give reasons for the views that they tacitly advocate; they persuade ... at a deeper and darker level by exploiting the conventions of the medium in ways that sometimes contrive to play on our vulnerabilities" (Novitz 1997, 248). Novitz argues that rational persuasion directly addresses our vulnerabilities and can make us defensive, while art that uses *anesthetization of emotion* works through a "nonrational and non-threatening form of persuasion: a form of persuasion that entices by touching the right emotional chords, but that never threatens or corrects" (ibid.). Novitz claims that this type of persuasion is more successful in shifting people's beliefs and values. This is because they are not aware of what has caused the shift, and when the shifting was occurring. It should also be kept in mind that anesthetization of emotion only means that while one set of emotions is being anesthetized another set is being elicited, as happens in this film through juxtaposed shots, often close-ups of faces and full body shots that emphasize gait, posture, the way people stand, what they do with their hands and so on. Some of this is very theatrical, and provides graphic, elaborate, detailed access to a huge repertoire of the body language of emotion through which one can more or less accurately read the imprimatur of inner states of mind.

For example, close to the beginning of *Pinjar*, the Amritsar sequence is framed by a voice-over which draws attention to the fact that children have died, though we have seen that many adults have also died. This non-diegetic insert (that is, commentary for the viewer's benefit, not internal to the story) in Gulzar's voice describes the children this way: "children whose innocent hands had not yet begun to write their *aleph* (a) and *bey* (b)," and who will never have the chance to write *pey* (p) *tey* (t) *sey* (s) and so on. One is invited to enter into not categorial identities of these children so much as a situational identification with their teachers and parents. The visual accompanying the non-diegetic insert foregrounds Sikh children with their little turbans, and the alphabet is clearly Persian. The montage in this segment, and other segments, is *intellectual montage,* as it juxtaposes on the basis of story development, orientation in terms of location, affect, perspective, subject position and so on. Because of the inherent juxtaposition (of intellectual montage), the cinematic depiction of Partition violence in this film is not sentimental or melodramatic, but affective in the way space and time are fused to compose poetics of emotion. This opening segment is shot from a high angle, which distances it to anesthetize horror, fear and hurt, or a sense of personal harm through emotional investment in the viewer's ethnic or religious identity. The visual perspective is of the overseeing eye of the camera itself, which will become a motif in the film and will assume an almost sublime, iconic significance in units of montage dealing, later, with Hindu refugees fleeing from Rathoval. For many of these long and medium shots, with very few close-up shots, emotional and moral perspective is established by non-diegetic, elegiac strains of "ek noor se sab jag aaya/sab kudrat ke bande" (from one light all came to be/every creature, a devotee of that light). The light is the light of nature, not of a particular deity. The soundtrack accompanies the kafila like an overseeing eye. The calming music distances fear, sense of harm, hurt, even reactive emotion to injustice and cruelty (of fate and man) by enveloping traumatic history in an incandescence of poetry that combines Sikh, Sufi and Upanishadic concepts of divine light, its unseen stewardship of life on the earth. Needless to say, the stewardship in real time has failed. The cinematic purpose, however, is to offer *palliative appraisal*; that is, a construal of a life situation that facilitates "intra-psychic coping" by "constructing situational meaning structure in such a fashion that the situation is appraised more favorably, less harmfully, and more tolerably than the actual state of affairs warrants or imposes in the first place" (Frijda 2007, 420–421).

As the early voice-over had cautioned, the *batwaara* (partition) of the country has extinguished the hearth fires of the metaphorical *sanjha chulhaa* (common kitchen); it has divided the common courtyard (*aangan*) of the Punjab. Home has become a wilderness. The familial referents (the common kitchen and courtyard of the traditional joint family) used recurrently in dialogue, commentary and song underscore public perception of harmonious relations between communities and outrage at their severance. Here it is important to point out that David Novitz and others who speak of art and emotion do not have in mind a mere folk theory of emotion, but a scientifically researched theory of emotion: the cognitive appraisal theory. Different from theories of emotion that consider only the somatic and affective aspects of emotional experience, appraisal theory views emotion as a communicative and interpretive strategy that gives meaning to affective and somatic experience, and plays, though not an exclusive, yet a significant causal role in eliciting emotion: somatic as well as psychological. To this effect, Richard Shweder claims that:

> emotion terms are names for interpretive strategies – such as "remorse," "guilt," "anger," "shame" – or a particular story-like, script-like, or narrative kind that any people in the world might or might not make use to give meaning to their somatic and affective "feelings."
>
> (Shweder 1994, 32)

According to cognitive appraisal theory of emotion, emotions are always about something; there is always an object, an event and a pattern of reasoning involved. However, events and objects do not in themselves elicit emotions, but our appraisal of events, with regard to their impact on our goals and plans, and relation to objects, elicits emotion. Appraisals are often more complex than what one might think, and sometimes the appraisal process can involve masking, or avoidance emotions. That is, one set of emotions, which may pose a greater threat to life or self-concept, may be avoided by choosing to focus on another set. For instance, attribution emotions are used in all kinds of social interactions to establish culpability or immunity from culpability to real or imagined agents when a subject is trying to avoid debilitating emotion (Ortony *et al.* 1988, 77–88). Among literary genres, this category of emotions plays more of a structural role in revenge drama, heroic epic and modern journalism, and less in elegy, though the Miltonic elegy (such as *The Lycidas*) resorts to it. It is no wonder, therefore, that poetic sub-genres used in *Pinjar* draw more on folk literature, the poetical forms of the *Heer, kirtan,* Sufi *qawali, bhajan* and *ghazal*: various forms of devotional song and romantic lyric.

Using diverse artistic resources, the song lyrics in *Pinjar* define perspective through synchronization of lines of verse with visuals in order to distance the viewer from identification based on the categories of Sikh, Hindu and Muslim and to motivate identification on the basis of what a characters' situation and inner states of mind are. Here, a more precise definition of categorical and practical will clarify the tie to emotion and ethics in relation to *Pinjar* as an artistic chronotope. Drawing on social and cognitive research, Patrick Hogan talks about the significance of categorial identity and practical identity in postcolonial theory and literary criticism. Briefly, categorial identity is a self-concept formed "initially not through introspection," but in relation to social discourses that hierarchize people and lead, inevitably, to some form of essentialization (Hogan 2004, 244). Contrarily, practical identity refers to ordinary "practices, or internalized cognitive structures that underlie action." Both build on situational identification based on a perception of "group or individual sameness based on actional or communicative presuppositions" (Hogan 2004, 251–254). It is important to keep in mind that in *Pinjar*, perception of sameness of Punjab's culture across divisions of religion is important for the elicitation of a mournful compassion. At the same time, an existential focus on the individual (such as Puro, or Rashid) in his or her metaphysical aloneness is important for the constitutive role played by remorse (a form of *dard*) and courage (*himmat*). The courage that is associated with retaliatory action is referred to as *loha* (steel), and/or the *palda* of one group, due to numbers (or something else) outweighing the other. *Himmat* is different from these and is exemplified by Puro's *himmat* all along, and Rashid's in the middle and the end. Rashid's courage that enabled the abduction of Puro in the beginning is referred to as *jurat*; that is, daring. None of these words are mentioned in the poems, because the work of lamentation and mourning does not require any of them.

The following discussion divides the song lyrics into three sections. The "maar udaari, ne kugiye, maar udari" (fly away, O! little bird) and "charkha chalaati Ma" (spinning at the wheel, mother sings) fall into the first category because they serve to thematically superimpose the unnatural and forced migration of populations (due to partition) on conventions of patrilocal marriage. In other words, displaced populations are like girls sent to permanent exile from their natal homes to marital homes. Populations not displaced are like boys who get to inherit the home. Following social rules about change of name, identity, change in affiliation and attachment, the auspicious occasion of the departure of the bride from her father's home (her journey into the unknown) marks a regrettable moment of exile. This chronotope, memorialized in countless Hindi movies as a genre micro-script, as film theorists define them, is used here for sorrow arising from displacement, separation and severance of attachments (Smith 2003, 48–61). It is an important genre micro-script because it is a specific feature of Hindi cinema. While the *batwaara* (partition) of the *sanjha chulha* (common kitchen fire) of the traditional extended family becomes a cognitive metaphor for partition of the Punjab, attention is drawn to patriarchal conventions and their invisible, systemic injustices that the historical trauma has bared to the bone. This too is a *pinjar*, a skeleton in the most hidden closet of the home, and must be examined. The next section will take up a discussion of cross-cutting in narrative and spatial montage matched to the diegetic, devotional song marking the Baisakhi festival (a spring festival): "darda maara maayiya/mere darda mitaa" (no longer able to endure it/I call upon you to remove my pain!), as well as the non-diegetically inserted "ek noor..." hymn mentioned above. This section will conclude with a discussion of the ghazal, "haath chhoote bhee to rishte nahi chhoota karte" (hand may slip from another's hand/does that mean relations have ended"). This song's last line is a fervent prayer that friendship between people of the two communities may not be torn asunder, even if a hand is slipping out of the grasp of another's hand. According to cultural norms that attach more value to concrete social networks and less to national entities, not only is *this* partition seen as unnatural but also division of the earth into nations and states is seen as regrettable. The final section will focus on the "Watana Ve" farewell song, addressed to the Punjab, the region that gets its name from being tended by the waters of five rivers.

Migration, exile and patrilocal marriage: *Maar Udaari* and *Charkha Chalaati Ma*

As mentioned above, *Pinjar is* an adaption by the director, Chandra Prakash Dwivedi, of Armrita Pritam's novella *Pinjar*, translated into English as "The Skeleton." The film follows the basic plotline while altering micro-events, characters and some of the setting. The events covered in the novel stretch from the early 1930s to the fateful events of 1947. The film compresses time to about a year. Briefly, Puro is kidnapped by Rashid in response to pressure from his Muslim family due to an ancient grudge. In the film, however, Rashid is also attracted to her prior to the abduction. In both the novel and the film, the abduction occurs days before Puro's wedding to Ramchand, the son of a prosperous farmer from the neighboring village of Rathoval. After the abduction, Puro is kept in a remote hut at the edge of the village from where her escape is not easy. When she manages to escape and reaches her father's house, they reject her. Like Sita of the epic, Puro is first kidnapped by an "enemy" of her family and then repudiated by her own people. As she adjusts to her new life, her new name, Hamida, tattooed on her arm after a formal *nikah* to Rashid, August 1947 rolls around and the Partition of India occurs. One of the girls abducted by rioters in Rathoval is Lajjo, the sister of Puro's intended bridegroom Ramchand; Lajjo is now married to Puro's brother Trilok. Puro asks Rashid to rescue Lajjo. At the Wagah border Puro's ex-fiancé Ramchand and her brother come to receive both women when the two governments join to restore kidnapped women to their respective homes and countries.

Some of the key changes in the film script clarify the logic of cinematic persuasion through the anesthetization of emotion. In the novel Puro has had a child with Rashid, Javed, and now has her second (adopted) child, and her fiancé Ramchand has married her sister. In the film, Ramchand refuses to marry a substitute bride; Puro has a miscarriage and Hindus of Sakkardali do not return the orphaned child to her. In other words, she is free to return to India and marry her fiancé; yet she *chooses to stay*. In the novel her final words are a bland statement: "My home is now in Pakistan" (Pritam 1987, 49–50). In the film she says to Rashid, "ab tu hi meraa sach hai; yahi mera ghar hai" (now you are my truth; this is my only home). The singular second person pronoun, "tu," signifies familiarity and intimacy. Within the vast repertoire of Partition history chronotopes, Puro's connection to the celebrated story by the Urdu writer, Sadat Hassan Manto's "Toba Tek Singh," is very significant in considering the role that the anesthetization of emotion plays in how people deal with trauma and the limits they will go to in order to defy dispensations. Briefly recounted, Manto's story is a story of exchange, not of women but of mad people in asylums in both countries. The artistic chronotope nature of Manto's story is evident here, because during his *time* in the asylum Bishan Singh, the protagonist as person becomes identified with *space*, his village, Toba Tek Singh. As Partition draws near, Bishan asks everyone whether the village of that name is now in Pakistan or in India, No one among the insane can give him a satisfactory answer; even the sane guards are confused about which village ended up where. Nevertheless, Bishan Singh is now playfully called Toba Tek Singh. At the Wagah border where the insane are gathered and sent to their respective countries, Bishan Singh for the last time wants to be told exactly where Toba Tek Singh is. When he is told, officially, that it is in Pakistan but he has to be transferred to India, he refuses to move. Night passes like that and when sun comes out, "from the throat of the immobile and immovable Bishan Singh [comes] forth a sky piercing shriek." Following Bakhtin's train of thought on the chronotope, one might say for this liminal being time thickens and becomes space because "In between on a bit of land, that had no name, had fallen Toba Tek Singh" (Manto 1999, 196). Puro is not mad like Toba Tek Singh; yet, in their defiance of the logic of Partition, they are similar. Puro chooses her practical home over her technical nation; Bishan Singh chooses his *village*, making *nation* as his domicile irrelevant. Anesthetization of emotion does not help Bishan Singh to cope; his psyche is already broken. Yet, it enables him to make a statement and through him the author makes a statement about the insanity of Partition contrasted with Bishan Singh's clarity of thought, even though, medically speaking, it is he who is mad.

It may seem that Bishan Singh takes his categorial identity more seriously in identifying with his official domicile: Toba Tek Singh. Yet, one has to bear in mind that attachment to land and animals has stayed in his disturbed brain as the more enduring space-time script. In the asylum, Bishan Singh is known for reiterating a single nonsense sentence with many variations by changing its final clause, which is its only comprehensible clause. It begins with "moong kee dal (the soup of the moog lentil) of...." As a staple item in a typical meal, it signifies the everydayness of nurture. At one point Bishan thinks he has solved the Partition riddle as it, sadly, affects him when he says, "moong kee dal of Toba Tek Singh government," expressing a contorted wish that if Toba Tek Singh had a government, no one could displace him (Manto 1999, 192). In the end, the impossibility of Toba Tek Singh having a government of its own penetrates into the tragically fogged mind and his final formula for the last clause is: "moong kee dal of Toba Tek Singh and Pakistan." This is Bishan Singh's declaration that he is a citizen of Pakistan. When his constitutional right is denied, the narrator describes him as an uprooted tree in an earthquake or a statue that has been toppled, as he lies "face down" on the strip of land where there is no village with a name, over which no nation and government has jurisdiction (Manto 1999, 196). At the same Wagah border, exchanges of a different kind take place when usurped women are being retrieved from abductors and sent home. Among these Puro is neither a statue, nor an uprooted tree; she is a sapling who has claimed her roots.

Puro has come a long way from the opening song sung in her honor as bride-to-be. The song serves to embed the story of Partition in two culturally specific patterns of exile and melancholy associated with them. First, the song celebrates a girl's reaching of puberty when she has to be given in marriage so that she can be a wife and a mother. In terms of the Bakhtinian chronotope, this is a "living human being moving through space" as he or she "endures the game that fate plays" (Bakhtin 1981, 105). The second is the cultural practice of patrilocal marriage. Following a consistent compositional principle, the poetic lines are calibrated with montage motivated by an emotion theme. The costume design of flowing clothes of leaf-green and yellow, the colors of a *maina*, or some other colorful bird, long shots showing her floating figure may overdo the comparison; yet the fusion of (anticipated) time (of flight) away from the rooted space (of home) constitutes the chronotope, with the repeated graphic matches of Puro and the cage hanging in the porch with a restless bird inside. In Chattovani, much later, her mother's shriek of instant pain at the news of her daughter's abduction is followed by an artfully framed *mise-en-scène* in the dark blue light of the shadowy evening as a counterpoint to the celebratory early morning song in Amritsar. Against the outline of a solemn tree seen from the balcony the hanging cage with the bird inside is a visual accompaniment to the mother's sense of disaster. This painting-like *mise-en-scène* clarifies what has happened. The impending historical narrative of exile, migration and the displacement of Hindus from Pakistan and Muslims from India has been superimposed on the cultural script of a young bride's departure, her disinheritance and exile. That *bidai* (departure of a bride) is graphically linked to the idea of *batwaara* (partition).

In *Pinjar*, a commonly accepted marriage practice is defamiliarized first when Puro does not get to marry in the conventional way and depart for her new home.

She is taken without proper ceremony, like a bird or a deer caught by a hunter in the woods. When Rashid first spots her in the fields, she is fanning her beautiful red dupatta (with a green border), holding it over her head and shoulders like a canopy. Seen from behind, from the perspective of others who are in the frame, it is spread over her shoulders like the wings of a bird as she holds it tightly and deftly. Rashid falls on his bicycle; the red dupatta is blown away. It collapses like an umbrella and covers his entire face. The movement and stillness in this montage ends with a point-of-view shot of her, a long shot, with Rashid and his bicycle on the ground. The idyllic nature of the shots of frolicking girls in the fields is, then, juxtaposed with the jerky movements of the bicycle. This narrative sequence serves as a preface for the abduction episode where Rashid confidently rides his horse, and lifts her up from the same fields. The contorted movements of Puro's life through time-space dwarf her figure next to the closed iron gate of her parental home when she was able to return to them. A full shot of her father, from a slightly higher angle from where Puro and her mother are, shows him with the *laltain* (kerosene lamp) in his hand, his back slightly bent, looking down upon Puro groveling on the ground. This gestalt emphasizes the categorial rather than practical identity of a father, whose experience of the moment is not guided by introspective access to feelings but rational considerations. Ironically, the sequence of shots of Puro's father, groveling in Rashid's uncle's home, begging for a return of his daughter before the abduction became publicly known, establishes a parallel. In his subjugation he is feminized; in his own home he is a sentry who must keep out the now defiled daughter. Puro beats her head against the tall gate and sits on the ground. For a moment the camera angle is high, as it was for scenes dealing with the dead on the streets of Amritsar earlier. She *is* like those little kids; familial crimes are no less severe than political crimes. A zoom-in highlights streaks of mud and sand on Puro's forehead, an obverse of facial decorations of a bride. A muddy, miserable abjection codifies Puro as dead to her family, the dispensable *pinjar* (skeleton). With staggering steps, Puro walks away from this scene of repudiation. Various long, full-body shots, featuring her fully now, emphasize her determination (for a brief moment it is her determination to die) but eventually to live. The non-diegetic strains of "charkha chalaate ma" (spinning at the wheel mother sings) begins when the mother stands up and pleads with Puro to leave. At this time, the song foreshadows *batwaara* (partition) of the country. Many girls will suffer worse fates, men will die, and the poet will sing of the violation of many Heers of the Punjab and deaths of many Ranjhas. For now, it is only Puro's fate and the calamity of dishonor that has struck her family. Interiors of the house covering this interval are shot in *film noir* dark.

Montage associated with the diegetically inserted "chharkha chalaate ma" (spinning at the wheel mother sings) has earlier acquainted the viewer with the mother's awareness of systemic injustices towards girls. Now, the lines of the song are either recalled by the characters or serve as non-diegetic, interpretive comments on the situation. Once again, the song does not contribute to melodrama because of the high camera angles that dwarf Puro. There are no medium-shot close-ups of her face looking straight into the camera. The song anesthetizes any dramatic emotion one may have in response to such an occurrence by reflecting upon conditions of life that are larger than this one girl. The verse line "jag main janam kyoun letee hai ladki" (why is a girl brought at all into this world) is synchronized with Puro as the mud-streaked castaway; the shot coincides with "beton ko detee hai mahal atariya, beti ko deti pardes re" (mother gives to the sons houses and palaces/to the daughter she apportions banishment). This is Puro's banishment because she is a girl, its inherent injustice brought out by her putative defilement. In ideological terms, the parallel with Bishan Singh of Manto's story is also striking here. Bishan Singh was not allowed to stay in Pakistan, the nation where his village Toba Tek Singh is; Puro is now the liminal woman, similarly slumped outside her father's gate in the vicinity of the well where Rashid is waiting for her in the shadows. He knows family honor will prevent her acceptance by her parents.

In the establishing shot, which introduces the song and anticipates its emotion-eliciting and emotion-masking asthetic, the mother is singing the song as she rocks her much-prized baby boy. This sequence creates deep and wide space in the house, with mother in alternating close-ups and zoom-ins, and father at the upper balcony looking down into the inner courtyard. There is one frontal close-up of mother with the two older sisters as they come to her and she embraces them. At the emotive climax of the song, the sisters stand at different corners of the house like spectators. One line in the earlier *maar udaari* song had likened Puro to a *chingaaree* (an ember) about to fly way. In the "charkha chalaate" sequence, her blurred image, with a light in her hand, composes her in the semblance of a still flame or a blaze (like a portrait painting) that provides perspective for the mother's lamentation. Everyone in the family participates in the cinematic action of the *maar udaari* song in Amritsar; in contrast the *charkha chalaate ma* song is a mournful solo. Looking down from the high angle at his wife and son, but not at the daughters, the father's perspective dominates this cinematic emotion episode. He too is moved to tears. Paternal culpability is graphically matched to his vulnerability, evident in his staggering gait (much like his daughter's) when he had returned chastened and empty-handed from Rashid's home. This sequence uses back lighting. In front of him is darkness; behind him the wide street is lit. He sits down in a deserted street in the middle of the night and bewails the fate of his daughter. The full body shots of the father and daughter are very similar. In his defeat and shame he is feminized; in her defeat and shame she is who she is: a woman.

At the other end, an easy condemnation of Rashid is put aside by foregrounding his attentiveness to Puro as he tries desperately either to feed her, or to rub her feet and forehead with oil. In these shots he is like a mother to a child, not a threat to her. In fact, when Puro's father returns from the Sheikh home and says to his wife, "mar gai teri Puro" (your Puro is now as good as dead), an abrupt cut to Rashid, rubbing herbal oil on Puro's forehead and saying, "Puro, hosh main aa" (Puro, wake up, please) establishes an oppositional parity between Puro's mother, father and Rashid through intellectual montage. From a more culturally oriented perspective, the viewer cannot help but be reminded of the song about Sita's fire ordeal, "Sita ko dekhe sara gaon" (the entire village sat watching Sita), ironically sung by Puro's fiancé, Ramchand as he practices with his sister in their Rathoval home. There will not be an honest fire ordeal for this Sita, as there was not for the legendary Sita. Nor will Puro implore the earth to absorb her back into her limbs, as Janaka's daughter, miraculously sprung from the earth, does. Like the mythical bird, the phoenix will rise from her ashes. Unlike Sylvia Plath's protagonist in "Lady Lazarus," a poem about female anger, Puro will not rise to "eat men like air," but to live with this man who is no longer a destroyer of her life, only a catalyst for change. Perhaps the point is that displaced populations will do the same: commit themselves to their new truth and new home, anesthetizing harmful emotion and renegotiating identity through substitution.

Retrospectively, the dirge in "charkha chalatee ma" was no more than a palliative appraisal of a life event, rite of passage, attachment and its severance, as Puro's mother was preparing for her firstborn's wedding. Yet it became emblematic of displacement and exile due to partition. In contrast to the material substitution of brides in Puro's home, when Puro is married to Rashid, at the time of the *nicah* (Muslim wedding) she seeks imaginary substitutions, hiding behind an anesthetizing reverie of her marriage to Ramchand. This sequence is almost like a film within a film and Puro split in two. When she says yes to her nicah to Rashid, the imaginary Puro is marrying Ramchand. But, of course, the Hindu rites don't require her consent; she will be given by father to husband. Here, Puro answers the question clearly three times in front of witnesses. In the wedding assembly, Aslam, who had been an instigator in her kidnapping, registers surprise, and takes note of Puro's definite and clear "yes." Multiplicity of subject positions to which the *nicah* montage provides access, inscribes into *mise-en-scène* an inner state of mind (of Puro) juxtaposed with external realities. At a different wedding in Chattovani, her brother Trilok uses palliative reverie to superimpose Puro's bridal face on his younger sister's face. The close-ups in Trilok's reverie focus on details of facial decoration and ornaments, and the long shots of Puro walking around the sacred fires of a Vedic ceremony. As reveries play out what might have been, narrative juxtaposition between a Vedic ceremony and a *nicah* ritualizes the two emergent selves of Puro-Hamida: the new woman India's Partition has given birth to.

Poetics of shared pain: *darda maara mayiya, mere dard mita*

In the aftermath of the Partition violence, when Hamida infiltrates Rathoval to rescue her sister-in-law, the Muslim name becomes an enabling talisman as she masquerades as the *khes* (bedsheet) seller. What had been an inscription of categorial identity allows her to carry on practical dealings (buying, selling and haggling over price) with Alladita's mother so that she can complete a mission of rescue. At the same time, while the branding of a new name (and categorial identity) on Puro's arm was done with brusque bluntness, without ceremony, her sisters and sister-in-law in Amritsar, celebrate the Baisakhi fair, having their names tattooed on their arms for fun. At this time, no one knows that Lajjo will also be saved by the tattoo. Puro will be able to identify her and it will make the rescue work easier. Conversely, when the task of tattooing "Hamida" on Puro's forearm has been completed, and her distress has been registered through a long close-up of her face, an abrupt cut to Trilok at the Gurusher Singh District Magistrate's office in Amritsar shows him making a long-distance call to Lahore, asking about his sister: "Sir, her name is Puro." The juxtaposition of the old name spoken into an indifferent phone and the new name inscribed on Puro's arm embodies ironies surrounding personhood. How can the Lahore police find a girl named Puro when she has become Hamida? Space-time configurations, brought together in a chronotopic alignment, delink identity from place of origin and affiliation.

The concern of the two songs to be discussed in this section is not with categorial identity of anyone but the common pain of all. In the Sakkardali house, as Puro's reclining figure disappears from the frame, Rashid's face in medium shot bending over her fills the screen. This domestic space, linked through a voice bridge to the public square in Sakkardali, where the musicians are and from where the song emerges, foregrounds Rashid's anxiety, while Puro's face shows lingering anger and distance. Synchronization of sound and image, and the fast cross-cutting from Rashid's house and the bed where she is, to a place where the singers are seated makes it seem as if the pain, for a moment, emanates from a gestalt of Rashid's experiential self. He is the first grammatical referent for the "I" and "my" used in the first line. The arrangement of temporal and special relations in this sequence ties this not-yet-home to the public square. In addition, through the cross-cutting of shots this segment knits the Sakkardali Baisakhi festival and song, which is filled with anxiety and foreboding, to the Amritsar sequence which is light-hearted, inviting the celebrants to dance the *gidda* (the girls' dance) and *bhangra* (the boys' dance) under the shadow of a peepal tree. The melancholy and despair on Puro's brother Trilok's face is at odds with the environment and connects him to the foreboding at Sakkardali. The opening line, "darda maara mayiya, mere dard mita," as has been pointed out, is matched to the long-extended close-up of Rashid's face; the parallel in facial expressions of dejected brother and anxious husband, in their affective juxtaposition, composes another intellectual montage. The haunting figure of the madwoman is part of this montage. The second line of the opening couplet that refers to "kismet andhi, baavari" (a fate that is blind and insane) follows the moving figure of the madwoman of Sakkardali until she sits in a corner near the pond. For a moment she defines visual perspective and subject position. The implication is not that she is fate, but that she is what indifferent fate can do to a person, and the appeal, "mere haal bana" (change my life or the condition of my life), applies to her. Baisakhi is a seasonal festival marking a definite change in the weather. The reference to this change, however, when matched to narrative development, is ambivalent. The stanza "mausam badla choli/rang basanti aaye/main bhee pelee ho gai/aisaa rang uthaa" (the season has changed its clothing/blouse/into a greenish yellow/I too became yellow/so well did the color rise (this year) is timed to the sequence of shots capturing the account of Puro's miscarriage even as Rashid is praying for her and his child's safety. A long shot captures Puro lifting a heavy basket, cuts to when she drops it, with close-up shots of her face, her figure leaning by the wall as the stream or blood around her foot mingles with the rich, yellow grains of wheat, shown in a close-up so sharp that one can count them. The line "main bhee peeli pad gai" (I too became yellow) is synchronized with the action of her lying down on the cot.

The color words, *basanti* (yellow-green) and *peelee* (in plural case and also marking adjectival feminine gender), at once refer to the earth and to Puro. Basanti as a color term is related morphologically to the word for spring season, *basant*. In contrast, the word *peelaa* or *peelee*, though it means yellow, as *peelee sarson* (yellow mustard blooms), can also refer to jaundice. *Peeliya* is a commonly used word for this condition owing to the yellowing of the skin as a result of jaundice. As we know, jaundice can also cause stillbirth and miscarriage. Paleness of the face due to the sudden loss of a huge quantity of blood is implied as well. Idiomatically, the expression, "peelee pad gai" also refers to instantaneous physical fear. The final line, though not without ambiguity, changes to something, at least provisionally, upbeat: "aisaa rang chadaa!" (so well did the color rise, or take!). The immediate atmospheric reference is to the yellow blooms (e.g., mustard) and wild flowers, erotic passion and female fertility, as well as the dyeing of garments for festive occasions, such as this festival, *baisakhi*. Like Hamida, the madwoman, who is part of this montage, is also pregnant. Unlike Rashid's wife, the madwoman will later deliver the child safely, though she will herself die in the process. Suggestions of death and new growth cannot be missed in this symbiotic connection between the pagli (madwoman) and Puro-Hamida, as well as the pathetic fallacy of atmospheric gloom at the joyous coming of spring.

Following this semantics and asthetics of mourning, subsequent lines wonder what grief has seeped into the verdant foliage this season ("kaisa sog laga hai/ abke hariyaali main?"). "Kaisa rang chada", and "kaisa sog laga" (how the color has risen, and what grief has seeped in) work together as point and counterpoint. This line is synchronized with a montage of the extreme physical pain of Puro as she is attended by a group of women. Thus, the semantic and visual signs compose an emotion episode of shared pain that, in being shared, has become infused with love and not hate. In the same stanza mention is made of an empty swing tied to the branch of a mango tree, evoking memories of people who have already left (for India), leaving behind absences. The singular noun and verb imply absence of one particular person noted by another person, suggesting the disruption of attachment bonds between particular people. The final anthropomorphic image of the walkway (*pagdandee*) that forks in a certain direction and disappears, calling out "my" name (*mud jai pagdandee/meraa naam bulaaye!*) has further resonance. It refers to memory, the sorrow of parting and separation. Just as the chorus in Greek tragedy sings out the pain that a character may feel but not express, this song is a summative comment on all that Puro must have felt for months as she went about her new home, doing daily chores, being friendly with Rashid's relatives. Her husband, though worried about her, cannot have access to this inner world of irrecoverable loss; no one can. The personal pronoun at once particularizes and universalizes the sorrow of partition, of the absences left by it. It invokes not statistics, not numbers, not data, not police reports made or and unmade (in Chattovani, Puro's father had to bribe the police to withdraw the report which Puro's brother had filed), but memory schemas of particular people in Sakkardali, Amritsar, Chattovani, Rathoval, Lahore, Toba Tek Singh, for that matter, and a thousand other places throughout India and Pakistan. The reason this sorrow is at once particular and universal is that it focuses on practical identities of people, their commerce with each other as human beings living together through the cycle of seasons, poverty and wealth, drought and rain, plenty and scarcity, childbirth, its joys, sorrows and travails.

The story-world implication of this montage, though nostalgic, is that some-thing of a bridge between Rashid and Puro has been created. When he enters her room she is like the sickly yellow of the song, while the song itself resonates with Virgil's image of autumn leaves that began this discussion. The loss of her child will later be substituted by the madwoman's orphaned baby, binding the pagli to Puro in joint motherhood. In the novel there are other girls, the Hindu girl Kammo and the Muslim girl Taro, in whose sorrow and pain Puro takes interest. In the film Puro relies wholly on her husband and the focus is on this emergent family unit, produced by the atrocities of Partition. When Puro finds the madwoman dead and her baby perhaps alive, she does not rush to another woman but to Rashid, who does what a midwife would do and cuts the umbilical chord. In a gentle and respectful gesture he closes the eyes of the corpse.

All these activities foreground practical identities, actions, behaviors of people, and depict life events that are common to all. Quite consistently, anes-thetization of emotion and palliative appraisal avoid elicitation of outrage, horror, terror, fear and disgust, by foregrounding how the dignity and integrity of life is preserved in horrible circumstances. At the shrine, very large flower canopies, mostly white flowers with specks of rose, are offered and they become associated with collective dardaa: everyone's pain. In addition, images, shapes, colors, words, rhythms, the rise and fall of tone, along with expressive gestures of the choric singers diminish differences and hierarchies, using angles of framing, *mise-en-scène*, montage, to offset ethnic and religious divides (even gender-based separations) and foreground introspective experiences of grief. Ordinarily, the madwoman is seen pursued by street urchins who mock and deride her as she repels them with curses, or she is followed by women who urge her to put some clothes on. In this sequence she is properly clothed, not pursued by cruel children, seated where she can safely listen, be a part of the festival to the extent that she can. Prior to this, the very first shot of Puro in Sakkardali shows her offering food to the madwoman. When Puro offers food, she is not standing and looking down at the beggar as might be more typical of a middle-class housewife. Instead, Puro puts away her broom, goes inside, brings out food, sits next to the madwoman, very close to her, looking into her eyes, offer-ing several dishes neatly arranged on a platter. It is a guest-and-host relationship, not housewife-to-beggar relationship. The madwoman's surprise and delight is apparent. Her deprivation and deficit is of a radically different kind than that of Hamida. Nevertheless, there is a common bond of pain and shame, of not only the abduction, but of rejection by Puro's family.

Mourning for love lost: *haath chhoote na*

In terms of poetic genre, the *dardaa mariya* song is a prayer following at least partially the style of a kirtan (hymns sung in Gurudwaras, places of worship for Sikhs) mixed with elements of a Sufi kawali and a choric song. It is clearly diegetic, while the ghazal, *haath chhoote*, is non-diegetc. It organizes Puro's long reverie, or daydream, as she journeys to Rathoval from Sakkardali with Rashid's old aunt. In Amrita Pritam's novel, the coachman and the *aapa* (the aunty) remark on how Hamida slept the whole way and that even the *baraat* on the road (a wedding party) did not wake her. In the film she does not fall asleep but is in a sort of trance imagining what her wedding to Ramchand would have been like. Puro's marriage party would have traveled the same road. The different moments and stages of her aborted wedding are systematically synchronized with couplets of the ghazal: "haath chhoote bhee to rishte nahi choota karate/vakt kee shaakh se lamhe nahi choota karate" (hand may slip from another's hand/does that mean the bond is dissolved/moments do not fall down (like autumn leaves) from the tree of time). The mindfulness of the journey on a country road, with her black burka in place, face uncovered, allows Puro to take recourse to substitution on a grand scale. The refrain *haath chhoote* is, as one has come to expect, timed exactly to her outstretched hand at the point where Puro, as a bride, would extend her hand to hold Ramchand's hand. The gap between reality and dream is made clear. On the road, there is nothing but empty space to meet Puro's outstretched hand. The intoxicating effect of a daydream anesthetizes Puro's sense of loss and lack. Moreover, *haath chhootana*, hand slipping out of another's hand, is a conceptual metaphor in Hindi-speaking areas that suggests loss of friendship and kinship support due to circumstances.

The daydream continues through their arrival at the shrine, as they get down from the *tonga* (a horse-drawn carriage) and intersects through cross-cutting with what is "real" in story time. When they wash their faces, in Puro's imagination, she is washing her face before the haldi ceremony (when a turmeric mask is used to beautify the bride's face). Vivid details of clothes, cosmetics, jewelry, hairdo, things that would delight any 15-year-old, and things she would have bought for herself with great enthusiasm in Amritsar, are included. It is apparent that the solitude of the journey to Rathoval has put life back into an abandoned life plan as if water has been poured to revive a withering bouquet of flowers. The culmination in a close encounter between bride and groom has Ramchand walking over a row of peacock feathers. In accompaniment to this fanciful montage, the poem speaks of the beloved having come and gone, without leaving the marks of his footsteps on the ground, so that the seeker cannot trace those footsteps. Intoxicating and pleasurable as it may be, Puro's reverie is no more than a bouquet of flowers; it is not shrubbery and plants rooted in the ground anywhere. While they are in Rathoval, Puro does, however, look in Ramchand's fields and finds him one day. The real encounter, as one may imagine, is not like the one induced by a day-dream. She does not reveal who she is and returns home, though he suspects that this was Puro. In broad asthetic terms, the song is not only about Puro's lingering love for her fiancé, but a dirge for not only love between man and woman, but all kinds of love and friendship – the bonds that are torn asunder when populations are displaced. Since it is a ghazal, the logical structure is tight, with the central poetic thesis contained in the second line: "moments do not fall (like autumn leaves) from the tree of time." Insofar as they belong to internal consciousness of time, moments are emotion memories. One does not remember all the moments of one's life, only those that have emotive significance. These will often be lived moments that through rumination attain an episodic structure, an iconicity that leads to the formation of emotion scripts. The celebrated line from a Sanskrit play, Bhavabhuti's *Uttararamcaritam*, "*çiram, dhyātva, dhyātva*" (moments that become iconic due to reiterative recall) links emotion memory to rumination. Cognitive theorists think of emotion scripts in the same way. In our consciousness, emotion scripts link the past with the present through elaborative encoding in which senses and lived life play a significant role. Forced displacement, migration and exile destroy habitats of lived life, memory and identity. In this case, however, Puro's reverie has nothing of memory in it. It is only fantasy. She and Ramachand never had a chance to make memories, while memories are being formed daily in her unglamorous, colorless home in Sakkardali. It is important to keep in mind that the mad-woman's death and motherhood take place subsequent to Puro's journey to Rathoval, and this journey occurs soon after her miscarriage. The *dardaa mariya* song and the *haath chhoote* ghazal follow each other as they thematize not only broken bonds but the forming of new bonds.

In Sakkardali when the Hindu council is intent on appropriating the mad-woman's baby, Puro says: "I made *panjiri* to distribute among the Muslims of the village so that the child would not have to live with a hurtful memory that no one celebrated his birth. Where were the Hindus of the village then?" From Puro's subject position, the child belongs to the woman who celebrated his birth and warded off shadows of death, not to those for whom his mother was a *pinjar*, a skeleton, an unsightly shadow. Up until this point Puro may have continued to think that, for Rashid, she was no more than a *pinjar* (skeleton) covered with an attractive padding of flesh; she can no longer think that. The word *pinjar* accu-mulates different meanings as the narrative progresses. Literally, *pinjar* means a cage and *asthi pinjar* is a skeleton. The ubiquitous cage with one bird in it is seen prominently in Puro's natal homes in both places, Amritsar and Chattovani. It becomes part of *mise-en-scène* recurrently in reference not only to the absent Puro who has flown away but to all human bodies, *pinjars*, living, dead and exiled, the demographic baggage of the Partition which must be transported, exchanged, accounted for in one way or another. What Rashid has provided for Hamida is not a cage but a nest. As the dreaded event of Partition draws near,

Rashid and Hamida's little nest represents some degree of sanity in the middle of insanity. Although its violent foundation was causally linked to the categorial identities of Hamida and Rashid, it evolves into a kind of *habitat for humanity*. The domestic chemistry is benign, unthreatening, based on cooperation. Rashid does not react in any way to Hamida's accusation that she has borne the burden of his sin. His pain does not turn into anger; it merges with the lament offered as a prayer. Hamida's reaction to the bad news that her brother may have set fire to her husband's harvest is honest and finely calibrated to the newly emergent nuances of their relationship. She registers shock and distress combined with some elation at the fact that her brother is thinking of her, as well as anxiety that, if found out, the brother will be punished. The family elder in Chattovani accepts this affair ultimately as Rashid's "family affair" (*uske ghar ka maamlaa*). His stern warning that no one from their family will have anything to do with the growing dissension between Hindus and Muslims once again shows the disavowal of categorial identity by the same family elder who had used it to exact revenge. Now that a Hindu girl is his nephew's wife, he has entered into the structure of kinship with Puro's brother and understands his rage. When Aslam challenges Rashid to react to the retaliatory offense of his crops being burnt down, Rashid says: "if your sister had been abducted, what would you have done?" At home in Sakkardali, he says to Puro: "One minute you are feeling sorry for the one whose harvest has been destroyed, the next minute you worry about the one who may have done this deed." For himself, he says that this is his punishment and, as such, brings him relief. He assures the joint family at Chattovani that he will relinquish his share of the next two harvests to make up for the loss. That is, he will be responsible for his brother-in-law's action. Establishing equivalences in contractual, moral and emotional accountability, this emergent family is all about human bondage based on the sharing of pain and obligation. If only India and Pakistan, as countries, had done the same post-Partition!

Mourning for the country: *watana ve!*

Palliative appraisal is never more needed than when the dreaded Partition actually occurs and chaos reigns in villages and towns. An extreme long shot of the full profile of an exaggeratedly huge man aiming his sword at a very fragile, young girl, pale and trembling in fear, followed by a cut to blood flowing down as if it is the blood of a sacrificial animal, stands out as summative commentary on what is happening. The girl is a very tiny thing, malnourished, almost a skeleton, like an autumn leaf trembling in the wind, while the man is like the force of nature, an anthropomorphic image of history lapsed briefly into savagery on both sides of the border. The Ratthoval refugees camp in Sakkardali. Ramchand and his mother are among them; his sister has been kidnapped and his father has disappeared (most likely killed). In representing this history, again, camera angles distance the viewer enough to anesthetize debilitating emotion, and the elegiac musical motif "ek noor se" (from one light), as mentioned above, inserts a metaphysical distance from history through the invocation of a transcendent unity of man with nature through divine grace that pervades the universe. The farewell dirge in the story world is sung by Ramchand as he relieves the night watch. Interestingly, this happens immediately after Ramchand's second encounter with Puro who has come under the pretext of selling food to refugees. Once again, practical identities of people are foregrounded in this economic exchange between Sakkardali villagers and the Rathoval refugees. Even though the exact terms of this commerce are not fair, with the villagers accepting only gold ornaments in exchange for food because money will change soon and will be of no use; still it is commerce that posits people as buyers and sellers, not as Hindus and Muslims. Hamida comes to the camp to deliver a girl who she found hiding in the sugar cane fields, another *pinjar*, subjected to rape but able to run away from her captors. In *mise-en-scène* reminiscent of Nargis offering Raj Kapoor water in *Jagate Raho*, Hamida offers water to Ramchand. This shot establishes her ascendancy and advantage over him and the Rathoval refugees. She is standing, looking down at him. When Ramchand looks up he recognizes her, having seen her in Rathoval. It is clear that Puro has lifted up Ramchand's spirits simply by her being immune to Partition violence. She promises to find his sister. His farewell apostrophe is to the land that has been left behind, not to the woman who has been left behind, not even to anything like the "airy crowd" seen by Aeneas in the underworld.

In the midst of loss the mournful *Watanaa Ve, Meriyaa Watana Ve* (Oh country, my beloved country) strain sung amidst somber shadows of the night in the camp, with camera angles alternating between high, almost aerial-like shots, as if the perspective is of the sky above and Ramchand below, on the earth, to low-angle shots where the perspective is of someone who can look at him at eye level on the camp ground, anesthetizes fear, anger and despair. The sequence is composed through alternating distance shots and close-ups. Perspective is established visually, of the people who pass by at the edge of the camp, guards and others, and aurally, through those who do not see the singer but can listen to the song, be comforted by it, wherever they are and whoever they are. The camera pans all across the camp, showing people huddled in heaps at different places, on tops of trucks, wherever there is space. In Amrita Pritam's novel the narrator comments on how deeply the refugees were able to sleep, even though grave dangers lurked. In the film there is an emphasis on a meditative mindfulness. The dominant element in the song that offers palliative appraisal is that country, the *watan*, is imagined not as mother, or father, but as a child. Country is neither fatherland nor motherland, but the fertile earth of the Punjab. The poet and singer wonders who, addressing his fields in Rathoval as "you," "will ask if you need water; if you are parched or just dry/When is the best time to water your crops." He wonders: "When we are not here, who will turn your wilderness into a habitation" (*ham na rahe to kaun basay'egaa teraa veeranaa*). The transfer of subject position is from the refugee to the country he is forced to leave, an avoidant emotion to distract from the shame of disinheritance. The idea that love survives separation is the underlying idea here, as it is in the *haath chhoote* song.

The legendary, star-crossed lovers, Heer and Ranjha are mentioned once again in the lament: "your Heers have been violated and your Ranjhas killed."

The viewer is reminded of an earlier, happier episode in Ramchand's life, when he bicycled through Chattovani (perhaps to catch a glimpse of his intended), and one of her friends jokingly called out to him: "Are O, Raanjhe, tu Ratthoval ka Ramchand hai na?" (Hey, you Raanje, you would not happen to be Ramchand of Ratthoval?). The folklore identity of Ranjha postulates that a man is prototypically a lover who has to part from his beloved. He is not a warrior who will fight for his beloved. Addressing the beloved earth, the poet says: "Mud ke ham na dekhenge/tu bhi yaad na aana" (we will not turn to look back/ you too should not visit our memories). Shifting to the theme of friendship, he continues, "we have divided up our play things and ended this game." Like the *sanjha chulha*, the joint family's kitchen that was divided, the playthings have now been divided. An antidote to the lamented end of friendship will be suggested later when Rashid and Ramchand embrace at the Wagah border, each feeling indebted to the other. At the beginning Rashid stole Ramchand's fiancé; at the end he restored his sister to Ramchand. The debt of gratitude and the gift of forgiveness will maintain a tie of friendship, of *yaari*. A heroic epic too seeks palliation for pain and shame, but does so through either revengeful or reconstructive heroic action; what is lost has to be regained. As an elegiac chronotope, *Pinjar* uses cinematic technique to outline an ethos of situational parities and identifications, capitalizing on stylistic features that depict human subjects in existential moments of coping when they seek palliatives for their physical, emotional and moral suffering. At the level of interpretation, it adds up to a philosophical conviction that the lives of communities and regions (nations are composed of communities and regions) should be grounded more in practical identities of people, and minimally in their categorial identities. Amrita Pritam's Puro asks a rhetorical question about outbreaks of brutality and savagery: "Could the earth soaked in blood produce golden corn? Could maize remain fragrant if its roots were fed with stinking corpses? Would women, whose sisters had been dishonored, bear sons for the despoilers?" (Pritam 2001, 35).

It is exactly this kind of residual anger, outrage and disgust that the film, *Pinjar*, wishes to exorcise through the cinematic meditation of historical trauma. The film argues for disinvestment in all types of categorial identity and greater investment in practical identity. Working through anesthetization of emotion and not exploitation of emotion, the film succeeds in touching the "right emotional codes" and uses a form of persuasion that does not threaten or correct, but that shifts perspective (Novitz 1997, 248). Rashid's culpability, as an individual person, plays a key role in this process. It engages him in ways that can be ideologically and morally reconstructive. From his rubbing oil on Puro's feet to rescuing his wife's sister-in-law, to paying respect to a dying Hindu outcast, to not taking offense when his fields are burnt down, his redemption is not even needed. He has an introspective self-concept that can change, and that can work out some sort of a humanitarian miracle in the midst of a humanitarian catastrophe of gigantic proportions. Not a hero-savior but a simple peasant, he is able to accomplish this feat simply, gradually, by *minimizing* pain and *maximizing* healing. Hamida's question in Pritam's novel is purely rhetorical. The earth does not care, but men and women should. The earth soaked in blood continues to produce golden corn and beautiful rice. Maize can allow its roots to be richly fertilized by stinking corpses. But a woman's son is her son, as Amrita Pritam herself shows in Hamida's growing love for her son Javed. From her initial hate love is born, and she is said to have "settled in as if she had always belonged to the village" (20). The two neighboring nations in South Asia have much in common. Can they not share a legacy of pain instead of competing over whose pain is greater and who is more to blame; can they not repair the damaged fabric of their *yaari*, their residual friendship? This is the question at the heart of this film.

Bibiography

Bakhtin, M.M. *The Dialogic Imagination: Four Essays*, translated by Caryl Emerson and Michael Holquist. Austin, TX: University of Texas Press, 1981.

Dwivedi. *Pinjar*. Directed by Chandra Prakash Dwivedi, 2003.

Frijda, Nico. *Emotion*. New York: Cambridge Univeristy Press, 1986.

——. *The Laws of Emotion*. London: Laurence Earlbaum, 2007.

Hogan, Patrick C. *Empire and the Poetic Voice*. Albany: State University of New York Press, 2004.

——. *Understanding Nationalism: On Narrative, Cognitive Science and Identity*. Columbus: Ohio University Press, 2009.

Manto, Sadat Hassan. "Toba Tek Singh," in *Intermediate Hindi Reader*, edited by Usha R. Jain and Karine Schomer. Berkeley: University of California Press, 1999.

Mitra and Maitra. *Jagte Raho*. Directed by Sombhu Mitra and Amit Maitra, 1956.

Novitz, David. "Anaesthetics of Emotion," in *Emotion and the Arts*, edited by Metter Hjort and Sue Laver. New York: Oxford University Press, 1997.

Ortony, Andrew, Clore, Gerald and Allan Collins. *The Cognitive Structure of Emotions*. New York: Cambridge University Press, 1988.

Pritam, Amrita. *Shadows of Words (Akshron ke Saaye)*, edited by Jyoti Sabharwal. New Delhi: Macmillan, 2001.

——. *The Skeleton; and That Man*. New Delhi: Sterling Publishers, 1987.

Roy, Bimal (dir.). *Bandini*. 1963.

Shweder, Richard. "'You're not Sick, You're just in Love.' Emotion as Interpretive Strategy," in *The Nature of Emotion: Fundamental Questions*, edited by Paul Ekman and Richard J. Davidson. New York: Oxford University Press, 1994.

Smith, Greg M. *Film Structure and the Emotion System*. London: Cambridge University Press, 2003.

Varma, Bhagyashree. *Amrita Pritam: Life as Literature*. New Delhi: Prestige Publishing, 2006.

Virgil. *The Aeneid*, translated by Robert Fagles. New York: Penguin, 2006.

——. *The Aeneid*, translated by John Dryden, Vol. 13. Boston, MA: Harvard Classics, 1697.

9 Return and retake

Stardom meets post-Partition trauma in Bengali cinema

Rini Bhattacharya Mehta

Postcolonial Bengali cinema corresponded for three decades with significant historical traumas, including one major famine and two separate geopolitical partitions. The impacts on the broader middle class – the Bengali class most directly connected with the mainstream production of literature, art, and cinema – of the Bengal Famine, the Partition of India, and the Bangladesh War have only recently begun to be studied. In the realm of cinema, a large part of the impact roughly concurred with the two most important and overlapping moments in the social history of Indian cinema(s) in the 1940s and 1950s: the decline and demise of the studio system and the rise of star-centered production. Within the study of Indian cinema, there is clear consensus on the systemic shift into star-centric production and its impact on the genres and content of films on the one hand and the modalities of "stardom" itself in the Indian economic context of restricted growth and movement of capital on the other, though the majority of the studies have been based on Hindi cinema produced in Bombay. The deeper implications of the impact of the star-centric production on Bengali cinema, especially on its relationship with the print narrative sources, have not been adequately examined to date. This chapter on cinematic representations of Partition in Bengali star-centric melodrama thus trains its focus on the intersection of two critical questions that have arrived belatedly in the wider field of Indian cinema studies: the modalities of Bengali star-centrism's interactions with social history and the sublimation of significant historical traumas in romantic films, via popular literature. The nexus between Bengali cinema and its narrative sources – frequently referred to in this chapter – is something of a regional characteristic. While all Indian cinemas have to varying degrees derived their narrative impetus from popular and literary texts, both Bengali filmmakers and viewers have arguably placed more emphasis on textuality. What many scholars and filmmakers had rightly pointed out remains true to this day: the fact that Bengalis frequently call a movie *boi* (book) highlights the Bengali's vested interest in the narrative source of the film. It would perhaps be possible in a much more detailed study to see the relationship between the print and the cinematic narratives evolve and transform.

The textuality of Bengali cinema has direct relevance to the main body of films examined here: films starring Suchitra Sen (1929–2014) and Uttam Kumar

(1926–1980) – the best-known romantic pair in Bengali commercial cinema – that have direct or indirect references to Partition. The two primary films discussed – *Nabaraag* (*New Hues*, 1971) and *Alo Amar Alo* (*My Guiding Light*, 1972) – were based on popular romantic novels set against the backdrop of post-Partition Bengal and published in the late 1960s. The films were made in the mold of romantic melodrama, with the conscious choice of casting Sen and Uttam Kumar in the leading roles. The interjection and the eventual sublimation of the trauma of Partition into the romantic fantasy that this on-screen couple embodied were part of a complicated passage of the plots from the novels to the films. Within the confines of the genre of melodrama in the golden age of Bengali cinema, these two films' turning the experience of Partition into an uncanny tool of disorientation and alienation may be used to dig into the larger context of Bengali melodrama's approach towards the immediate postcolonial socio-political milieu, and how there persisted within the dominant form of melodrama a contrapuntal presence of desolation, resilience, and ultimate triumph of the repressed. My reading of the above two films as 1970s "Partition melodrama" follows a comparative path, employing thematic and contextual parallels with three earlier films – *Sabar Upare* (*Above All Else, 1955*), *Bipasha* (Bipasha, 1962), and *Shilpi* (The Artist, 1956), with an eye on the shift in the relationship between private desire and anxiety on the one hand and the political expression of the same on the other.

The Suchitra-Uttam star-text

In the 22 years between 1953 and 1975, Suchitra Sen (1929–2014) and Uttam Kumar (1926–1980) played the lead roles in about 30 Bengali films produced in Calcutta. Both had adopted screen names for their career in cinema. Suchitra Sen was Rama (pronounced Roma) Sen, married into a wealthy Calcutta family; Uttam Kumar – the eldest son in a middle-class family – was born Arun Kumar Chatterjee, and he worked as a clerk for the Port Commissioners in Calcutta before his screen career took off. Out of these 30 films, those made in the 1950s and the 1960s form the definitive core of the "golden age" in Bengali cinema. Bhaskar Sarkar in his recent significant work on Partition cinema sheds crucial insight on the ontology of the star power of the Suchitra–Uttam duo:

> The characters that Sen played exuded a poise that was essentially iconographic. In this respect, Sen's characterizations were rather similar: they were all smart, active, gorgeous creatures who nevertheless remained curiously frozen through the narratives, rarely posing a serious challenge to the status quo.... Her coupling with Uttam Kumar, undisputedly the most popular star of the Bengali screen, allowed for the projection of a certain fantasy: the adhunika could now desire, and even express that desire within limits imposed by the narrative. Of course, the heroine's passion for one particular star-hero across so many narratives served to rein in feminine

desire, domesticating it within a monogamous ambit, even de-eroticizing it by investing it with the aura of "true love."

(Sarkar 2009, 149)

The "*adhunika*" (the current, modern woman) that Sen portrayed for more than two decades was extremely effective in battling and defeating notions of "bad modernity." The "bad modernity" has been projected in both Bengali and Hindi cinema in broad strokes by "overtly" Westernized women (and men) whose sole narrative function was to attack "tradition" and therefore indirectly affirm the triumph of tradition through their own defeat and humiliation. Sen broke that mold, and her roles opposite Uttam Kumar overwhelmingly projected "agency" within the patriarchal overarch of melodrama. Even if her characterization remained, as Sarkar claims, "curiously frozen through the narratives, rarely posing a serious challenge to the status quo," she was perhaps the first star in Bengali and Indian Cinema to have more agency than her male counterpart in most of her films. And within the limits of melodrama, which pretty much defined Sen's artistic sphere, "serious challenge to the status quo" was barely the priority of either the producer or the viewer. To the awestruck Bengali audience of the 1950s and 1960s, her unmatched ascendance was unique and remarkable in a profession where actresses, irrespective of their star power, still walked in the shadows of the male stars. In the "superhit" Uttam–Suchitra films, Sen's name appeared first and Uttam Kumar's second, and the amount of concern Sen showed in the presentation of her work before it rolled out of production was atypical of stars in commercial cinema, to say the least. The persona that she created of herself as the mysterious, reticent artist beyond the reach of journalists, interviewers, and admirers added to the mystique, effectively producing a professional and artistic legend.

The legend however took considerable time to develop. If the monogamized, domesticated "true love" between successive characters played by Uttam Kumar and Sen was hypnotic for the "mass audiences," it was found to be syrupy and overdone by critics and journalists, who for a long time refused to accord to the two actors any claim even to artistic success. Common nicknames for Uttam Kumar and Suchitra Sen included "flop master general" and "dumb doll," respectively. The 1950s and 1960s were as politically turbulent as the pre-Independence decades in Bengal; wounds inflicted by the Bengal Famine and Partition still visibly oozed. Sen and Uttam Kumar had colleagues in the industry with strong ties to various leftist movements in literature and culture; Bengali films with openly political content were quite common, and Art cinema had already come into existence. Suchitra–Uttam's rise to stardom through kitschy melodramas – concurrent to the "progressive" wave – may be easily deciphered as a convenient turn to the Right, a fade-in into a reactionary dream. This sort of judgment actually does justice to most films that starred Suchitra and Uttam in the leading roles: "[t]he fantasies afforded a kind of vicarious pleasure that was a welcome respite for mass audiences reeling from the hardships of quotidian life in post-Partition, postfamine Bengal" (Sarkar 2009, 156). But it is also easy to see in the fractured space and ideology of quite a large body of these "melo-dramas" how the narratives and their visual representations often appear undone at the seams, how Partition and Famine and the downward spiral descent of the villages of Bengal often scream at the audiences over the mellifluous dialogues and songs. A slightly askew yet equally valid view can lead to a different per-ception: the screams of Partition, of Famine, and the destitution of villages actu-ally drown in the mellifluous dialogues and songs about the moon, fragrant flowers, the heroine's beauty, and eternal love. A journey worth taking therefore is the one that leads us between the layers of images and meanings in seemingly innocuous and romantic narratives in search of traces of traumas that could not speak their own names.

A significant shift occurs in the star texts of the pair in the two films *Nabaraag* and *Alo Amar Alo*, from several earlier, especially two earlier "Parti-tion" films: *Bipasha* (Bipasha, 1962) and *Sabar Upare* (Above All, 1955) which were chronologically beyond the circle of influence of the second Partition (the Bangladesh War). In spite of the then newly instituted "star-centeredness" of the 1950s melodramas, *Bipasha* and *Sabar Upare* are more representative of "social realism" than "romantic melodrama." Partition is mentioned only once in *Sabar Upare*, but its impact on the female lead and her approach to life and its chal-lenges is significant. *Bipasha* has a more direct and extensive approach to Parti-tion and covers, quite unusually for a Bengali film, the Partition of the Punjab. In both the films, the female lead played by Sen has an unusually proactive role in the narrative, and that role practically redefines the coordinates of the woman as a citizen of the newly formed nation-state. The contrast between the proactive role of the "refugee" woman in the earlier films and the petrified, stylized char-acterization of the same in the films of the 1970s is an important factor in the argument I present. In an attempt to extract the interpellation between narrative realism and cinematic melodrama's use of star-power, I also keep a discerning eye on the novels which provide the story in each of these films.

The taming of the profligate: class struggle meets melodrama in *Nabaraag* and *Alo Amar Alo*

Nabaraag and *Alo Amar Alo* appear toward the end of Sen and Uttam's common oeuvre. Released in 1971 and 1972 respectively, the films were obviously shot, edited, and produced in Calcutta at a time of high socio-political and economic turmoil. Immediately relevant to the subject of the films were the incidents leading to the Bangladesh War (or the "second Partition" as Bhaskar Sarkar calls it). Refugees poured in across the eastern border of India for the second time in 25 years, as Calcuttans witnessed a replay, on a lesser scale, of 1947. Following the Great Partition of the British Indian Empire into independent nation-states of India and Pakistan in 1947, West Bengal – the partitioned one-third of Bengal that remained in India – had been reeling in the aftermath of the Partition riots, the refugee influx problem, and a broken agro-economy of which the 1945 famine had been one of the many manifestations. The Communist Party of India that was banned by the British and sidelined by the Nehru government had split into two separate parties in 1965: the Communist Party of India (CPI) and the Communist Party of India, Marxist (CPI-M). Both parties were involved in various stints at power-sharing in West Bengal's state government, and in the process had lost their revolutionary rhetoric, inching toward the mainstream. The most prominent political phenomenon that in various social histories has been recognized as the righteous outburst of the post-Famine and post-Partition generation of Bengalis was perhaps the Naxalite movement of the late 1960s and its many offshoots. In what may be surmised as a commonplace political irony, Indian's federal government led by Indira Gandhi played savior to the East Pakistani rebels and provided military help to forge the state of Bangladesh while ruthlessly suppressing the Naxalite rebellion within India's borders. Bengali mainstream literature has quite a few memorable texts that reflect on Bengal's inexhaustible ordeals in the twentieth century alone: Samaresh Majumdar's *Kalbela* (Doomsday) focused on the Naxalite movement; and Sunil Gangopadhyay's *Purba–Pashchim* (East–West) remains to this day the definitive masterpiece covering the Partition, the Naxalite Movement, and the Bangladesh War.

In both *Nabaraag* and *Alo Amar Alo*, Uttam Kumar plays an industrialist with old money (and new), ensconced in Calcutta's high society; Suchitra Sen in both films is a refugee from East Bengal, a newcomer in Calcutta. The similarity in roles is significant not just because of the closeness in terms of time of production, but for the fact that in most (commercially successful) films featuring the couple thus far, Sen has played the rich heiress and Uttam Kumar an underprivileged and struggling young man (and, in at least two films, of a caste lower than the heroine's, which becomes a mitigating factor in the narrative). In *Jiban-Trishna* (Thirst for Life, 1957) Uttam Kumar plays a rich legatee for a change and Suchitra Sen a struggling artist, though at the end Uttam Kumar's character willingly hands over his wealth when his long-lost half-brother – the legal inheritor of his father's wealth – appears. In the bourgeois patriarchal scale of power in most earlier films, Uttam Kumar figures lower than Sen, so much so that their union at the end resolves – in the typical style of the melodrama – many thorny questions regarding economics, women's agency, and such conflicts as tradition/ modernity, domestic/professional, etc. In an insightful essay on *Agnipariksha* (The Trial by Fire, 1954), Dulali Nag has suggested that the conflicts and their resolution in the Uttam–Suchitra films must be understood in the unique context of the "modernist–nationalist ideology" of post-Independence Bengal:

> The centrality of the female figure in these narratives can now be understood in a context different from the universal tradition of the melodramatic genre or the functional necessity of catering to a predominantly female audience. To the extent that popular films present a collectively desirable image as a dream resolution to some real social-cultural crisis, the image of Suchitra Sen offers such a resolution to the crisis if nationalism, caught between the contradictory demands of the familial and the public sphere, in defining gender roles. The centrality of the female figure is doubly determined within

this schema. She is an agent of modernity for her educated status, she is also the focal point of the family drama … this popular image of a desirable woman subverts the elite nationalist construction of a woman as the repository of cultural authenticity.

(Nag 1998, 780)

The phrase Nag uses in her work – to describe what Sarkar in his book calls Suchitra Sen's "iconographic poise" – is "an excess in her characters." This element is so powerful that it can easily turn the *femme formidable* into a surrogate father(figure) without compromising her feminine charm. Situating this unique element in the context of the Bengali cinematic tradition, Nag writes:

> While for Pramathesh [Barua] the woman was always an image of the sexually inaccessible but nurturant [sic] mother (hence the whole narrative of unrequited love followed by tuberculosis), for Uttam Kumar she rather fulfilled the lack of a father figure, a protective father he had lost in leaving the village. (In almost all their successful films including "Agnipariksha", the death or loss of a father figure for Uttam Kumar precedes his union with Suchitra Sen. In other cases the father is simply absent from the narrative.) Suchitra Sen, on the other hand, while most of the time seen with a loving father figure, has either an extremely strained relation with her mother ("Agnipariksha") or is marked by the absence of one ("Shapmochan", "Sagarika", "Sanjher Pradeep", "Chaoa Paoa", "Harano Sur", "Surja Toran"). Their eventual union in a marriage seeks to correct this imbalance in their respective psychic order.
>
> (Nag 1998, 781)

The two films in which Suchitra Sen has an involved mother figure – *Shilpi* (The Artist) and *Saat Paake Bandha* (The Wedding Vows) – end with the hero's death in one film and a divorce (almost without precedence in Indian cinema) in the other. Interestingly, *Nabaraag* and *Alo Amar Alo* mark a distinct shift from the above formula of gender and power. Both of the characters played by Uttam Kumar – Bipul and Nilendu – are unambiguously secure in their (male) authority, while the Sen characters – Narayani/Rina and Atashi – are strangely unhinged individuals devoid of familial authority or support. Narayani/Rina's lives are a world apart from Bipul and Nilendu's cocoons of privilege, and they lose their dignity (to varying degrees) in the relationship. Atashi's predicament is considerably worse because she has to suffer Nilendu's violence and her own father's betrayal. Both films end with transgressions neutralized by either consent or discipline, but what is contained is not the excess of the female protagonist but that of the male. The excessive and arrogant authority of the elite bourgeois Calcuttan male (one who is not déclassé like his East Bengali migrant counterparts) is strangely tamed and tethered in by the irresistible charm of the refugee.

Nabaraag is based on a novel *Natun Tulir Taan* (New Brushstrokes) by Ashutosh Mukhopadhyay, one of the most popular novelists of his time; the novel was first published in 1968. While his contemporaries – the great Bando-padhyay trio (Manik, Tarashankar, and Bibhutibhushan) – have long been inducted into the literary canon of post-Tagore Bengal, Mukhopadhyay has primarily been acknowledged as a best-selling author of racy yet engrossing novels. He was noticeably more frank in depicting sexual situations and feelings than both his more "literary" contemporaries and his "popular novelist" col-leagues. He frequently constructed a pathology of desire between an exceedingly beautiful "fair-skinned" woman and a successful, powerful, and overtly libidi-nous man. In this sense, Suchitra Sen is the embodiment of every heroine ever created by Ashutosh Mukhopadhyay: a woman so beautiful that no man can resist her. In every one of Suchitra Sen's films there is direct diegetic reference to the physical beauty of Sen's character: in most cases she is simply called "the most beautiful woman" to her face and she either smiles in agreement or does nothing. In *Nabaraag*, her character Narayani has been chosen to be the wife of the rich and powerful Bipulananda because of her beauty. Nothing else of her identity has ever mattered to her husband; her archaic name Narayani is replaced by the more contemporary and fashionable "Rina." She has been given private instruction in English, ballroom dance, and the piano; and she uses her unschooled intelligence to keep up with the pretensions of her role. The novel begins with Rina voluntarily drinking alcohol at a party for the first time in her life; the film skips a few steps and introduces her as a gloomy drinker ill-at-ease and capable of losing control, in contrast to her husband who holds his drink with elegant ease. The unsurpassable difference between the two characters is made clear in a flashback to the couple's courtship; the rich industrialist's son shown to be awestruck by the beauty of a simple East Bengali village belle who has taken refuge in an uncle's house in Calcutta.

The crisis in *Nabaraag* is revealed in two parts. Narayani aka Rina feels uprooted from her village in East Bengal; she tells Bipulananda when they first meet that she hates Calcutta because she cannot see the horizons as she could in her village. She has a deep feeling of alienation in her marriage and has an uneasy relationship with the wealthy lifestyle of her husband's family. Second, she is uncomfortable about the upbringing of her son Raja under the over-indulgent attention of her husband Bipulananda. Bipulananda's power and wealth are depicted as immense and untamed by pre-global India's regulatory governance, and fill Rina with an almost erotic dread. She yields to her husband but wishes to assert moral control over her only son, and when she fails repeat-edly, she withdraws into an alcoholic gloom. She is shaken out of her resigned stupor when Nanda-da, a childhood acquaintance, visits her, seeking financial help for his orphanage. The last third of the novel and the film takes a sudden turn toward the mysterious when the son goes missing, and the reader and the viewer alike are left to wonder why he has been kidnapped and by whom. Bipu-lananda uses his power to mobilize the police, and the usual suspects, including the disgruntled members of labor unions in his various factories, are rounded up and harassed without result. Desolate and desperate, he takes to driving through and roaming the streets of Calcutta searching for his son. Rina on the other hand appears stricken but remains strangely silent. The second turn in the narrative comes with the news of the discovery of the son in a remote ashram operated by Nanda-da. Bipulananda arrives there with the police, only to hear that Raja was sent here by Narayani herself. He learns that Narayani has been a benefactor for the ashram, and has even visited her son a couple of times over the past few days. When Bipulananda meets Raja, he sees a transformed boy: happy, humble, and full of life, obviously enjoying his time in the ashram. An exchange between Narayani and her trusted servant informs the reader/viewer that she may have to face the wrath of Bipulananda when he returns. While her servant advises her to leave the house to escape the consequences of her action, Rina chooses to stay, half expecting her husband to turn violent. Bipulananda returns as a changed man, informs Rina that he has decided to keep Raja at the ashram for another month, and he apologizes to her for his overindulgent spoiling of their son. He addresses Rina as Narayani for the first time in their marriage, and expresses the hope that the upbringing of their son will be on the right track when he comes home; and the film ends with the customary embrace that came at the conclusion of most Suchitra–Uttam films.

The expression for upbringing used by Bipulananda at the end of the film and by Narayani several times in the novel is "manush haoya," literally "becoming a human being." In Bengali bourgeois colloquy, the meaning includes a good education (school, college, and university), securing a salaried job (or becoming a professional), and retaining the moral stipulations of the *bhadralok* class. Being a *bhadralok*, for instance, did not necessarily mean being wealthy or even financially comfortable, as the majority of the *bhadraloks* have traditionally received meager salaries from the time of the class's inception during the East India Company's administration of Bengal.[1] There has been something strangely indeterminate about *bhadralok*ness in Bengali language; translated as respectability, and used frequently in both literary and colloquial expression, it has absorbed in its signification the ambitions and anxieties of the aspiring Hindu *petit bourgeoisie* rather than the established upper and upper-middle classes. With every political and economic contingency that plagued modern Bengal – from the numerous mass movements in the nineteenth century to the Great Partition in 1947 and beyond – *bhadralok*ness has recurred in public discourses as a regressive concept, representative more of the discriminatory privileges and the anxiety of losing them rather than a unified class identity. The anxieties of the postcolonial, post-Partition Bengali *bhadralok* thus have a predictable focus. Bhaskar Sarkar has convincingly argued that the Bengali anxiety with *bhadra*-ness in the cinema from the 1950s through the 1970s was intricately related to their fear and loathing of the East Bengali refugee "other." The concept of "manush haoya" in the context of *Nabaraag* however refers to a different element, though complementary to the class anxiety of the *bhadralok*s: a yard-stick holding one and all to the presumed standards of a high-flying bourgeois morality. Bipulananda is a powerful individual with burgeoning resources, and it pains Narayani/Rina to see him bringing up his son without "moral values" – translated by her as discipline, humility, and respect for the impoverished and laboring underclass. The insensitivity of Bipulananda and his class is shown in the film by juxtaposing two scenarios: one of Raja's birthday celebrated by the roof-top pool, and the other of strike posters and striking workers of Bipulananda's various factories. The political posters announcing the impending strike and the workers' demands are shown in rapid succession to the tune of "Happy Birthday" playing in the background. When Nanda finds and visits Narayani in Calcutta, he expresses his inability to eat the elaborate spread of snacks and sweets she brings him, as he thinks of the 50 orphans he has under his care who eat boiled rice every day without any side dishes. Narayani/Rina writes a check for his orphanage and promises to visit him. When she finally visits the place for a few days, she feels she has gone back to the idyllic days of her childhood in her village in East Bengal; she plays hide-and-seek with the boys, shares their sparse meals, and seems to have found, for the first time in her married life, an understanding of her own personality and a purpose to her life. The orphans in Nanda's care live in close proximity to nature, eat meager food, have plenty of physical exercise, receive an education, and begin their days with prayer in assembly. The training model for young children (especially boys) described here closely resembles the colonial-nationalist recipe for education – a three-way combination of missionary, British boarding schools, and the Indian Brahmanical idea of "brahmacharyashrama" (the period of apprenticeship spent in celibacy and strict discipline in the Guru's residence). Devastated by Raja's sudden disappearance, Bipulananda discovers and embraces a new compassionate side to his self as he reinstates the jobs of the sacked workers, and comes to acknowledge them as fathers to children of Raja's age. Bipulananda's education is complete when he sees his son's transformation under Nanda's tutelage, when the police discover Raja in Nanda's orphanage. The profligate is finally taught a lesson in humility and morality by the déclassé Nanda and, more significantly, by Narayani – the seemingly helpless trophy wife who could be living her life in silent appreciation of security and privilege.

The political message or the lesson of the film is undoubtedly stronger than that of the novel. The cinematic exposition of the contrast between Narayani's youth in a village in East Bengal and the life that her marriage brought her is starker, for example, than what the novel projects. The film uses Sen's iconic presence in its articulation of Narayani's change through her steep and sudden social climb. While the star factor mentioned earlier predisposes the overall effect of the film, there is an undeniable connection, if somewhat masked, to the social realism of the 1950s and 1960s. And it is this connection that sets both *Nabaraag* and *Alo Amar Alo* apart from the pervasive, very consciously depoliticized lyricism of Indian cinema of their time.

Romancing the other: *Alo Amar Alo*

As opposed to *Nabaraag* which more or less stays faithful to Mukhopadhyay's novel, the 1972 film *Alo Amar Alo* adds several twists to an already problematic novel of the same name by Pratibha Basu, published in 1967 (Basu 1967). Uttam

Kumar plays the rich and arrogant Nilendu Mitra, who donates his spare time and money to just causes and in secret keeps pimps who bring in a steady supply of new and "fresh" women, who are "returned" to their homes when they cease to pique Nilendu's curiosity. In both the novel and the film, Nilendu remembers a traumatic childhood, mainly because of a philandering and perpetually drunk father. The novel mentions the father's mistreatment of his mother (who died relatively young) and uses it to explain the misogyny which underlies Nilendu's general attitude towards women. The film bypasses this, and emphasizes the widower father's crude insensitivity towards him. In a scene meant to provide an insight into Nilendu's pathology, he looks out of his window one night at a poor homeless couple tending to their sick child; a flashback shows Nilendu as a young boy, sick and alone in the night, wandering out of his room in a stupor to find his father carrying on business as usual, with alcohol and another strange woman by his side.

The novel however begins not with Nilendu; it does not even begin with Atashi who becomes the last victim of Nilendu's sadistic curiosity. The intro-ductory pages of the novel provide the reader with two intertwining threads, both about Gaganendra Haldar, a *bhadralok* patriarch turned into a helpless pauper by Partition. One is about Gaganendra's blind rage in response to a perhaps inap-propriate/indecent proposal (the reader learns what it actually is only halfway through the novel) that has come from a slimy creature named Mahim Sarkar, who was once one of the many dependants living with Gagenendra's family in East Bengal, but is financially better-off in the topsy-turvy post-Partition world of Calcutta. The other thread makes the reader privy to the collective predica-ment of Gaganendra's family in a long, winding narrative about the past opu-lence of three generations of Haldars in East Bengal. An impoverished Gaganendra lives in Calcutta in a colony – optimistically named *Nabajiban* (New Life) Colony – of makeshift houses built by refugees, under the leadership of Manab Mitra, an ex-revolutionary from Dhaka. Gaganendra has nine children, the eldest of whom is Atashi. His wife is bedridden; his second daughter Malati is an invalid as a result of an untreated injury; the adolescent third daughter Champa is rapidly going astray; his eldest son Partha is weak and ailing. The only members of the household to put up resistance in the face of the downward spiral of hunger, humiliation, and destitution are Atashi and two of her youngest siblings. Chameli and Arjun attend a free public school, study hard using bor-rowed books, and never complain. Gaganendra and Atashi are the only two char-acters in the novel with interior monologue; the other characters are revealed as observed by them.

The proposal that has driven Gaganendra to rage comes from a slimy Mahim Sarkar, who incidentally had been employed by the Haldars years ago in East Bengal. Mahim Sarkar now lives in Calcutta, and works as a pimp for Nilendu Mitra. Gaganendra has a classist and caste-ist attitude towards Mahim (Gaganen-dra being a Brahmin landlord and Mahim a Kayastha commoner in pre-Partition Bengal), which turns into hatred and fury when Mahim proposes that Atashi spend a few weeks with Nilendu in exchange for several thousand rupees. The unimaginable act of selling one's own daughter horrifies Gaganendra but nevertheless consumes his imagination. In a momentary lapse of moral judgment he leads an unsuspecting Atashi through a dark alley into the clutches of Mahim Sarkar who waits with Nilendu's driver and a car for an opportune moment. Atashi puts up a fight in the car, is eventually subdued, and is delivered to Nilendu in an apparently unconscious state, and this is where the novel takes a turn towards the bizarre. She recovers under the personal care of Nilendu's physician, but exhibits symptoms of amnesia, and mistakes her abductor Nilendu for a doctor. Her only recollection of the past seemed focused on the fact that she had left her house in search of a doctor for her ailing brother. She calls Nilendu "daktarbabu" – the most common Bengali way of addressing a physician – and Nilendu plays the role thrust upon him, nurturing her with attention and indulging her every whim. The last third of the novel is about the bizarre transformation of the prospective abductor/rapist into a gentle lover. There are a couple of moments when Nilendu comes close to violating Atashi, but he retreats each time. When Atashi's memory returns, she feels a vague sense of reproach towards her father, and a dark reckoning about her predicament; she knows that she cannot return to her family. The novel never goes back to narrate the family's condition once Atashi is abducted (only one reference is brought up by Mahim Sarkar – more about that later); the only scenario the reader is told about is the life of Atashi and Nilendu in the insulated asocial situation being played out in Nilendu's house. The novel ends with Nilendu suggesting to Atashi that he will visit Atashi's father and ask for her hand in marriage. A story of trauma, abduction, and rape thus takes a strange and happy turn towards the fairy-tale ending, with the prospects of a marriage between the prince and the refugee.

The writer of the film's screenplay makes a distinct political choice, by creating a narrative space for the social and legal consequences of the abduction. In the film, Atashi returns home after recovering from her amnesia, and Gaganendra commits suicide. Atashi files a police report under apparent pressure from the local political activist Manab Mitra, following which Nilendu is arrested. During the trial, Atashi faces Nilendu in court and refuses to accuse him of any wrongdoing; he is thus acquitted. A changed man, Nilendu returns to his house and is preparing to leave Calcutta for a long, indeterminate journey when Atashi appears (this is her second entrance into Nilendu's house and her first by choice), and tells Nilendu she will not let him leave. She embraces him in a reconciliatory gesture, signaling also the customary ending, as mentioned earlier, of the Uttam–Suchitra romances.

Alo Amar Alo as a novel is typical of Pratibha Basu's oeuvre, a love story in which romance comingles with trauma and suffering. In several of Basu's novels, the protagonists experience emotional and sometimes physical torment often owing to an older male relative's act of betrayal, an act that is disclosed to the protagonists much later in the narrative. Her novels also frequently feature a rescuer who bears little or no relationship to the female protagonist's immediate reality. It may be argued that the dual elements of "torment" and a "knight in shining armor" were what made Pratibha Basu's novels enormously popular among Bengali middle-class adolescents and young adult readers; the sanitized sado-masochism offered the reader a "thrill" otherwise not found easily in the literature intended for *bhadralok* consumption. It is difficult to guess the "selling points" of Basu's novels, especially considering her mostly teenager readers; very little data of *bhadralok* teenager reading habits divided along gender lines exist. It should be taken into account that Pratibha Basu was after all part of a close-knit literary circle of poets, scholars, and authors, her own husband being the indomitable Buddhadev Bose, founder of the first Department in Comparative Literature in India, a brilliant essayist and critic but a mediocre poet and novelist. If Buddhadev's novels were overtly cerebral, Pratibha's were entirely sentimental, the redeeming quality in both being the minute details served in a language that was at once sophisticated and visceral, analytical and poetic. Interspersed with phrases from Tagore's songs and poetry (the title *Alo Amar Alo* is the opening phrase in a popular song by Tagore), Pratibha Basu's novel presents all the horrors of Partition but at the same time couches it in the sanitized lingo of bourgeois romance.

Despite its limitations, *Alo Amar Alo* as a novel makes a crucial breakthrough: it is one of the rare Bengali novels where the déclassé, dehumanized *bhadralok* "sells" his daughter. The ways in which the father's guilt catches up with him are significantly different in the novel and the film, and perhaps shed light on the political bent of the respective texts. The novel contains several references to the "refugee" forming a new class of the exploited, refugee women in particular falling prey to sexual predators and pimps. The misogynistic and predatory Nilendu recalls seeing women visiting the soldiers' barracks, exchanging sex for food. The novel's only reference to Gagan Haldar's state after he betrayed Atashi is in the spiteful words that Mahim Sarkar directs to the amnesiac Atashi: Mahim says that while Atashi has been playing the forlorn drama-queen in Nilendu's mansion, her father Gagan waits outside the soldiers' barracks in the dark, searching for Atashi among the women who come and go. Mahim also suggests that Gagan may have disposed of the money in disgust, as his family live in the same squalor as they did while Atashi was there. In the novel, Atashi does not go back to her parents; Nilendu sends her home with a check for 10,000 rupees, but she turns around and comes back to Nilendu. Nilendu has the last word, literally: he promises to take her home and officially "ask" her father for her hand in marriage. Atashi's silence perhaps imparts the happy ending to the novel: all is well again, and dignity is going to return to the Haldars in the unlikely form of Nilendu Mitra. The film, however, ventures into a more complex space. Atashi actually goes back, and her father commits suicide as a result of the overwhelming guilt he has been suffering. Atashi is led by Manab Mitra to take legal action against Nilendu, but absolves him in court, and returns to him of her own free will. It is Atashi who has the last word, as she seals the relationship with genuine affection. Bhaskar Sarkar provides some crucial insights on the film's approach to the complex post-abduction scenarios in the aftermath of Partition:

Since the rich industrialist is made to face the law, the film upholds the democratic ideals and institutions of the state. However, the possibility of punishment is enough, as the romantic hero cannot be punished: in court, Atashi admits voluntarily that Nilendra [*sic*] never forced himself on her and actually took care of her in captivity. This admission implicates her with her tormentor, much to the consternation of her family. Here, the narrative clearly plays on the confusing experiences of women abducted during Partition; in captivity, many of them formed tender attachments with their abductors; when the Indian and Pakistani governments arranged for mass exchange of these women, many were unwilling to go back to their original families. The families also harbored mixed feelings about their "tainted" women. By placing the generic union of the romantic leads under the cloud of familial and social disapproval, the film unambiguously commiserates with those unfortunate women and restitutes to them a certain dignity.

(Sarkar 2009, 64)

Sarkar continues to make an illuminating point as to "how a fantasy of plenitude associated with a pair of stars, once invoked as an antidote to Partition blues, is refigured for subsequent critical purposes" (Sarkar 2009, 165). It is possible to be in overall agreement with Sarkar on the film's shedding light on the continued everyday horror of the aftermath of the abduction and still scrutinize the film's refiguring of the romance and the trauma from a different angle. Using Said's approach to Jane Austen's treatment of slavery in *Mansfield Park*, there is considerable scope to interrogate – in the context of both the novel and the film – the narrative function of Partition and the cooptation of the trauma by the master-plot. Given the typical elements of the sub-genre of romantic novels that characterizes Pratibha Basu's oeuvre and the directorial choice of casting Uttam–Suchitra in the lead roles, how exactly do we read the encoding of Partition into generic bourgeois/*bhadralok* romance that ends in a respectable, socially sanctioned union? The "fantasy of plenitude" seems less of an uninterrupted celluloid reverie than a state of bourgeois hopes, fears, and dreams prone to entropy when observed over a longer period.

The inheritance of injustice

In the 1962 film *Bipasha*, the eponymous heroine (played by Sen) is introduced as a ward of a Christian mission; the film opens with Bipasha passing her college examination. She travels to New Delhi to visit a friend and interview for jobs, and meets Dibyendu Chatterjee, an engineer working for Damodar Valley Corporation, one of the mega-dam-building projects undertaken by the Nehru government in the 1950s. They meet again as Bipasha finds employment with the Tribal Welfare Mission in Panchet, close to the dam. Dibyendu moonlights as a poet and music-composer, and he begins wooing Bipasha who feels attracted to him as well; they are engaged to be married. On the day of the wedding Dibyendu receives a letter from his maternal uncle and, instead of driving to his friend's house where Bipasha and the officiating priest await his arrival, leaves town and disappears. Bipasha refuses to be labeled "lagnabhrashta" (literally "one who missed the moment": the inauspicious nomenclature in Bengali Hindu upper-caste tradition for women whose weddings are canceled at the last minute), declares herself as Dibyendu's wife, and begins to search for him. She visits the places Dibyendu mentioned to her, and realizes that, in spite of her close friendship with Dibyendu, she knows next to nothing about his life – only bits and pieces narrated by him. She finally finds him in Allahabad, but he refuses to acknowledge her or their relationship, in the light of his recent discovery of a "damning truth," the fact that he is "a bastard" whom his mother's lawful husband refused to acknowledge. His mother was abandoned by the father (who married a British woman in England), and is probably still living an ignominious existence somewhere in Allahabad. Dibyendu's maternal uncle had informed him of this fact in a letter that reached him on his wedding day, therefore prompting him to flee the scene to avoid "tainting" Bipasha with his own shame. Bipasha is unmoved by this history and tries in vain to make Dibyendu shake off his outmoded sense of identity. Turned away by Dibyendu, a distressed but optimistic Bipasha begins her own investigation into Dibyendu's family history; she meets his maternal uncle, as well as a lawyer who represented Dibyendu's father in the divorce case filed by his English wife. Events take an overtly dramatic turn at this point, as Dibyendu attempts to commit suicide but is saved by a Hindu "Swami," who turns out to be the none other than Bipasha's long-time guardian. After Bipasha narrates Dibyendu's history to him, the Swami is forced to revisit his own past, as he discovers that he is Dibyendu's father who had deserted his family to marry an Englishwoman and had falsely accused Dibyendu's mother of infidelity. Both the film and the novel end with Dibyendu being reunited with his mother, who had been living a secluded life for over a decade.

In *Bipasha*, both Bipasha and Dibyendu are professionally involved in projects of nation-building, and both have traumatic pasts that are gradually revealed to the viewer. Bipasha – the daughter of a Punjabi mother and a Bengali father – had crossed the blood-drenched frontiers of the newly formed Pakistan to reach India. Her mother long dead, Bipasha had left Sialkot with her father, but he was killed in an ambush by rioters looking to rape and kill, and Bipasha had saved herself by jumping off a ridge, sustaining only minor injuries. She was awakened from her unconscious state by an elderly Sikh man, who persuaded her to join him and his son on their trek across the border. In India, she was given refuge in a Christian mission, and received the support of a Hindu Swami (who eventually turned out to be Dibyendu's father) to pursue higher education. In the novel the Mission is presented in a less than perfect light; the nuns try continually, albeit gently, to persuade Bipasha to convert to Christianity, an attempt which only makes Bipasha's received belief in Hinduism stronger. This issue is bypassed in the film, wherein the Mission's Tribal Welfare project is almost a mirror-image of the dam-building project, both geared towards the organization of hitherto untapped resources of the nation.

The film *Bipasha* evokes an earlier film with an almost identical cast: *Sabar Upare* (Above All, 1955). Shankar (played by Uttam Kumar) is a young defense lawyer who learns after winning his first case that his father (who Shankar thought died long ago) is serving a life sentence for a murder he did not commit. Shankar travels to Monghyr, tries to visit his incarcerated father (played by Chhabi Biswas) but learns that he has been exhibiting signs of insanity and is now housed in a solitary unit. Shankar begins his investigation into the murder and the subsequent trial that happened seven years before, and meets Rita, a schoolteacher who lives alone (deemed unusual for a Bengali bourgeois woman in the early 1950s). Rita's response to Shankar's own shame – "I am a dishonored woman from East Bengal" – is a subtle yet sharp reminder of the subliminal presence of the Partition trauma in the everyday life of the *bhadraloks*. But, as Sarkar notes in his book, "the admission becomes a romantic gesture, occurring in the narrative at a point where the two are getting closer ... Partition trauma figures all too briefly in order to establish a strong bond between two individuals of dubious origins" (Sarkar 2009, 162). Rita helps Shankar build his case against the corrupt prosecutor and find the real murderer; she also provides Shankar with moral and emotional support during the uphill legal struggle that Shankar wages. The exoneration of Shankar's father – that Shankar fought for and finally won – is described by Shankar as the triumph of justice and truth. However, the rhetoric Shankar uses in his description establishes the concept of truth not in an abstract realm but in the law of the state. It is the firm optimistic belief in the nation-state that is underscored in the film. It is worth noting that the original (and fraudulent) trial of Shankar's father had occurred in 1942 – a year remembered for its intense confrontations between the colonizer and the colonized in British India, and for the commencement of Mohandas K. Gandhi's "Quit India" movement. The retrial takes place in approximately 1949 (Shankar's father is mentioned as having been incarcerated for seven years), two years after Indian Independence and the Great Partition. The reference to redressing the wrongs of the past recurs during the trial, and a portrait of Mahatma Gandhi hangs behind the judge's chair in one of Indian cinema's earliest uses of such iconography in the representation of the "law of the state" as a corollary of the triumph of the nation.

Bipasha and *Sabar Upare* – notwithstanding the dramatic twists in the narratives and the overall subservience to the comic trope – have a grounding in realism that is conspicuously absent from the pair's later films. Compared to the pair's other films from the 1950s and 1960s which foreground the romantic relationship, its trials, and its various negotiations with normativity, these two films highlight the archeology of justice; they demonstrate unequivocally the redemptive possibilities of the postcolonial nation-state.[2] The gross injustices suffered by the characters have occurred either during the colonial period or during the violent conclusion to that past: Partition. In *Bipasha*, Bipasha experiences the trauma of her father's violent death and her sudden destitution during the Partition riots; Dibyendu's father is an anglicized wretch, and Dibyendu's familial past is severely disrupted during the British colonial period, owing to his father's philandering and the regressive stigma consequently attached to Dibyendu.

The everyday subject of history

There are no more than a handful of discussions about the legacy of the Bengali melodrama of the 1950s in the context of Indian cinema in general. Even rarer are discussions relating Bengali mainstream cinema with Bengali parallel or art cinema. We are, therefore, on uncharted territory as we think of the Partition narratives folded into the creases of Bengali popular cinema as serious stake-holders in the legitimate aesthetic/discursive articulation of the event. Ritwik Ghatak's much deeper and darker corpus of films seems like a world apart from the mellifluous excesses of romantic melodrama, but it is impossible to ignore certain common ground. For example, if there is one trait that the Uttam–Suchitra films discussed above share with a much deeper and darker corpus of films by the Director Ritwik Ghatak around the same time, it is the refusal to categorize "Partition" violence as overdetermined by sexuality and religious identity. Partition, as an event that disrupts the private and the public worlds of the *bhadralok*, is the aesthetic capital of Ghatak's films, and a complex "structure of attitude and reference" in the melodrama. I borrow the idea of the "structure" from Said's reading of Jane Austen's *Mansfield Park*, a kind of reading that can only add to the layers of collective cultural memory (Said 1993, 95). The ways in which melodrama sublimates the historical and the political are often how bourgeois collective experience encodes the same. Given the magnitude of the Bengal Famine and the two Partitions, it is difficult to imagine any significant segment of viewers left untouched by either of the two events.[3] The subliminal presence – in mainstream texts, including the novels and films discussed above – of the violence of hunger, destitution, and exploitation of various kinds needs to be examined as assiduously as these presences are noted in non-mainstream texts. This is where the Bengali preoccupation with "textuality" (the idea of a film as "boi" or a book) can be taken into account. The embourgeoisment of experience in the universal context of development of the novel as a genre and the very particular Bengali connection between the novel and the film in the golden age of Bengali cinema call for attention to the encoded details found in the works discussed above. An effectual history of postcolonial Bengali cultural collectivity must include such texts as these in order to be complete.

Notes

1 Both Partha Chatterjee and Sumit Sarkar have written about the clerks and other low-level officials and professionals who made up the majority of the *bhadralok* population in Calcutta. For further reference, see Chatterjee (1993) and Sarkar (1993).
2 Commercially successful films that mythologized the romantic pair are: *Agni Pareeksha* (Trial by Fire, 1954), *Shapmochan* (Breaking the Curse, 1955), *Sagarika* (1956), *Harano Sur* (the Lost Melody, 1957), *Pathey Holo Deri* (Delay, 1957), *Indrani* (1958), *Chaoa Pawoa* (1959), *Saptapadi* (The Wedding Vows, 1961), etc.
3 *Shilpi* (1956), one of Suchitra–Uttam's earlier films, has Uttam Kumar play the role of an artist from an impoverished village who falls in love with the daughter of his rich guardian in Calcutta. The artist loses his penchant for creating beautiful works of

art when he witnesses the devastation caused by the Bengal Famine. His beloved (played by Suchitra Sen) discovers a series of hauntings sketches of sick and starving bodies. This is the one rare film featuring the duo in which Uttam Kumar's character dies.

Bibliography

Agradoot (dir.). *Agnipariksha*. Produced by M.P. Productions, 1954.

——. *Sabar Upare*. Produced by M.P. Productions, 1955.

Agragami (dir.). *Shilpi*. Produced by Agragami Productions, 1956.

Basu, Pratibha. *Alo Amar Alo*. Calcutta: Bharabi, 1967.

Bose, Bijay (dir.). *Nabaraag*. Produced by S.M. Films, 1971.

Chatterjee, Partha. *The Nation and its Fragments: Colonial and Postcolonial History*. Princeton, NJ: Princeton University Press, 1993.

Mukherjee, Pinaki (dir.). *Alo Amar Alo*. Produced by Charu Chitra, 1972.

Mukhopadhyay, Ashutosh. *Natun Tulir Tan*. Calcutta: Deys Publishing, 1968, 1993.

Nag, Dulali. "Love in the Time of Nationalism: Bengali Popular Films from 1950s." *Economic and Political Weekly*, April 1998, 779–787.

Said, Edward. *Culture and Imperialism*. New York: Random House, 1993.

Sarkar, Bhaskar. *Mourning the Nation: Indian Cinema in the Wake of Partition*. Durham, NC: Duke University Press, 2009.

Sarkar, Sumit. *Writing Social History*. New York: Oxford University Press, 1993.

Sen, Asit (dir.). *Jiban Trishna*. Produced by Badal Pictures, 1957.

Index

eBooks
from Taylor & Francis

Helping you to choose the right eBooks for your Library

Add to your library's digital collection today with Taylor & Francis eBooks. We have over 50,000 eBooks in the Humanities, Social Sciences, Behavioural Sciences, Built Environment and Law, from leading imprints, including Routledge, Focal Press and Psychology Press.

Choose from a range of subject packages or create your own!

Benefits for you
- Free MARC records
- COUNTER-compliant usage statistics
- Flexible purchase and pricing options
- 70% approx of our eBooks are now DRM-free.

Benefits for your user
- Off-site, anytime access via Athens or referring URL
- Print or copy pages or chapters
- Full content search
- Bookmark, highlight and annotate text
- Access to thousands of pages of quality research at the click of a button.

Free Trials Available

We offer free trials to qualifying academic, corporate and government customers.

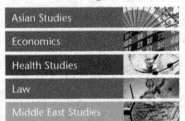

eCollections
Choose from 20 different subject eCollections, including:

- Asian Studies
- Economics
- Health Studies
- Law
- Middle East Studies

eFocus
We have 16 cutting-edge interdisciplinary collections, including:

- Development Studies
- The Environment
- Islam
- Korea
- Urban Studies

For more information, pricing enquiries or to order a free trial, please contact your local sales team:

UK/Rest of World: **online.sales@tandf.co.uk**
USA/Canada/Latin America: **e-reference@taylorandfrancis.com**
East/Southeast Asia: **martin.jack@tandf.com.sg**
India: **journalsales@tandfindia.com**

www.tandfebooks.com